This book proposes a radical alternative to dominant views of the evolution of language, and in particular the origins of syntax. The authors argue that manual and vocal communication developed in parallel, and that the basic elements of syntax are intrinsic to gesture. They draw on evidence from areas such as primatology, anthropology, and linguistics to present a groundbreaking account of the notion that language emerged through visible bodily action, and go on to examine the implications for linguistic theory and theories of the biological evolution of language.

Written in a clear and accessible style, *Gesture and the nature of language* will be indispensable reading for all those interested in the origins of language.

GESTURE AND THE NATURE OF LANGUAGE

GESTURE AND THE NATURE OF LANGUAGE

DAVID F. ARMSTRONG

Gallaudet University

WILLIAM C. STOKOE

Gallaudet University

SHERMAN E. WILCOX

University of New Mexico

CAMBRIDGE
UNIVERSITY PRESS

Published by the Press Syndicate of the University of Cambridge
The Pitt Building, Trumpington Street, Cambridge CB2 1RP
40 West 20th Street, New York, NY 10011–4211, USA
10 Stamford Road, Oakleigh, Melbourne 3166, Australia

First published 1995
Reprinted 1996

Printed in Great Britain at the University Press, Cambridge

A catalogue record for this book is available from the British Library

Library of Congress cataloguing in publication data

Armstrong, David F.
Gesture and the nature of language/David F. Armstrong, William C. Stokoe, Sherman E.
Wilcox.
p.   cm.
Includes bibliographical references and index.
ISBN 0 521 46213 4 (hardback) – ISBN 0 521 46772 1 (paperback)
1. Gesture. 2. Sign language. 3. Biolinguistics. 4. Grammar, Comparative and general –
Syntax. 5. Language and languages – Origin. I. Stokoe, William C. II. Wilcox, Sherman,
III. Title.
P117.A75   1995
417'.7 – dc20   94-6456 CIP

ISBN 0 521 46213 4 hardback
ISBN 0 521 46772 1 paperback

TS

Contents

Acknowledgments

The authors wish to thank Dr. John Bonvillian, Dr. Walter Adams, and an anonymous reviewer for reading and commenting on drafts of this book. The authors are, of course, entirely responsible for all opinions expressed herein and any errors of fact or interpretation.

Figures appearing on pages 207 and 208 are reproduced by permission of the University of Chicago Press from *Language and species* by Derek Bickerton, © 1990 by the University of Chicago.

Figures appearing on pages 75, 76 and 77 are reproduced from an article in *Sign Language Studies* by Scott Liddell and Robert Johnson © 1989 by Linstok Press, Inc. and appear with the permission of the Editor.

Portions of this book appeared previously in an article by the authors published in *Current Anthropology*, under the title "Signs of the origin of syntax," © 1994 by the Wenner-Gren Foundation for Anthropological Research.

Introduction: language from the body

> A curious thing about the ontological problem is its sim-
> plicity. It can be put in three Anglo-Saxon monosyllables:
> "What is there?" It can be answered, moreover, in a
> word – "Everything" – and everyone will accept this
> answer as true. However, this is merely to say that there is
> what there is. There remains room for disagreement over
> cases; and so the issue has stayed alive down the centuries.
>
> Willard Van Orman Quine, *From a logical point of view*

Language, like the physical universe, in all likelihood cannot be
known fully by an observer in one place at one time. Language
theorists and linguists, like physicists, must acknowledge uncertainty. In a masterful summing up of his philosophy of language
and much else, Kenneth L. Pike (1993) explains how, as long ago
as 1959, he wrote of "Language as Particle, Wave, and Field,"
borrowing this three-part label for the principle of complementarity from the work of physicist Niels Bohr.

Complementarity and uncertainty go together: it is only by
understanding the limitations on a single point of view or system
of mathematics that one can begin to see further. Since
Heisenberg, physicists have known that if one can locate a particle precisely, its action (as part of a wave of similar particles) will
escape detection, and that if one studies the wave action, individual particles disappear. Field theory states the necessity of looking at both wave and particle. Neither way of looking by itself
suffices, and each requires premises and methods appropriate to
itself.

In the present book we turn this competing but complementary
manner of viewing nature onto a genus of language that must
quite literally be looked at. This genus contains primary sign

1

languages of deaf communities as well as alternate sign languages, used by people who can hear. It is related of course to the common human practice of making visible gestures to signify and communicate, and as we will show, to the equally common human practice of making invisible but audible gestures in the throat and mouth for the same purpose.

Much discussion of language has focused on particles; at first identified as words, later as morphemes, then segments, and ultimately, distinctive features. Less plentiful discussion has described how these particles merge and lose their distinct identities as they function in the waves of continuous speech sound and sign language movement, and more basically, in the waves of neural and muscular activity that produce them. More recently, a branch of formal reasoning, sometimes called "fuzzy logic" (McNeill & Freiberger, 1993), has emerged that invites us to see the world as consisting of classes of things that merge into one another, rather than as perfectly distinct categories. From this evolving field we will make use of concepts such as linguistic classes built around gestural prototypes rather than contrast among the defining elements of class membership.

Just as field or quantum theory transcends the arithmetic of particle counting and the calculus of wave form analysis, so in language as particle, wave, and field, the concept of field implies that the distinctions made at the particle and wave levels lose their categorical significance or take on a new significance when conceived of as field phenomena.

Viewed as particle, a visible gesture includes what seem to be nothing but physical features; for example, the look of the movement a hand and arm make. It is also quite obvious that many such particular gestures differ in just these physical features. What is not at all obvious is how to determine precisely what and how much difference must be introduced to change one such particle into another. That determination cannot be made simply by comparing the appearance of the gestures, no matter how fine-grained the examination becomes. It requires instead finding out by careful procedures (e.g. ask no leading questions) how the makers of the gestures and those at whom they are directed understand them, and it results in finding that sometimes the change is so small as to be all but imperceptible to the uninitiated, at other times large and clear, but it also transpires that gestures grossly different in appearance (or sound) may be interpreted as carrying the same message.

Of course, this difference between particle and wave, better known in linguistics as (phon)etic and (phon)emic difference, has long been recognized. The difference between this and a field view, however, is not so well known. What will emerge in the chapters below is that even the commonsense and fundamental difference between word and sentence, if it does not disappear, takes on a new meaning when the full implications of field, wave, and particle are grasped.

To state the differences baldly here, anticipating the exposition in several chapters, the word-sentence distinction cannot be made at the physical level of sound or sight. Words are for representing classes of things and actions (and for doing certain grammatical chores); sentences are for representing very basic relationships:

actor-to-action
actor-to-action-to-undergoer
experiencer-to-state

Because of the nature of language sound and the mechanism of its production in a spoken language, there is usually a gross physical difference between a word and a sentence; but because of the nature of visible gestures and the mechanism for producing them, a word and a sentence in a sign language often look identical, except to a native user of that language.

The wave/particle metaphor is a central metaphor of science, but we do not want to overextend it. Nevertheless, we observe that many current theories of language have not fully escaped the limitations of the particulate view. Pike's tagmemic theory has been displaced by speculation about a mutation-produced language organ in every human brain, with or without separate modules for different grammatical operations. We take the view that language is based in gesture – that is, bodily movement to which human beings attach meaning. While the analysis of language into formal, particulate categories has led to productive results, it has resisted explanation in terms of organic evolution.

We propose an approach that takes into account the evolutionary history of the human organism and its social relations.

Chapter 1 suggests a taxonomy of gestures and gesturing. Chapter 2 explores the similarities and differences of the visible and invisible (vocal) gestures used to express language. In Chapter 3 the crucial physiological and linguistic differences between spoken and signed language are examined. The philosophical basis of various language theories are reviewed in Chapter 4 in the light of recent physiological and neural evidence. Chapter 5 looks at tests of the hypothesis that humans have a genetically programmed drive to acquire language. Chapter 6 turns to the necessary social dimension of language emergence, acquisition, and use. In Chapter 7 we explore more fully the identity, at the field level, of gestured/visible word and sentence as the probable origin of syntax. Finally, Chapter 8 puts the study of language from the body into an evolutionary perspective and completes the explication of our central image: language comes from the body.

CHAPTER 1

The universe of gesture

For if we are to do the biology of language at all, it will have to be done by tracing language to its roots in the anatomy, physiology, and social environment of its users. Only in this way can we hope to arrive at an account of language perception and production fitted to animals rather than machines.

Michael Studdert-Kennedy, *Perceiving phonetic events*

1.1 SIGNED AND SPOKEN LANGUAGES

Linguistic, psycholinguistic, and sociolinguistic research on American Sign Language (ASL) over the past three decades has established without question that ASL is a natural human language. Studies of several other indigenous signed languages have led to the same conclusion: primary sign languages, those used (mainly) by deaf people, are fully developed human languages more or less independent of the spoken languages of the linguistic communities in the same region. One of our purposes here will be to explore just how independent of each other these signed and spoken languages are. Several questions occur to us.

First, what is the relationship between spoken and signed languages? Are signed languages merely analogues of spoken languages, the linguistic equivalent of the bat's wing (evolved quite differently from the bird's wing)? Or are they true homologues, biologically related, as the human lung is to the swim bladder of fish? One objective of this book is to frame the study of signed languages in terms that will lead to answering the question of relationship. Specifically, it will explore a model that describes both spoken and signed languages as systems of gestures.

Second, what can the study of signed languages tell us about the human capacity for language? Linguists have not hesitated to propose theories of "human language" based on data drawn only from spoken languages. But by considering all natural human languages – both signed and spoken – we can gain a better understanding of how language is represented in the brain, how it evolved, and how its use is conditioned by natural limitations on the organs of articulation and the sensory mechanisms for perception.

The general model encompassing both spoken and signed languages to be presented here assumes that the key lies in describing both with a single vocabulary, the vocabulary of neuro-muscular activity – i.e. gesture.

The development of a phonological description of ASL (e.g. Stokoe, 1991) has demonstrated clearly the problem in distinguishing between gesture and language. Consider, for example, the ASL sign for 'gun.' According to the phonology of ASL, this sign involves a handshape in which thumb and forefinger make an "L." As well as being a standard ASL sign, the sign is also known and used by all hearing Americans. In fact, the sign is universally understood in all parts of the world where handguns are known, among both hearing speakers and deaf signers. A vocal sign having a similar (but perhaps more universal) status is the lip buzz or "raspberry," signifying breaking wind. Perhaps a more appropriate example is that of the "chug-chug," "choochoo," or "chut-chut" sound signifying 'train.' In fact, words for train in some languages involve this sound, despite the disappearance of locomotives that make such sounds.

These examples may be used as an entering wedge into a taxonomy of human gestures. This taxonomy takes an evolutionary perspective and does not ignore but includes in its levels the finer-grained taxonomies made by, e.g. Goffman, Ekman and Friesen, Kendon, Argyle, and McNeill. In this taxonomy, at least four levels can be identified. First, there is a primate (or perhaps mammalian or even vertebrate) level that contains the gestural primitives common to all people and in some instances all primates or all mammals. Examples are gestures implying bigness as signs of threat or intimidation, and gestures implying smallness as signs of submission. Loudness and softness in vocal communication have the same import. In this context, Givens (1986) has called for a "paleontology of gesture."

Second there is the level of the 'gun' sign, which is so salient and transparent that it will be understood wherever people have experience with handguns, although it has no inherent, pan-specific meaning. Third is the level of the gestural pool unique to but universal within a particular social group. In the case of English-speaking Americans, these would be gestures understood by both hearing and deaf people, but not by people outside of the American culture. Finally, there would be a level of gestures, spoken or signed, again in the case of English-speaking Americans, unique to the spoken and signed languages of the hearing and deaf communities respectively. At this level would be gestures, spoken and signed, that are mutually unintelligible between deaf and hearing people. A closer examination of spoken (acoustic) and signed (optic or visible) gestures at this level is provided in Chapter 2.

There is a much broader issue at stake here, and this concerns the question whether "gesture" – especially manual gestures – can be considered independent of speech. The position taken by some linguists, that speech has no significant relationship to the (primarily) manual gestures that accompany it, has been challenged recently (Kendon, 1991; McNeill, 1985,1992). These gestures are thought to be ancillary to speech, to be metalinguistic, or to express emotion, but to have no explicitly referential communicative function. McNeill (1985) claims that this is not a legitimate distinction, and that, in fact, the gestures that ordinarily accompany speech can and often do serve referential functions. Some of these gestures may be incorporated into the primary signed languages of the deaf people within the particular region. In an obverse sense, Padden (1990) has observed that the lip movements associated with certain spoken words may, in effect, be incorporated as signs of a primary signed language. Factors such as these tend to blur what might appear to be a clear cut distinction between language and gesture, as McNeill has suggested: "We tend to consider 'linguistic' what we can write down, and 'nonlinguistic' everything else; but this division is a cultural artifact, an arbitrary limitation derived from historical evolution" (1985: 351)

Frequently what we can write down is stripped of its emotional content and much of its communicative intent. We maintain that a gestural approach to analyzing communication events will help us overcome such arbitrary distinctions.

1.2 SPEECH AS GESTURE

Oddly, much more work has been done to describe speech than to describe signing in gestural terms. The psychologist Ulrich Neisser, for example, has noted that it is possible to describe speech as "articulatory gesturing, and to treat speech perception as comparable to perceiving gestures of other kinds" (1976: 159). Michael Studdert-Kennedy, a speech researcher with the Haskins Laboratories, has suggested that speech can be characterized as "subtly interleaved patterns of movements, coordinated across articulators" (1987: 74).

Such description of speech as gesture contrasts with the traditional description of speech by analysis into abstract linguistic units. In the traditional framework such units of language – segments for example – have three properties: they are discrete, they are static, and they are context-free. Speech is consequently seen to consist of the sequential ordering of discrete states (or targets) of vocal tract activity.

Problems develop when we consider how these abstract units are realized as articulations; i.e. physiological activity. First, speech as actually produced is not discrete and context-free; segments influence each other in a process known as "coarticulation." The influence has been observed to extend up to three segments in either direction; for example, consider the word *spoon*. In their canonical forms, the segments /s/, /p/, and /n/ do not have lip rounding. Coarticulation operates in a right-to-left fashion on the /s/ and /p/ of *spoon* and left-to-right on the /n/; i.e. the lips are rounded even as pronunciation of *spoon* begins and remain rounded until it ends, even though only the vowel segment theoretically calls for rounding (Daniloff & Hammarberg, 1973). Second, the vocal tract is rarely if ever in stasis. As Carol

Fowler, a speech researcher at the Haskins Laboratories observes: "if segments are only achievements of vocal tract states . . . then most of the talking process involves getting to segments, and less of it is involved in actually producing them" (1985: 240).

Problems with formal categories also arise in the study of speech perception. It seems that human beings do not always perceive speech sounds as static targets. Winifred Strange (1987) manipulated sequences of segments, typically consonant-vowel-consonant (CVC) sequences, to test whether perceivers rely on information for canonical, "target" formant frequencies, or for transitions. Because of coarticulation there is a period of time during the transition from C to V and from V to C when the segments influence one another. Strange took a word such as *bab*, electronically attenuated to silence the middle two-thirds of the vowel (but leaving in the surrounding consonants and the co-articulated transitions) and asked subjects to identify the vowel. Subjects had no more difficulty in doing so than when the vowel sound was fully audible. On the other hand, when the coarticulated transitions were attenuated, subjects experienced difficulty in identifying the vowel. These results led Strange to propose a model of speech perception in which vowels are characterized as gestures, the acoustic consequences of which are perceptually relevant.

Fowler's synthesis (1987) of these findings from speech production and perception provides an insight into how these results may apply to signed language. She proposes that listeners "focus on acoustic change, because changing regions of the sound spectrum best reveal the gestural constituency of the talker's utterances." By extension, we might hypothesize that sign language viewers focus on optical change (movement) because changing regions of the viewers' visual field best reveal the gestural constituency of the signer's utterances.

Browman and Goldstein are pioneers in developing gestural models of speech. They point out that:

Much linguistic phonetic research has attempted to characterize phonetic units in terms of measurable parameters or features. Basic to these approaches is the view that a phonetic description consists of a linear sequence of static physical measures, either articulatory configurations or acoustical parameters. The course of movement from one such configuration to another has been viewed as secondary. We have proposed an alternative approach, one that characterizes phonetic structure as patterns of articulatory movements, or gestures, rather than static configurations. While the traditional approaches have viewed the continuous movement of vocal-tract articulators over time as "noise" that tends to obscure the segment-like structure of speech, we have argued that setting out to characterize articulatory movement directly leads not to noise but to organized spatiotemporal structures that can be used as the basis for phonological generalizations as well as accurate physical description. In our view, then, a phonetic representation is a characterization of how a physical system (e.g., a vocal tract) changes over time. (Browman & Goldstein, 1985: 35)

Mowrey and Pagliuca (1988) propose a model of speech as gesture to account for phonetic evolution. In their model, words are "complexes of muscular gestures which are temporally ordered, but not in the serial segmental fashion familiar from classical [linguistic] theory." Rather than representing static or canonical vocal tract targets, their model represents the muscular activity that produces vocal tract movement. Thus their model resolves a basic incompatibility between traditional (segmental) models of speech and its instantiation as neuromotor activity:

Bursts of muscular activity move the articulators along a trajectory and hence are more appropriate for describing the transitions between targets than the targets themselves. Enlisting the most dynamic aspects of articulation to describe the most static ends – targets – mistakenly equates movement with states. (Mowrey & Pagliuca, 1988)

The Mowrey and Pagliuca model has been tested experimentally using electromyographic (EMG) measurement of speech errors (e.g. slips of the tongue, such as "alsho share" for "also share"). Speech errors have typically been offered as strong evidence of the reality of segments (Fromkin, 1979). The traditional claim is that segments are transposed in the erroneous production because of anticipations or perseverations. Mowrey and MacKay (1990) present evidence clearly indicating that individual muscular components of articulatory gestures are transposed in speech errors, thus contradicting claims that language production planning takes place at a segmental level.

1.3 SIGNING AS GESTURE

The notion that signed languages could be described in terms of muscular gestures seems too obvious to have been the occasion for serious debate. As noted, however, very little research has proceeded in this direction. A likely explanation for the lack of interest in the neuromotor activity of signing is that signed language researchers have had to argue for the recognition of signed languages as human languages and against strongly held but unsupported opinions to the contrary (Wilcox & Wilbers, 1987; Armstrong, 1984). Consequently the thrust of much sign language research has been to demonstrate that currently accepted linguistic theories can be applied productively to the study of signed languages and that the observed structure of signed languages confirms the theories. This has led precisely to the argument that signed languages cannot be studied as organized systems of gestures. While understandable, this conservatism is tenable only if the central dogma underlying theories of speech organization is valid. As we have suggested above, increasing numbers of researchers are questioning this dogma.

The result of this dominant theoretical posture has been the devotion of considerable effort to identifying signed equivalents (or analogues or homologues) of the theoretical elements of speech. Linguists have proposed various candidates as signed segments, among them movements and holds (Liddell, 1984), movements and locations (Sandler, 1986), movements and positions (Perlmutter, 1988). Others have taken the different tack of proposing that the common ground shared by signed and spoken languages will be found at the level of the syllable (Wilbur, 1987). Still others have proposed that signed languages simply do not have segments (Edmondson, 1987). So far, there has been little serious consideration of the possibility that signed words, like spoken words, may be analyzed as complexes of temporally ordered muscular gestures, not as imperfect representations of abstract formal categories.

1.4 SEMANTIC PHONOLOGY

Stokoe (1991) proposes a radical alternative to sign "phonologies" developed as analogues to those descriptive of spoken languages, such as those that we have just described. What is radical about this approach is that semantic phonology calls into question, by making it unnecessary, one of the most cherished elements of the central dogma of structural linguistics, namely the concept of duality of patterning. Duality of patterning is seen by some as a pivotal achievement in the evolution of language (Pulleyblank, 1986). Armstrong (1986:121) defined it in the following terms:

> The human vocal apparatus is capable of producing a vast array of sounds, just as the body as a whole is capable of producing an enormous number of visible movements. Each language, signed or spoken, incorporates a small and relatively fixed number of these sounds or movements, respectively. The sounds or movements, so incorporated, differ from language to language. The rules in a given language for generating morphemes from the stock of phonemes are independent of the rules for generating meaningful utterances (words and sentences) from the stock of morphemes. This is the general statement of the principle of duality of patterning.

This concept has been applied productively to signed languages as well as spoken languages. However, Stokoe (1991) calls into question complications introduced by the need to deal with production in three dimensions in sign language phonology. As a response to "autosegmental, metrical, and . . . lexical phonology," Stokoe proposed semantic phonology, which draws directly on gestural analysis, and which will be more fully explored in Chapter 7. According to this concept, a word (sign) of a primary sign language may be seen as a marriage of a noun and a verb. In semantic terminology, the sign is an agent-verb construction. The agent is so called because it is what acts (in signing as in generative semantics, see Chafe 1970), and the verb is what the agent does. Stokoe (1991: 112) continues:

> The usual way of conceiving of the structure of language is linear: First there are the sounds (phonology), these are put together to make the words and their classes (morphology), the words in turn, are found to be

of various classes, and these are used to form phrase structures (syntax), and finally, the phrase structures, after lexical replacement of their symbols, yield meaning (semantics). A semantic phonology ties the last step to the first, making a seamless circuit of this progression. The metaphor for semantic phonology that jumps to mind is the Möbius strip: the input is the output, with a twist.

Stokoe proposes terminology descriptive of the physical actions of the gestures themselves. Critics may say that this system is both too simple and too pretentious. In particular, the issue of notation will arise: how can the necessary anatomical terminology be expressed in notation that is simple enough? We would respond as follows: is notation in the traditional sense any longer necessary in the scientific study of language and gesture? It is doubtful that linguistics would ever have emerged as a separate discipline if spoken languages had not long before been reduced to phonetic notation in two dimensions on a flat surface. It took human beings a very long time to develop a system to represent speech (at least some of it) on tablets or panels or papyrus or vellum sheets. It is testimony to the non-obviousness of phonetics that this invention may have happened completely only once. And even the invention of phonetic writing left the intonation and most of the other phenomena of face-to-face vocal communication out of its reckoning, including most of the phenomena indicative of the emotional state of the speaker.

Inevitably, linguistics became a way of first describing and then explaining segments – the parts of language that letters represent in phonetic writing systems. Efforts to reduce signing to something like phonetic writing (e.g. Stokoe, 1960; Stokoe et al., 1965) or radically different two-dimensional representation (e.g. Labanotation) have been numerous but never quite satisfactory. The reason is well expressed by Hockett (1978) in terms of the dimensionality of signing and the possession by humans, as primates, of unusually well developed abilities to perceive and process visual input in three dimensions. Looking back, it appears that linguistics was made possible by the invention of writing. Looking ahead, it appears that a science of language and communication, both optic and acoustic, will be enabled, in all probability, not by refinements in notational systems, but by increasing sophistication in techniques of recording, analyzing, and manipulating visible and auditory events electronically. We will be particularly concerned with the implications of this observation for visible communication events, but we believe that it has equally profound implications for auditory ones as well.

Semantic phonology is appropriate in another way to a gestural view of language. The linguistic sub-discipline of phonology may well be the most elaborated of any in the social sciences, for not only do phonologists continue to posit more and more sublexical levels but they disagree widely also on the number, nature, and name of the categories at each level. Given the axiom that language must have both words and sentences, it is not unreasonable to suppose that early language was simpler than language now. When the word-level units of a language can be identified as two elements – an action and something acting or acted upon – there is obvious simplicity. But simplicity is not incompleteness: such a system contains both words and sentences, for the words can be symbolically, SVO (subject-verb-object).

The pattern is syntactic, but its elements, as agent, action, and the optional patient, are semantic terms. Of course, there is the normal linguistic requirement that different agents and actions (or verbs) be easily and clearly, even automatically, distinguished one from another, but this is a matter of gestural control and visual perception: which muscles contract, precisely when, and to what degree? (Just so, speech recognition is a matter of the same kind of knowledge about other muscles.) According to semantic phonology, just below the SVO elements of a sign language word lie strictly physiological phenomena, not tiers and tiers of logical and/or psychological constructs.

Much has been written about a kind of word found in sign languages called either a "size and shape specifier" (Klima & Bellugi, 1979) or a classifier (Wilbur, 1987) – the latter a category of word found in many spoken languages but not in English (Allan, 1977; Kantor, 1980). This kind of word serves as a pronoun with certain specifically limited referents; e.g. a person, a long thin object, a heavy compact object, an animal, a vehicle, etc. In ASL this kind of word, known by the handshape alone, also

gloss	VEHICLE	GO-AROUND	PERSON
syntax	S	V	O
signs	noun (verb)	verb (noun)	noun (verb)
DASL			
notation[a]	3	<	G $^\wedge$

Figure 1.1 Description: Unrotated forearm with thumb and first two fingers extended moves (upper arm extension, slight inward rotation and wrist bending) past and around upright index finger of other hand.
a. Stokoe et al., 1965

has a unique privilege. When used as subject in a sentence its handshape can substitute for the normal handshape of the ASL verb used with it, retaining the verb's normal sign action. Hence, using upper and lower case allows the formula in Figure 1.1 to symbolize a sign sentence (English glosses shown above the syntactic and the semantic-phonological symbols).

In this way, the two basic functions of language – to make words and to make sentences of words – are satisfied very economically by gestures performed in full view. To keep linguistics from confusion, it has been customary to insist on a separation of levels, particularly the semantic, syntactic, and phonological levels; but the semiotic function, interpreting the meaning in a sign, moves freely through all levels. Something (let us say the particular configuration of a hand and arm), which participates in signifying a word, also performs the function of sentence subject, and hence has the general meaning of agent, something acting. From long looking at these relationships, it is easy to see semantics, syntax-cum-morphology, and phonology in signed languages as far less complex than a long tradition of linguistics based in written texts has made them appear. It is impossible to see the same interrelation of phonology, syntax, and semantics in spoken languages, not only because most of the gestures producing speech are invisible, but also because of the difference between the perceptual and productive modes used for speaking and signing.

1.5 LANGUAGE AS GESTURE

Investigation of signing as gesture in the sense described above was begun by Wilcox (1992), as an extension of his research on fingerspelling. Fingerspelling was chosen because, as an artificial visible system that differs from natural signed language, it allows us to highlight significant processes. It has several unique parallels with speech, but it operates on the alphabetical level. It is a method of representing the individual letters of an English word by means of an alphabet of hand configurations for the letters. With the exceptions of 'J' and 'Z' (which are movements of other configurations), fingerspelling is viewed as consisting of as many static hand configurations (targets) as there are letters. Fingerspelled words are thus described as the sequentially ordered production of these static hand configurations. (Hand alphabets that caption drawings of stationary hands with letters have been in circulation since printing with movable type began and help to preserve this view.) As with speaking, however, fingerspelling in actual production is dynamic, continuous, and coarticulated. The results of the Wilcox study support the notion that fingerspelling is best understood as patterns of movement coordinated across articulators. Coordination seems to be organized around peak velocities of the articulators – during the movements between hand configurations rather than during the time target configurations are visible.

We will be particularly concerned here with the question of coarticulation, that is, the extent to which individual elements in fingerspelling (letters) are influenced by other elements before or after them. Original research that will be reported in Chapters 2 and 4 is used to investigate the question whether from a neurological perspective, language is represented in modular fashion in the brain. In general, the study of spoken and signed language production as temporally ordered muscular gestures makes it possible to begin a search for the neural basis of human communication in general. Neurolinguistic and speech-reception research suggests that such a search can succeed (Edelman, 1987, 1989, 1992; Fowler, 1987; Kimura, 1976, 1981; Strange, 1987).

A.M. Liberman, a pioneer in modern speech research, noted that:

[T]he key to the phonetic code is the manner of its production. [To understand it] requires taking account of all we can learn about the organization and control of articulatory movements. It also requires trying, by direct experiment, to find the perceptual consequences (for the listener) of various articulatory maneuvers (by the speaker). (Liberman, 1982: 165)

Liberman's remarks can be applied with equal force to the study of the "phonetic" basis of signed languages (as we have suggested in the discussion of semantic phonology above), and so of language: the key lies in understanding the organization and control of articulatory movements – whether vocal or visible – and finding their perceptual consequences. We will be concerned in addition with examining the evolutionary history of the biological substrate of language and gesture.

1.6 AN EVOLUTIONARY PERSPECTIVE ON LANGUAGE

In this endeavor, we take an explicitly evolutionary (selectionist/ adaptationist) approach. The governing theoretical framework is the theory of organic evolution by means of natural selection. The application of this theory to linguistic evolution has been under attack for some time (e.g. Piattelli-Palmarini, 1989), and we will explore a series of antinomies that have arisen as a result. Further, we will propose ways to resolve these antinomies given a non-formalist (gestural) approach to the study of language.

We contend that traditional formalist approaches to understanding the evolution of language have started with formal categories and argued backward to possible precursors as well as to alleged brain mechanisms to explain their existence. We believe that this introduces a further level of circularity into a domain that already has circular tendencies. Our approach will be to start with the raw materials of communication as they are exhibited among both humans and relatives of humans. We will be concerned as well with the fossil evidence for communicative capabilities in the evolving hominid lineage.

In all of this, one dominant theme will govern the development of our arguments, and that is that the primary human adaptation is social first and then technological. The notion underlying this observation is fairly simple: it was life in social groups that gave early hominids a selective advantage in new habitats. First attempts at tool making supplemented this advantage. The key to successful social life is communication – which among primates is both visual and vocal. In this regard, however, we note that the primary sensory adaptation of primates is visual. Consequently, we argue that language-cum-syntax may have come naturally from an analysis of visible gesture. Finally, we note that the fundamental *anatomical* adaptation of the hominids is to support bipedal locomotion, an adaptation that frees the forelimbs for non-locomotor activities, including carrying and (most important from our perspective) gesturing.

Within this general evolutionary framework, a more specific, gesture-oriented framework naturally emerges. This framework can be expressed as a series of assertions:

(1) Language has the primary purpose of supporting social inter-action and cooperation (Armstrong, 1989). Competing theories stress the priority of support for the development of technology as the primary selective force driving the evolution of language (Davidson & Noble, 1989; Dibble, 1989). A theory that derives language from gesture provides support for the former position, as we will argue throughout this book.

(2) The neurological organization of language in the brain is not modular (Edelman, 1992). Neurolinguistic research on deaf signers has been used both to support and refute modularity. We believe that a gestural interpretation of signed language organization leads away from the notion of a modular organization.

(3) Language acquisition in children is organized along general principles and is not guided by a language acquisition device. The problem of separating language from gesture is seen most

clearly in the study of language acquisition, especially the communicative interchange between mother and infant.

(4) The earliest linguistic units may have been either visible or vocal gestures or, quite likely, both. We will explore the notion of visible signing as a basis for subsequent linguistic evolution.

(5) The earliest linguistic units are likely to have been large and semantically complex.

Because of our interest in signed language and visible gesture, we will emphasize the importance of hands, the visual system, and upright posture in the development of language. We believe, in particular, that an analysis of the physical structure of visible gesture provides insights into the origin of syntax, perhaps the most difficult question facing students of the origin and evolution of language (see a recent review of several books on language origins and the cognitive abilities of non-human primates by Lord Zuckerman, 1991). It is the origin of syntax that transforms naming into language, by enabling human beings to comment on and think about the relationships between things and events, that is, by enabling them to articulate complex thoughts and, most important, share them with others.

We cannot accept the opinion of many (e.g. Lieberman, 1991; Edelman, 1992) that language originated from and resides in a three-part system composed of the brain, the vocal tract, and the auditory system. We believe not that brain, voice, and hearing constitute language but that the whole organism, and especially the visual and motor systems, are involved in language. The primate and mammalian trait of interpreting the visible actions of others, the development of true bipedalism, binocular vision, lateral upper limb, eye, and cerebral dominance – all these amply provide something that by means of natural selection could and presumably did evolve into language.

Language in this scenario has two essential functions: first, to make words; that is, to symbolize, signify, communicate *things*, *events*, and other such isolates of experience as chimpanzees can operate with. Second, language must also – or else it is not language – symbolize, signify, and communicate *the relations between things and events*; that is, language makes sentences. Syntax has begun to emerge when the simplest sentences can be made.

There is, obviously, no doubt that vocal material can be used for making words – not just calls that have pre-existing relations to what they signify but also signs standing for classes that may have few or many exemplars. It is also obvious that such vocal words are made, and for many millennia have been made, into sentences; but the concomitant use of visible gestures and vocal gestures like intonation to form and classify sentences has too often been overlooked. The crucial problem is to find how sentence forming came about in the evolutionary history of our species. How might syntax have begun?

There is nothing in the nature of vocal words to help in this search. In fact, special devices have to be used in many languages to make clear whether a word is to be understood as a noun or as a verb; that is, can it be a subject or predicate, the primal elements of sentence structure? In English, given any word, from "anger" to "zero," we cannot rely on the word alone to state its function. We add affixes or concatenate:

His *anger* annoyed me. My annoyance *angered* him.
.
.
.
I *zeroed* in on the question. But my answer scored *zero*.

When we look at visible, particularly manual-brachial, gestures used as signs, it is not necessarily that way at all. Such a gesture can be and is (and always was and could be) both or either a word or a sentence. When a signer tells us something, we may in response bend our right hand and touch our forehead with the fingertips. The signer understands from the action and from facial and other evidence that we have responded: 'I know that.' Obviously, we have signed a whole sentence, but if you look for a hand touching the forehead with the fingertips in one of the usual picture books published as sign language dictionaries and you are lucky enough to find that pictured, it will be listed as a word, glossed KNOW, and, as that gloss implies, an ASL verb.

Like other languages, ASL has its special devices to make clear when one of its words – "signs" in common parlance – is a verb or a noun. It took a deaf and a hearing linguist working together to point these out (Supalla & Newport, 1978). Similar devices also make clear to signers when a certain action performed or seen or both is a word or a sentence. Sign language linguists have produced many volumes of description of the phonology and morphology of signs and the syntax of sign languages. But, despite all their striving to show that sign languages and spoken languages obey the same universal rules, no one has pointed to the fascinating reason why devices are needed to distinguish a signed word from a signed sentence. By itself, without added facial or head or eye actions, an action of the hand and arm (or hands and arms) has the potential for symbolizing *either* a word *or* a sentence.

Whether one means to say 'I know' or simply 'know' or 'knows' or 'knew', the hand and arm perform the same action. We stress the arm, because in descriptions of sign languages, dating from the beginning of their use in education at the end of the eighteenth century to current linguistic descriptions, the attention has focused on the hand and fingers and what they do. Describers of sign languages have said, in more or less these terms: "The hand (in such and such a configuration or handshape) touches the head." So it appears to the observer, but if one is to get at the source of language from the body, one needs to realize that the hand touches the forehead because a message from the brain has gone out to muscles that make the hand bend at the knuckles and keep the fingers in contact along their sides and the thumb alongside out of the way. Then, a fraction of a second later, other impulses go to muscles in the arm to make it flex at the elbow and extend at the shoulder. Thus, the hand is largely and its fingertips entirely are passive entities moved by neuromuscular action until this particular action ends, making contact with the forehead.

1.7 GRASPING SYNTAX

For a long time there has been – even now there is – reluctance to accept this action and its visible result as part of a language, largely because it seems overly transparent to observers: they see at once that it *means* 'know' because the hand touches the head and because they think of knowledge as inside the skull. This sign, as Saussurians would say, is motivated or iconic, and the inference is that being so openly linked to one feature of its meaning it must be a "natural" and not a linguistic sign. But suppose one means 'catch' or 'grasp,' and moves the hand in a somewhat different way and with a different result. This time the hand begins less bent or even fully open; the flexion at the elbow is less; and the upper arm instead of extending rotates at the shoulder joint to bring the forearm and hand across the front of the body until the moving hand closes around the upright forefinger of the other hand. This too might be called a motivated sign. As just described, it means 'catch'; its iconicity is even more obvious than in the sign for 'know.' The active hand caught or grasped the finger of the other hand.

Here, we could almost rest our case. The iconicity now is not between a sign and a single thing or action it signifies but between the whole gestalt of something acting, its action, and the result, the patient it acts upon. In other words, this manual-brachial gesture meaning 'grasp' or 'catch' is also a complete transitive sentence: It has a subject, a verb, and a direct object, or, in semantic terms, an agent, action, and patient. Iconicity – resemblance of some kind between signed and signified – may not have impressed Saussure as important in *langue* or *parole*, but it is a condition of all kinds of communicative behavior, both linguistic and nonlinguistic. To dismiss it as unimportant is to miss its obvious part in the evolution of consciousness, of concept formation, and of behavior mediated by what the brain has learned and stored, once its neural material – its wealth of circuitry – has grown sufficiently complex. Not only do visible gestures, whether of sign languages or not, often resemble what they signify, they also are likely to have originated because a two-legged primate with hand-eye coordination evolved during ages of arboreal living, but now endowed with hindlimbs of a very different kind suddenly or gradually discovered that certain actions observed were, and others could be, mimicked with manual-brachial actions. This is not to say that vocalization and facial expression were not involved in making sense in face-to-face interaction. It is to say, however, that nothing so far seems to have as much potential as visible gestures involving an actor and its action for guiding hominids to the act of symbolizing *relations* as well as *things*. Simply put, with visible signs it is possible to make sentences as well as words, to evolve syntax as well as a knack for naming things.

All of this suggests a scenario for deriving syntax from visible gesture. At this point it is important for us to state why we are primarily interested in the origin of syntax. Our interest arises from the assertion that syntax is the most difficult aspect of language to derive plausibly from pre-human primate communication and cognitive systems – in this we agree with Lord Zuckerman (1991) and others (e.g. Bickerton, 1990; Wallman, 1992). We differ from some formalists by contending that it is difficult but not impossible. We have mentioned before that chimpanzees show well-developed abilities to conceptualize and to name objects and events, certainly two fundamental prerequisites for language, but they appear to have relatively poor ability to express relationships through signs. As we develop our scenario, we will be relatively unconcerned with the timing of threshold events or with trying to define precisely what linguistic capabilities particular ancestral species may have possessed. We recognize that there is evidence that chimpanzees can form very simple sentences (Greenfield & Savage-Rumbaugh, 1991), however, their abilities in this regard appear quite limited. What is certain is that members of the species *Homo sapiens* can produce complex sentences, and chimpanzees, our closest living relatives, cannot. This in turn implies that the earliest hominids could not do so either.

We propose that there was continuity with our prehuman ancestors, and this implies an interest in deriving syntax incrementally – precisely what many grammarians insist cannot be done. We believe that Edelman (1992) has provided a theory of neuronal architecture that makes possible just such an incremental scenario. We must briefly discuss Edelman's Theory of Neuronal Group Selection (TNGS). Edelman sees the ontogeny of neural structures as involving the selection of preexisting elementary neuronal groups and their assembly into increasingly complex structures. The selection process comes about through the organism's interactions with its environment, so that no two individuals have precisely the same end-state neural structures. This ontogenetic theory also clearly has a phylogenetic analog. To the extent that more complex structure confers selective advantage through the production of more behavior, complex structure could be built incrementally by means of natural selection.

We propose that visible gestural words/sentences could have provided the behavioral building blocks associated with neuronal group structures for constructing syntax incrementally, both behaviorally and neurologically. As we mentioned earlier, however, we differ with Edelman and others on the necessity for strictly simultaneous evolution of the human vocal tract and its interconnections with the neural mechanisms responsible for syntax. Our position is that embryo sentences are contained in visible, especially manual-brachial gestures. We have noted that the evolutionary development of the modern human hand began with the evolutionary development of bipedalism, the trait that characterizes the phylogenetic divergence of hominids and chimps. This can help us to understand the evolution of another characteristically human possession, a very large brain. We note that Perrett et al. (1989) have identified a neural substrate for perception of specific forelimb configurations in macaque monkeys.

The brain has experienced an evolutionary history not unlike what we would expect if language evolved incrementally; namely, it has increased in size fairly gradually from the australopithecines and *Homo habilis* through *Homo erectus* to *Homo sapiens*. If the arms and hands have provided raw material for the production of language since very early in the hominid lineage, and if language-cum-syntax has been built up from gestural embryo word-sentences, then it becomes possible to explain the evolution of a large brain prior to the appearance of the current configuration of the vocal tract. Explaining the large size of the brain and its staged increase prior to the appearance of anatomically modern *Homo sapiens* before the Upper Paleolithic is a major problem for those who believe that syntax arrived by mass mutation at that time.

We note also that there appears to have been gradual evolution
of the vocal tract from *Homo erectus* to anatomically modern *Homo
sapiens* (Laitman, 1985; Lieberman, 1991). To the extent that the
current configuration of the vocal tract is due to selection for
more efficient vocalization related to language, speech became
an increasingly important factor in human morphological evolution. We propose, however, that in the early stages of hominid
evolution, visible gestures took the lead.

Without positing incremental development of linguistic, i.e.
syntactic, capabilities, it is also more difficult to explain the *reorganization* of the brain that was apparently under way already
among the australopithecines. Although the cranial capacity of
australopithecines was probably not greater than that of chimpanzees, Ricklan (1990: 180) notes the following organizational
differences: "prominence of the inferior frontal convolution, forward placement of the brain stem, expansion of the parietal lobe
and reorientation of the cerebellum." All of these would be
implied in the elaboration of visual/gestural communication. It
has been suggested that there is evidence for Broca's area in
australopithecine endocasts. Although this remains controversial,
there is more general agreement that it is present in the first
representatives of the genus *Homo*; thus Tobias (1987: 753):

The presence of both a strong inferior parietal lobule and a prominent
motor speech area of Broca in the endocasts of *H. habilis* represents the
first time in the history of the early hominids that the two most important neural bases for language appear in the paleoneurological record.

We note that neurolinguistic research on deaf signers of ASL
(Poizner et al., 1987; Kimura, 1981, 1993) has shown that areas of
frontal and parietal cortex in the left hemisphere of the cerebrum
are critical to signing as well as speech.

We recognize that several other plausible scenarios have been
proposed for deriving language-cum-syntax from nonvocal behaviors. For example, Parker (1985) has proposed that visible/
gestural communication within the social group about subsistence activities played a major role in the evolution of language. That tool use and manufacture require cognitive

capabilities not dissimilar from those underlying language has been recognized by Holloway (1981), Gibson (1983), and others. We are in general agreement with these scenarios and with the hypothesis that language confers a selective advantage on social groups that have it. Nor do we deny that hominids have made use of the vocal tract for social communication from the very beginning. What we hope to add to the ongoing discussion is an understanding of the nature of the basic visible/gestural building blocks and a phylogenetic mechanism such as Edelman's TNGS for assembling them into complex sentences expressing complex ideas to interpretants capable of apprehending them. Throughout the course of this book, we will develop these arguments in support of a bodily basis for the origin and evolution of language.

CHAPTER 2

The nature of gesture

> The retinal image produced by the hand of a gesticulating
> speaker is never the same from moment to moment, yet the
> brain must consistently categorize it as a hand.
>
> Semir Zeki, *The visual image in mind and brain*

One way in which the central role of gesture in language can be understood is to consider gesture as a critical link between our conceptualizing capacities and our linguistic ability. This chapter will begin by exploring two opposing approaches to the study of language with special significance for how we might unify our understanding of spoken and signed languages. Next, we will explore the nature of gesture and how it is involved in the evolution and structure of human cognition. Then, we will demonstrate how visible gesture might link cognition to language.

In Chapter 7, we will develop the idea that visible gestures hold the seed of syntax. Here, we suggest that visible gestures played a pivotal role in the evolution of the cognitive capacities underlying linguistic competence. A critical function of the early conceptual abilities of hominids was to categorize an essentially unlabeled world of objects and events. Once we were able to categorize and conceptualize, visible (primarily manual) gestures – hands acting – were themselves categorized as prototypical *objects* and *actions* in the world. These capabilities led to the development of language and, once again, enabled us to marshall these concepts and articulators as linguistic symbols.

2.1 COMPARING SIGN AND SPEECH

Our claim is that gesture is a critical link running through the evolution of perception, conceptualization, and language. We also believe that linguistic description using the vocabulary of neuro-muscular activity or gesture can unify our understanding of signed and spoken language not only at the phonological level but also in their grammars.

Of course, we are not the first to attempt to unify signed and spoken languages. Where we differ with most previous attempts is in the manner of approaching the search for unity. In the following section we explore the most common alternative, the formalist approach.

2.1.1 The formalist approach: language disembodied

The most daunting barrier to unification of signed and spoken language is not to be found in lexicon, morphology, syntax, semantics, or pragmatics, but in the *actual substance* of the two language types. There is much confusion over this point. Sometimes speech is described in terms of the acoustic signal, other times in terms of the articulations which produce those signals. Likewise, signed languages are sometimes characterized as gestural (but rarely in the fine-grained articulatory phonetic detail which descriptions of speech enjoy), other times in terms of their visual perceptual characteristics. At the level of the proximal signal, spoken languages consist of acoustic signals which are perceived with the auditory apparatus; signed languages consist of optic signals perceived with the visual apparatus. At the level of the distal event, spoken and signed languages both consist of signal-producing gestures, but gestures produced by vastly different musculoskeletal systems.

Klima and Bellugi (1979: 39) claim that the modality difference – sound versus light – has structured signed and spoken languages in radically different ways:

Thus the lexical items of ASL and all other primary sign languages we know of appear to be constituted in a different way from those of spoken languages: the organization of signs [their sublexical or phonological organization] is primarily simultaneous rather than sequential. ASL uses a spatial medium;[1] and this may crucially influence its organization.

For the most part, current linguistic descriptions of ASL have relied on formalist linguistic theories. The predominant effort has been to demonstrate that ASL is indeed a language and can be described using theories of language developed for spoken languages. Further, it is often claimed that the findings of ASL linguistic research lend support to these theories of language.

These theories incorporate several powerful assumptions about the goals and expectations of linguistic investigation (cf. Langacker, 1991: 507–514). One assumption is that grammar is independent of meaning. From this assumption follows what Givón (1989: 94–95) calls three "pre-empirical postulates":

(1) Language is a separate module of the mind/brain, not part of "general cognition";
(2) Structuralism in the analysis of language; that is, language structure can be analyzed independently of its communicative function;
(3) The sign-relation between the linguistic code and its mental designatum is arbitrary, unlike the obvious iconicity seen in pre-human communication.

Another assumption is that the mental is independent from the physical. This leads to the view that linguistic units are mental things that cannot be identified with a set of articulatory, physical characteristics (Fowler, 1986: 9). This view is stated by Givón (1989: 95) as another postulate:

(4) Some abstract, idealized entity – be it *langue* or *competence* – is the "object" of linguistic analysis.

---

[1] Here, it seems, is yet another confusion over the nature of signed versus spoken languages. Spoken languages also use a spatial medium (cf. the vowel space and features such as [front], [high], and [back]). More precisely, Klima and Bellugi are referring to an optic versus an acoustic signal.

Concerning the phonology of spoken languages, the formalist approach assumes that speech can be segmented into a linear stream of phones, the actual acoustic substance. These phones are analyzed into sets of features and abstracted as relational entities or phonemes. Clearly, in undertaking such phonological description we are already engaged in categorization. The formalist approach relies on a long-standing and unchallenged set of assumptions about the nature of categorization which has been given the rubric of the "classical approach to categorization" (Edelman, 1992; Lakoff, 1987; Langacker, 1991). Taylor (1989: 22–29) outlines several basic assumptions of classical categorization as it relates to phonological description. The following are most pertinent to our discussion.

(1) **Categories have clear boundaries.** "A category, once established, divides the universe into two sets of entities – those that are members of the category, and those that are not" (Taylor, 1989: 23).

One especially significant claim about the structure of language related to this assumption is that language, especially in its phonology, is characterized by discrete as opposed to graded oppositions.

(2) **Features are universal.** The phoneme categories and features are intended to capture not merely the facts of one or several languages, but the sound-producing capabilities of humans (Chomsky and Halle, 1968: 297).

While this may seem a reasonable goal when we consider only one language type, it becomes less clear how a universal set of features is to be defined when we consider both signed and spoken languages. The physical substance of the two language types would seem to bar any universal inventory of features common to both. The solution to this dilemma is in the next assumption.

(3) **Features are abstract.** As Taylor (1989: 26) explains: "Features . . . can be thought of as representing the speech-

producing capabilities of man. And indeed, many of the features that have been proposed such as [vocalic] and [high], clearly make reference to aspects of phonation and articulation. Nevertheless, the features do not characterize the observable facts of speech, i.e. its generation in the human vocal apparatus, its acoustic properties, and its perception by the auditory system."

Instead, phonemes are seen as relational entities, independent of their material expression by human speakers and signers. It is "the relations between categories, rather than the physical properties of the members of the categories, which establish the value of any one category within the system. . . . [A]utonomous phonology splits off the act of speech as an articulatory, acoustic, and perceptual event from the abstract linguistic system . . ." (Taylor, 1989: 27).

Thus, the formalist approach to language provides the way out of our dilemma: if spoken language phonology must be described in terms of disembodied, abstract systems, so should signed language phonology.

Unfortunate conclusions result from the strategy of relying on the formalist approach to unifying signed and spoken languages. For example, a major conclusion of Poizner, Klima and Bellugi (1987) is that "language, independent of its transmission mechanisms, emerges in a . . . linguistically driven manner" (Poizner, Klima, & Bellugi, 1987: 23). It becomes clear in their book that these authors use the phrase "linguistically driven manner" to mean that language emerges in a formal, modular way, that is, that "language is amodal, taking a form which is independent of channel or of behavioral system" (Kimura, 1988: 375).

One problem with this position is that it assumes that the organization of language is independent of its motor programming (Kimura, 1988). Another is that it ignores the deep historical and neurological linkages between oral and manual gestures (Kimura, 1976, 1979), and between human movement, cognition, and language.

In fact, if language is truly amodal, independent of signaling channels, behavioral systems, and modes of production and perception, then we would predict that language would not exhibit any intermodal organization. However, there is strong evidence that language perception, production, and acquisition derive from just such an intermodal organization. Kuhl and Meltzoff (1982: 1139–1140), for example, remark that "it may be profitable to investigate infant speech perception as an inter-modal event. Studies of infants' intermodal organization of audi-tory, visual, and motor concomitants of speech may bring us closer to understanding the development of the human capacity to speak and comprehend language."

The point is significant not merely for the development of language in the child but also in the species. Commenting on the medium of amodality, Studdert-Kennedy (1986: 101) remarks that:

Characteristic motor systems have evolved for locomotion, predation, consumption, mating. Matching perceptual systems have evolved to guide the animal in these activities. The selection pressures shaping each species' perceptuomotor capacities have come, in the first instance, from physical properties of the world. By contrast, these per-ceptuomotor capacities themselves must have played a crucial role in the form of a social species' communication system . . . Certainly, specia-lized neuroanatomical signaling devices have often evolved, but they have typically done so by modifying pre-existing structures just enough for them to perform their new function without appreciable loss of their old . . . Language has evolved within the constraints of pre-existing perceptual and motor systems. We surrender much of our power to understand that evolution, if we disregard the properties of those sys-tems.

It is difficult to imagine how language – whether spoken or signed – could have ever developed in the human species in an amodal fashion. As B. F. Skinner (1957) noted, natural selection must operate on overt behavior, not on mental events. The via-bility of more substantive approaches to language has been dem-onstrated for spoken languages (Browman & Goldstein, 1990b; Bybee, 1985, 1992; Fowler, 1986; Givón, 1984; Mowrey & Pagliuca, 1988). The same approaches are also likely to be pro-ductive in signed language research.

The work of Carol Fowler provides an example of how we can avoid the mind-body dilemma which has been a barrier to developing a biologically and evolutionarily informed theory of language. It could also help us avoid the barrier to unification of signed and spoken languages that their actual substance imposes.

Fowler (1985) reminds us that language, whether planned or produced, is always realized in some physical medium. At the level of planning, this medium is neural; at the level of utterance, it is articulatory (gestural). There is no translation from mental to physical; there is only motor activity brought about by neural activity. This relation is shown in Figure 2.1a below (after Fowler 1985). Both signed and spoken languages are gestural; the difference is that spoken language gestures result in (primarily) acoustic signals, while signed language gestures result in (primarily) optical signals (Figure 2.1b; cf. Wilcox 1992 and Fowler & Smith 1986).

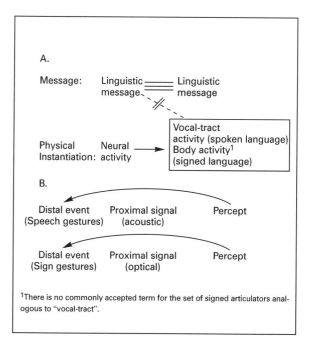

Figure 2.1

As Fowler points out, and we will discuss further in this and subsequent chapters, the relation of planned language unit to realization does pose problems. The properties of language forms at the message or mental level appear to be discrete, static, and context-free, while their realizations are coarticulated, dynamic, and context sensitive. When faced with these obstacles, one solution is to push back the problem. Thus, MacNeilage and Ladefoged (1976: 90) suggest that these abstractions are "too abstract to characterize the actual behavior of articulators themselves. They are, therefore, at present better confined to primarily characterizing earlier premotor stages of the production process."

Instead of upping the ante into the further reaches of mental abstractions, Fowler's counterargument places the game squarely in the realm of the physical.

Presumably, access to the neural activity going on as the message plan is constructed would offer no clearer picture of the critical properties of linguistic units than does access to vocal activity. Yet having witnessed the confusing neural activity, we would not conclude that "linguistic units should be recognized as too abstract to characterize the actual behavior of [populations of neurons] themselves" or that linguistic units are "better confined to primarily characterizing the earlier [preneural] stages of the production process." The buck has to stop somewhere. (Fowler 1985)

2.1.2 The cognitive alternative: language embodied

As the preceding discussion should make clear, we do not subscribe to the assumptions of the classical approach to categorization nor to an approach to the study of signed and spoken languages which relies on formalism and dualistic separation of mental or cognitive functioning from physical, embodied functioning. Rather, we prefer to look for the source of unification in the actual physical substance, in the acts of speaking and signing as articulatory and perceptual events.

It seems to us that language is not dualistically separated from its physical realization; rather, it is deeply rooted ontogenetically and phylogenetically in its bodily basis. Neither is grammar independent of meaning. This view is compatible with cognitive or functional theories of language such as those of Bybee (1985), Deane (1991), Givón (1989), Lakoff (1987), and Langacker (1987; 1991).

This alternative approach is certainly not new. Jesperson (1924: 17), for example, remarked that:

> The essence of language is human activity – activity on the part of one individual to make himself understood by another, and activity on the part of that other to understand what was in the mind of the first.

Deane (1993) outlines two broad approaches to language. The first stresses discontinuity between core linguistic abilities and other, broader domains: "Grammar is isolated and examined as an axiomatic formal system" (Deane, 1993: 8). The second view stresses continuity between language and other mental capacities: "Language is consistently placed in the context of its social and communicative functions. Linguistic structures, processes and categories are viewed as instantiations of the categories, processes and structures which comprise human intelligence."

Deane (1991) argues for this second view of language based on an elaboration of George Lakoff's (1987: 283) Spatialization of Form Hypothesis. According to the Spatialization of Form Hypothesis, grammar is ultimately spatial. Deane suggests that several predictions regarding the relation between grammar and cognition follow from this hypothesis (363–364):

> (i) According to the hypothesis, the acquisition of grammatical competence occurs when linguistic information is routed to and processed by spatial centers in the brain.
> (ii) Specifically, it is claimed that linguistic expressions are processed as if they were objects with internal structural configurations. That is, they are processed in terms of certain basic image schemas, namely part-whole and linkage schemas critical to the recognition of the configurations which define complex physical objects.
> (iii) But as Johnson (1987) argues at length, image schemas are basically embodied schemas, high level schemas which function as cognitive models of the body and its interaction with the environment.

In other words, the Spatialization of Form Hypothesis treats grammar as a form of image-schematic thought in which words, phrases, and

sentences are endowed with an abstract structure grounded in immediate bodily experience of physical objects. It therefore predicts an association between grammar and such cognitive abilities as object recognition,
spatial structure, and body awareness, especially modeling bodily movement and position in space.

Deane's proposal has important implications for many of the
claims we will be making. We will return to his theory of language
and cognition in section 2.9, where we discuss the role of spatial
cognition and visual perception in the origins of language.

In Chapter 7 we will describe in more detail a view of signed
language phonological structure which Stokoe has called *semantic
phonology*. Semantic phonology invites us to look at the signed
word in semantic terms as an agent-action construction.
Although many articulators are used in the act of signing, the
most salient are arms and hands. We suggest that human arms
and hands are – both phylogenetically and ontogenetically – prototypical and embodied complex objects. As we see it, semantic
phonology describes the "internal structural configurations" of
these objects as they are used to produce a natural language –
in this case, ASL.

But semantic phonology is much more than an alternative
approach to understanding the organization of ASL. It is, we
propose, a vital link in understanding how language could have
emerged from visible gestures. Thus, we propose a theoretical
position which makes the following assumptions:

(1) A linguistic theory must acknowledge the physically embodied
    grounding of language; in a very real sense, the body is in the
    mind (Johnson, 1987) – the essence of language is bodily
    activity.
(2) Physical, signal-producing gestures are the means by which
    signed and spoken languages are realized. While there are
    many differences between signed and spoken language articu-
    latory gestures, and indeed between linguistic and non-linguis-
    tic gestures, the key to understanding the human language
    capacity depends on exploring what unites them *qua gesture*
    (see Kimura, 1976).

(3) One further step in the pursuit of understanding the evolution of cognition, consciousness, and language is to recognize the key role played by the production and perception of visible gestures.

(4) Discontinuities of all types – language versus gesture, language versus general cognitive capacities (such as abstraction, categorization, judgments of similarity, etc.), language as amodal (independent of transmission system) versus language as intermodal (multiply linked to all human transmission systems) – are suspect; evolution prefers to build on prior systems rather than invent new ones (Gould, 1982; Hill, 1974).

Studdert-Kennedy (1985: 151) articulates a position compatible with ours in his discussion of phonetic perception as event perception:

If there is indeed a universal set of linguistic features that owes nothing to the nonlinguistic capacities of talkers and listeners, their biological origin must be due to some quantal evolutionary jump, a structure producing mutation. While modern biologists may look more favorably on evolutionary discontinuities than did Darwin, we are not justified in accepting discontinuity until we have ruled continuity out. This has not been done. On the contrary, the primacy of linguistic form has been a cardinal, untested assumption of modern phonology – with the result that phonology is sustained in grand isolation from its surrounding disciplines.

Semantic phonology challenges these assumptions not merely for signed language phonology but for what has been put forth as the very essence of language: duality of patterning. Not only does semantic phonology return phonology from its isolation from other disciplines, it also reunites it with the cognitive, perceptual, and motoric capacities of humans.

Other approaches to spoken language phonology have been put forth. They are, as would be expected, in tune with the arguments and assumptions we present in this chapter. Studdert-Kennedy (1985: 152) continues:

An alternative approach is to suppose that features and phonemes reflect prior organismic constraints from articulation, perception, memory, and learning . . . This work rests on a number of assumptions that might be challenged. Its importance does not rest on the correctness of its assumptions nor on the accuracy of its predictions. Its importance lies in the style of approach: substance-based rather than formal. For if we are to do the biology of language at all, it will have to be done by tracing language to its roots in the anatomy, physiology and social environment of its users. Only in this way can we hope to arrive at an account of language perception and production fitted to animals rather than machines.

2.2 WHAT IS GESTURE?

Notions about the nature of gesture abound but rarely are explicitly stated. Some writers clearly take gestures to be movements only of the hands and upper limbs; others include facial expressions. Some consider gestures as separate from (but sometimes cooccurent with) speech; others consider speech to be gestural. Gesture is also used to refer to many types of movements and posturing behaviors, not only in humans but in all moving creatures.

Gesture can be understood as neuromuscular activity (bodily actions, whether or not communicative); as semiotic (ranging from spontaneously communicative gestures to more conventional gestures); and as linguistic (fully conventionalized signs and vocal articulations). A common use of the term, perhaps the one most used in a lay sense, treats gestures as intentional, non-componential, symbolic structures: a single gesture represents a single meaning.

Several oppositions among speech, signs, and gestures are found in the literature. Some researchers would place signs and speech together as language, in opposition to gestures. This is the position, for example, of Burling (1993).

Burling distinguishes between what he sees as two fundamentally different forms of human communication: language and a gesture-call system. He asserts that it appears implausible that human language emerged as an elaboration or evolutionary outgrowth of our gesture-call system. As an alternative, he proposes that the place to look for the antecedents of language is in the cognitive abilities of primates.

We see at least two problems with Burling's analysis. First is the dichotomy between gesture and cognition. As we will demonstrate in this chapter, animal motoric activity, especially gesturing, was surely a critical element in the development of our cognitive capacities. Commentators on Burling's article also noted this problem. Parker (1993: 41), for example, counters with the following view: "First of all, minds are embodied rather than free-standing and therefore can only be apprehended through the actions of their bearers."

The second problem is the dichotomy between language and gesture-call. The single criterion for such an opposition, for Burling at least, is the principle of contrast. For example, Burling (1993: 28) writes:

Of the many features that distinguish the two main types of human communication, none is more important than the principle of contrast. The phonological system of a language, by imposing absolute distinctions on the phonetic continuum, is almost pure contrast, but we also can speak of words and even sentences as being in contrast . . . Graded intermediate positions between the distinct sounds, words, and sentences of a language are impossible. The result is a digital system of communication constructed of contrasting signals.

On the other hand, Burling continues, "the signals of our second form of communication vary, both in form and meaning, along continuous scales. This means that this kind of communication is not characterized by linguistic contrast and that it constitutes an analogical rather than a digital system." Human and animal gestures, Burling claims, "show pervasive grading, a feature that is missing from language."

It seems to us that Burling's claim that language does not show grading is overstated. Leaving aside the question of grading in phonology and the phonetic medium for the moment, there is abundant evidence of grading in language. Langacker (1991: 3) writes that "lexicon, morphology, and syntax form a continuum of meaningful structures whose segregation into discrete components is necessarily artifactual." Heine, Claudi, and Hünnemeyer (1991: 260) note that grammaticization chains (what happens on the way from lexeme to grammatical form) often behave like "continua with fuzzy boundaries" and "do not lend themselves to a taxonomic approach of language description in terms of discrete categories."

But Burling's strongest claim is that the basis of phonological systems is one of pure contrast. As we pointed out above, such a conclusion rests on the assumptions of classical categorization, namely that categories divide the universe into two, discrete sets. We have already been introduced to the unit of measurement for describing contrast under this view: the distinctive feature. It will be instructive to take a brief look at an alternative view as it pertains to distinctive features.

Bybee (1992) examines some of the problems of a view of phonology as pure structural contrast for spoken language phonology. She notes that distinctive features are not very useful in understanding the nature of phonetically conditioned processes such as coarticulation. As an alternative, Bybee proposes that "rather than abstracting away and regularizing in the name of establishing a small and coherent set of distinctive features, we must attend to the actual phonetic shape of linguistic units." Second, she notes that, like other componential features developed to model structure rather than substance, their constancy across realizations in different combinations is less real than imagined. This is important, because "words consist of real phonetic substance, in the lexicon [i.e., our mental representation of words] as well as in production and perception."

McNeill (1992) reports on an exhaustive study of gestures that accompany speech and comes to several conclusions about the nature of gesture. According to McNeill (1992: 41), properties of gestures (at least those that accompany speech) include:

(1) Global and synthetic. The meanings of the parts of a gesture are determined by the whole (=global), and different segments are synthesized into a single gesture (=synthetic). The global-synthetic property contrasts with the combinatoric linear-segmented property of speech and sign language.

(2) Noncombinatoric. Gestures don't combine to form larger, hierarchically structured gestures. Most gestures are one to a clause, but when there are successive gestures within a clause, each corresponds to an idea unit in and of itself.
(3) Context-sensitive. Each gesture is created at the moment of speaking and highlights what is relevant, and the same entity can be referred to by gestures that have changed their form.

The second property deserves special mention because it is often assumed that gestures of the type that McNeill describes and gesture-calls such as those described by Burling are not possible precursors to language because they lack a hierarchical structure. Later, we will explore ways in which it is possible to analyze these complex gestures as combinations of simpler gestures which are hierarchically arranged. Similar evidence of the underlying links between language, manual activity, and the ontogeny of hierarchically organized behavior is presented by Greenfield (1991).

Greenfield demonstrates a clear relation between the hierarchical organization in speech and language and combining objects with the hands. Through a review of several experimental studies of tool use in chimpanzees and children, adult and child aphasia, and object combination Greenfield finds solid support for a model which predicts that:

(1) The hierarchical organization of language and manual object combination is closely linked and interdependent in early development;
(2) The ontogeny of left frontal lobe circuits is implicated as the cerebral cortical basis for the hierarchical organization of speech and manual object combination.

Greenfield interprets this evidence to show that "the similarities between the ontogenetic development of combinatorial organization in language and manual object combination (including tool use) are homologous rather than analogous" (Greenfield 1991: 550).

For Greenfield and others, the seat of this homology is Broca's area. This interpretation flows from the belief that the essence of language is its hierarchical, structural organization. From our more substantive perspective, language is not essentially formal; rather, the essence of language is richly intermodal – it is motoric, perceptual, and kinesthetic. As we will see in section 2.9, Deane has proposed as the seat of grammatical competence a brain area which integrates just these modes – the inferior parietal lobule.

We are not the first to suggest a gestural origin of language. Hewes (1973; 1974; 1976) was one of the first modern proponents of a gestural origins theory. Kendon (1991: 215) also suggests that "the first kind of behaviour that could be said to be functioning in anything like a linguistic fashion would have had to have been gestural." For Kendon, as for most others who consider gestural origins of language, gestures are placed in opposition to speech and vocalization. Thus, as Kendon notes, the problem is to explain the change from gestural to vocal language:

All forms of language that we encounter today (with the exception of the relatively rare occurrence of primary, i.e., deaf sign languages and the even rarer development of alternative sign languages in speaking communities) are, of course, spoken. If language began as gesture, why did it not stay that way. . .? (Kendon, 1991: 215)

While we would agree with Kendon's strategy of examining the relationships among spoken and signed languages, pantomime, graphic depiction, and other modes of human representation, we are not convinced that placing gesture in opposition to speech leads to a productive framework for understanding the emergence of cognition and language. For us, the answer to the question, "If language began as gesture, why did it not stay that way?" is that it did.

2.3 SPEECH AS GESTURE

In contrast to those who seek to distinguish gestures from speech (and signs), a growing number of researchers are attempting to explain speech (but, oddly, not yet signs) *as gesture*. An early proponent of this approach was the cognitive psychologist Ulrich Neisser (1976: 156):

To speak is to make finely controlled movements in certain parts of your body, with the result that information about these movements is broadcast to the environment. For this reason the movements of speech are sometimes called *articulatory gestures*. A person who perceives speech, then, is picking up information about a certain class of real, physical, tangible . . . events.

Neisser rolls many important concepts into this rich passage. We will return in a later section to some of the points he raises, including the all-important link between the production and perception of gestures as real, physical, tangible events and the evolving capacity of human cognition as event perception.

According to Studdert-Kennedy (1987: 77), "the gesture is a *functional* unit, an equivalence class of coordinated movements that achieve some end." This view of gesture derives from the work of Kelso, Saltzman, and others (see, for example, Fowler et al., 1980; Kelso, Saltzman, and Tuller, 1986) who are developing a task-dynamic approach to speech. These researchers are attempting to unify linguistics, phonetics, and speech motor control by focusing on physical actions. For example, Kelso, Saltzman, and Tuller (1986: 31) write:

We outline a dynamic account of speech production that differs radically from views that characterize speech as a planned sequence of static linguistic/symbolic units that are different in kind from the physical processes involved in the execution of such a plan. Rather, we hypothesize that the coordinative structures for speech are dynamically defined in a unitary way across both abstract "planning" and concrete articulatory "production" levels.

A key concept in the task-dynamic approach is the *coordinative structure*. A coordinative structure is a functionally defined unit of motor action – an ensemble of articulators that work cooperatively as a single, task-specific unit. A related concept is synergy, functional complexes or ensembles which comprise classes of movement patterns or gestures. The notion of synergy was first described by Bernstein (1967), who recognized that there can be no one-to-one relationship between patterns of motor impulses and the movements they cause (Edelman, 1989). This lack of *invariants*, here between motor impulses and functionally defined units (gestures), will reappear in many forms throughout this chapter.

One of the most elaborated theories of speech as gesture is called gestural phonology (Browman & Goldstein, 1985, 1986, 1989, 1990a). According to Browman and Goldstein (1990b: 300), in gestural phonology:

the basic units are dynamically-defined articulatory gestures. These gestures are coordinative structures modeled in terms of task dynamics . . . [T]he gestures are defined in terms of speech *tasks*, the formation and release of various constrictions such as bilabial closure (for [b]). Such tasks typically involve the coordinated motions of several articulators rather than the independent motions of individual articulators.

Gestures understood as neuromuscular activity are present at various levels: several articulators *move* in a coordinated way to accomplish a *task*. But notice that the task is, for example, a bilabial closure, a [b]. The task at this level is merely a movement complex, it has no conceptual/semantic content and thus no symbolic function. Only when [b] is combined with other complex movement structures does it form a larger, bipolar structure which acts as a symbol – for example, a word.

In the gestural view of speech, words also are analyzed as gestural complexes: "words are not simply strings of individual gestures, produced one after the other; rather, each is a particular pattern of gestures, orchestrated appropriately in time and space" (Kelso, Saltzman, and Tuller, 1986: 31). Words are a "coordinated pattern of gestures . . . an articulatory program, or routine, composed of a few variable gestures" (Studdert-Kennedy, 1987: 78).

Sequentiality matters at all levels in such a description. Vocal fold vibration, glottis opening, lip closure, and so forth must follow a certain sequence in order to produce a [b].

Sequentiality also is involved in combining these gestures into larger ones (words, for example): 'bat' is not 'tab.'

Browman and Goldstein refer to gestural specifications as input to a gestural "score" that determines the actual trajectories that the articulators follow. Since these articulators are vocal tract articulators the result is the production of sounds. The output of all this is an acoustic signal. Browman and Goldstein call the relationship between gestural specifications and the acoustic signal "input-output relations."

The relation between gestures and the signal they produce is a critical point in understanding the organization of speech. As Browman and Goldstein (1990b: 302–303) explain:

Consider the case of a single gesture in isolation. Within the model, each gesture is a dynamical control regime that regulates the formation of a characteristic constriction within the vocal tract . . . The articulator motion determines, in turn, the time-varying shape of the vocal tract and thus the acoustic output . . . If the nature of multi-gestural structures in speech were such that the gestures were produced in strict, non-overlapping, sequence, the choice of input or output would not make a lot of difference . . . In real speech, of course, gestures overlap in time: they are coproduced. Thus, the acoustic output associated with a given gesture will vary as a function of other concurrently active gestures . . .

In Chapter 4 we will present evidence for precisely the same phenomenon in fingerspelling: the overlap of gestures in time as they are coproduced to form coarticulated fingerspelling. The point we wish to emphasize here is that gestural overlap of speech or signing poses a problem for perception, which is necessarily not of the gestures themselves *but of their consequences in the signal that they produce*. This fact is often overlooked in comparing gestures to speech: the difference is not in the form of production (both are articulatory movements of the body), but in the form of the signal. Some articulatory movements result in primarily acoustic signals. Others, including semiotic "gestures" as well as natural signed language, result in primarily optical signals.

2.4 THE TWO FACES OF GESTURE

In later sections we will implicate visible gesture in the origins of cognition and language. Naturally, the success of this task depends critically on what we mean by gesture. We do not disagree with researchers such as Kendon, McNeill, Burling, and others who demonstrate that there are grounds for distinguishing gesture from language, vocal-articulatory gestures from holistic gestures that accompany speech, symbolic from nonsymbolic gestures, and so forth.

But there are also deep links among these various classes of gesture. We believe that the only way to begin exploring the nature of gesture, and hence illuminate the role of gesture in the shadowy prehistory of human cognition and language, is by adopting a definition of gesture that allows us to link all types of functional movements. Our working definition of gesture is that of Studdert-Kennedy: *a functional unit, an equivalence class of coordinated movements that achieve some end.*

Our point of departure for understanding the nature of gesture is cognitive grammar. Langacker (1991: 2) states that "a linguistic system comprises just three kinds of structures: semantic, phonological, and symbolic (a symbolic structure residing in the relationship between a semantic and a phonological structure – its two poles)." Restating Langacker only slightly, we would analyze symbolic gestures as comprising three kinds of structures: conceptual, neuromuscular, and symbolic (Figure 2.2).

We conceive of gestures as complex structures at many levels. Whether a semiotic gesture (e.g. the "come here" gesture used in America) or a linguistic gesture (a signed word in ASL, such as FATHER), symbolic gestures are bipolar structures, combinations of substantive and conceptual (ultimately, of course, at the neuronal level even conceptual structures are substantive) structures. Their conceptual content is what gives them meaning. Their substantive content is what allows them to be shared (given that, as yet, we cannot transfer conceptual content directly from one mind to another). Their bipolar status is what gives them their communicative capacity.

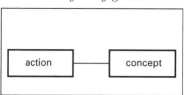

Figure 2.2

We analyze gestures even further, however, by examining their unipolar structure. That is, we recognize that both the neuro-muscular pole and the conceptual pole of symbolic gestures have internal structure. Here too, we find that gestures are complex structures, composed of smaller units.

Such an analysis is appropriate whether the larger structures we are examining are symbolic or non-symbolic gestures, and, if symbolic, whether the gestures are linguistic (signed or spoken words) or non-linguistic (gestures or gesture-calls). Again, for us, a gesture is an equivalence class of coordinated movements that achieve some end. Sometimes this end will never be symbolic at any level. In non-symbolic gestures, multiple articulators still work cooperatively to achieve a functional end – for example, the gestural task of a tree-dwelling monkey reaching for a vine. This end – reaching, grabbing, catching, holding, and releasing – is never precisely the same. Yet, the monkey must achieve it. Sometimes, the class of coordinated gestures will combine with others to form even more complex gestures which function communicatively – as when multiple vocal gestures (the coordinated movements required to produce a [b], for example) are combined with other gestures to form words, which then function as communicative (linguistic) gestures.

This realization can help us to resolve a bit of confusion about gestures. In the writings of researchers who study gestural communication (typically sociologists and anthropologists), gesture is often used to mean symbolic but non-linguistic structures. In the writings of speech scientists, phoneticians, and phonologists, gesture typically is used to refer to non-symbolic (unipolar), but nevertheless linguistic structures, which in combination form symbolic, communicative structures.

These many senses of the term gesture have usually been considered too distinct to be linked, either theoretically or biologically. In firm opposition to this view, we claim that it is critical to make such a link. In the continuity of gesture, its production, and its perception, we find potential solutions to several problems in the study of the origins of language.

2.5 PERCEPTUAL CATEGORIZATION

We have seen that the lack of invariants is a difficult barrier to overcome in understanding the relation between motor impulses and the functional gestures they produce. The precise selection and timing of the motor impulses necessary for a monkey to reach for and catch a tree limb while leaping are never the same, yet the monkey can reliably produce this functional gesture. And we can see that this ability would be under extreme selective pressure. An arboreal monkey that misses his grip is liable to be a dead monkey.

We also have seen that the relation between gestures (input) and the acoustic signal (output) is complex; there is no invariant relationship between gestures and the signals they produce. Studdert-Kennedy (1985: 142) explains:

If words are indeed formed from strings of consonants and vowels, and signs from simultaneous combinations of primes, we must suppose that the listener, or viewer, somehow finds these elements in the signal. Yet from the first spectrographic descriptions of speech[2] ... two puzzling facts have been known. First, the signal cannot be divided into a neat sequence of units corresponding to the consonants and vowels of the message. At every instant, the form of the signal is determined by gestures associated with several neighboring elements. Second, as an automatic consequence of this, the acoustic patterns associated with a particular segment vary with their phonetic context. The apparent lack of invariant segments in the signal matching the invariant segments of perception constitutes the anisomorphism paradox.

---

[2] In Chapter 4 we will relate this problem of perception in spite of variability to the perception of speech and sign and the claim of modularity. We note here that perhaps one reason this claim is even made for sign is the lack of anything like a spectrographic description (a description of the physical, optical properties) of sign.

The anisomorphism paradox exists not just for linguistic perception but also for visual (non-linguistic) perception. Consider the following problem. Look at some object in your environment, say a chair. Now get up, walk to another position in the room, and look at the chair again. You probably had no trouble recognizing the chair *as the same chair*.

As Biederman (1990: 42) notes, there would be very little problem explaining visual perception "if every time an instance of a particular class was viewed it projected the same image to the retina, as occurs, for example, with the digits on a bank check when they are presented for reading by an optical scanner." This is clearly not what took place when you looked at the chair from different locations. Biederman continues:

> But there is a fundamental difference between reading digits on a check and recognizing objects in the real world. The orientation in depth of an object can vary so that any three-dimensional object can project an infinity of possible images onto a two-dimensional retina ... Not only might the object be viewed from a novel orientation, it might be partially occluded behind another surface, or it might be broken into little pieces, as when viewed behind light foliage or drapes, or it might be a novel instance of its class, as for example when we see a new model of a chair. But it is precisely this variation – and the apparent success of our visual system and brain in achieving recognition in the face of it – that makes the problem of pattern recognition so interesting.

[handwritten marginal note: pattern recognition]

The recalcitrance of these and other examples of recognition in the face of variation can be grouped together as the general problem of perceptual categorization. Our environment is inherently ambiguous and unlabeled. "The number of partitions of potential 'objects' or 'events' in an econiche is enormous if not infinite" (Edelman, 1987: 3). The niche to which an organism must adapt is not partitioned according to logic into absolute, invariant categories. Rather, the problem for the organism is one of perceptual categorization, "a process by which an individual may treat nonidentical objects and events as equivalent ... in some sense, the problem of perception is initially a problem of taxonomy in which the individual animal must 'classify' the things of its world" (Edelman, 1987: 26).

The essence of all these problems is to explain "how perceptual categorization could occur without assuming that the world is prearranged in an informational fashion or that the brain contains a homunculus" (Edelman, 1987: 4). Edelman's solution to this problem, what he calls the Theory of Neuronal Group Selection (TNGS), is that the brain is a selective system operating on principles analogous to natural selection (Mayr, 1982). Edelman addresses one of the central problems we raise in this book: how to explain the emergence of language in an evolutionary, biological way. By so doing, Edelman also offers a glimpse into the nature of language as gesture.

2.6 THE ROLE OF MOTOR ACTIONS IN PERCEPTION

One result of adopting the definition of gesture that we have is that it encourages us to understand the connection between perceptual categorization, which plays a role in our cognitive capacities and our linguistic competence, and movement.

We start by noting Edelman's proposal that categorization must involve the operation of at least two separate sensory channels which supply signals to neural maps. Each channel independently samples a stimulus domain (Edelman, 1989: 49). Neural maps interact with each other in a process Edelman calls reentry, "a process of temporally ongoing parallel signaling between separate maps along ordered anatomical connections" (Edelman, 1989: 49). Still, this is not enough to explain perceptual categorization. Categorization requires multiple interactions among local maps resulting from sensorimotor activity. "This directs our attention to the moving organism, actively sampling its environment" (p. 54).

This final component Edelman calls a global mapping, a dynamic structure containing multiple motoric and sensory re-entrant maps that interact with non-mapped regions (such as the frontal lobes, the basal ganglia, and the cerebellum).

The concept of a global mapping takes account of the fact that perception depends upon and leads to action... the results of continual motor activity are considered to be an essential part of perceptual categorization. Neuronal group selection in global mapping occurs in a dynamic loop that continually matches *gesture* and *posture* to several kinds of sensory signals. (Edelman, 1989: 54–56) [italics ours]

Much the same point is made by others who attempt to describe how cognition is related to physical embodiment. Churchland (1986), for example, remarks that:

[B]rains are not in the business of pattern recognition for its own sake, and the nature of pattern recognition, as accomplished by brains, must be understood in the context of its role in how brains achieve motor control. Evolution being what it is, pattern recognition is there to subserve motor coordination... [I]f we ignore motor control as the context within which we try to understand pattern recognition, we run the risk of generating biologically irrelevant solutions... [A]s evolution solved the problems of sensory processing and motor control simultaneously, we may find it profitable – nay, *essential* – in shaping our theories, to mimic evolution and aim for simultaneous solutions as well. (473–474)

Similarly, Mark Johnson (1992: 349) relates our movement in and perception of an external, physical world to cognition and ultimately to language:

In order merely to survive we have to make an immense range of perceptual discriminations, identify recurrent objects and shapes, and move our bodies from one point to another. In other words, we have to discriminate figure/ground relations, objectify parts of our perceptual interactions, track objects through a perceptual field, exert force to move objects into various spatial relations (inside/outside, right/left, in front of/behind), and keep our balance as we move from one place to another. Among these sensorimotor activities just mentioned, we can recognize such recurring structures as object, figure-ground, source-path-goal, containment, compulsive force, and balance. Such recurrent patternings of our mundane bodily experiences are what Lakoff and I call image schemas. They are malleable, flexible patterns of perceptual and motor processes and activities.

It is important to recognize that the notion of image schema also relates to our previous discussion of formal versus embodied theories of language. Image schemata are not abstract relations between symbols and some objective, external reality. Rather, they organize our experience and understanding at the level of bodily perception and movement.

Varela, Thompson & Rosch (1991: 172) present very much the same argument in their attempt to study cognition not as the recovery of a pregiven, labeled outer world (realism) or a pre-given inner world (idealism), but as embodied cognition.

The notion of *embodied action* is intimately linked to the conception of language as gesture that we are developing here. By using the term *embodied* Varela, Thompson & Rosch (1991:173) draw attention to two important points:

Scaffolding

(1) cognition depends upon the kinds of experience that come from having a body with various sensorimotor capacities, and

(2) these individual sensorimotor capacities are themselves embedded in a more encompassing biological, psychological, and cultural context.

By using the term *action*, they imply that "sensory and motor processes, perception and action, are fundamentally inseparable in lived cognition. Indeed, the two are not merely contingently linked in individuals; they have also evolved together" (Varela, Thompson, & Rosch, 1991: 173).

They call their approach *enactive* and state that it consists of two major premises:

(1) perception consists in perceptually guided action, and

(2) cognitive structures emerge from the recurrent sensorimotor patterns that enable action to be perceptually guided.

In terms of the claims we are making, we may restate this by asserting that the cognitive structures that underlie language emerge from perceptually guided gestures, prototypically those made by the hands.

2.7 GLOBAL MAPPINGS, PRECONCEPTS, AND PRESYNTAX

Let us return to Edelman's theory of neuronal group selection for a moment. In the previous section we learned that global mappings in the brain match gesture and posture in the moving animal to several kinds of sensory signals. Edelman proposes that global mappings not only are necessary to explain perceptual categorization, but that they are also likely candidates for the brain structures responsible for concept formation. Among several properties of global mappings that lead Edelman to this conclusion, the following are important for our purposes:

(1) global mappings can correspond to objects, actions, and relations;
(2) by their nature, global mappings involve both spatial and temporal relations;
(3) global mappings can relate to classes of objects and movements.

Concept formation is thus linked evolutionarily and anatomically to perception, which itself depends on the organism's movements and gestures. Concept formation is driven by the organism's perceptual apparatus and corresponds to *things* and *motions* (Edelman, 1989: 141). "Ultimately, although concepts can be highly abstract, they are tied to objects (and actions) in the world" (1989: 146).

Once formulated, concepts can be placed in ordered relations. While clearly a precursor to syntax, Edelman argues that this new capability did not depend on anything like linguistic syntax: "a means of simply classifying, distinguishing, and temporally ordering event concepts and object concepts . . . would have represented a great evolutionary advance but would not have required symbols and grammar" (1989: 147). Edelman implicates reentrant mappings between temporal and frontal cortex and the basal ganglia as the basis for this new capability, which he calls presyntax.

In summarizing these proposals, Edelman (1989: 148) notes:

The view of concept formation and of presyntax presented here is closely tied through global mappings to the mechanisms of motor and perceptual sequences... [T]he structures underlying any conceptual functions must ultimately be tied to perceptual relations constrained by events in the world and the ability to identify such events.

2.8 EVENT COGNITION AND LANGUAGE

The next step is to link our ability to form concepts – especially concepts related to the perception of objects, actions, and relations – to language. Several linguistic approaches are suitable, including cognitive grammar (Langacker, 1987, 1991), cognitive semantics (Lakoff, 1987), and functional/typological frameworks (Bybee, 1985; Givón, 1984, 1989). In the following discussion we will rely primarily on Langacker's cognitive grammar.

Several tenets of Langacker's theory are important for our concerns. The first we have already seen:

(1) A linguistic system consists of only three kinds of structures: semantic, phonological, and symbolic, which is the relationship between a semantic and phonological structure. (Langacker, 1991: 2)

Langacker places several constraints on the types of structures that can be posited in a grammar. The most severe is the *content requirement*:

(2) Permitted structures are limited to overtly occurring expressions, to schematizations of permitted structures, and to categorizing relationships between permitted structures. (Langacker, 1991: 2)

Like the approaches pioneered by Fowler, Kelso, Browman and Goldstein, and Studdert-Kennedy to the study of speech, the content requirement forces the analysis to be grounded in physical substance, or in conceptualizations derived from the physical. Regarding the nature of the conceptualization process, Langacker notes:

These conceptualizations are not the result of processes carried out by an autonomous *faculté de langage*. Language is an integral part of human cognition; an account of linguistic structure must accord with what we know of cognitive processes. Language is embedded in the general psychological matrix and represents the evolution and fixation of structures having a less specialized origin. (Langacker, 1987: 13)

Finally, within the framework of cognitive grammar, grammar and meaning are not separate systems:

(3) Grammar reduces to symbolic relationships between semantic and phonological structures; grammatical structure is inherently symbolic and all grammatical constructs have conceptual import. (Langacker, 1991: 3; 1987: 282)

Most relevant for the present discussion is how cognitive grammar describes the conceptual foundation of grammatical structures. As an extended example, let us consider how cognitive grammar would ground the conceptual basis of two of our most basic grammatical categories, nouns and verbs, in our bodily experience of the world. Langacker offers what he calls the *billiard ball model* (1991: 13–14):

We think of our world as populated by discrete physical objects. These objects are capable of moving about through space and making contact with one another. Motion is driven by energy, which some objects draw from internal resources and others receive from the exterior. When motion results in forceful physical contact, energy is transmitted from the mover to the impacted object, which may thereby be set in motion to participate in further interactions.

Physical objects and energetic interactions stand in polar opposition to one another. To demonstrate this, Langacker analyzes the billiard-ball model into four components: space, time, material substance, and energy.

The essence of space and time is **extensionality**; together they provide a multidimensional setting within which the other two components are manifested. Moreover, we think of material substance as being manifested primarily in space . . . whereas energy is only observable through

change and thus requires time for its manifestation. I will therefore refer
to space as the **domain of instantiation** for material substance, and
time for change and energy. (Langacker, 1991: 14)

Physical objects are composed of material substance and thus
are instantiated in space. They are discrete – they have limited
spatial expanse. Finally, Langacker notes that objects are autonomous; their spatial existence does not rely intrinsically on
another object or on participation in an interaction.

Interactions, on the other hand, are quite different from objects
on these dimensions.

An interaction does not reside in physical substance, but rather in the
transfer of energy and the change thereby induced. Time and not space
is thus an interaction's domain of instantiation, and the domain in which
we think of it as being located. Also reversing what we observed for
objects, an archetypal interaction is discrete, compact and continuous
along the temporal axis, but spatially expansive: at the very least, its
spatial extension includes the locations of its various participants and the
trajectories they follow through its duration. Finally, an interaction does
not exist independently of its participants. Though we can perfectly well
conceptualize an object separately from any interaction involving it, the
conception of an interaction inherently presupposes some references –
however vague or schematic – to the entities through which it is manifested. (Langacker, 1991: 14)

Langacker (1991: 283) proposes that "the universality of nouns
and verbs and their centrality to grammatical structure stem
directly from the archetypal status of the billiard ball model."
Langacker's description of the conceptual underpinnings of grammar in physical objects and their interactions provides an integrated framework for understanding how language and cognition
might be derived from prior systems based on perception and
movement of the human organism. Langacker's notions of the
nature of grammar are also clearly similar to Stokoe's use of
syntactic structure in semantic phonology.

Langacker (1991: 284–285) also derives semantic roles from the
structure of embodied events:

I do not believe that semantic roles are first and foremost linguistic constructs, but rather prelinguistic conceptions grounded in everyday experience . . . In order to call attention to their primal status and nonlinguistic origin, I refer to these as **role archetypes** . . . These archetypes reflect our experience as mobile and sentient creatures and as manipulators of physical objects. The archetype **agent** is a person who volitionally initiates physical activity resulting, through physical contact, in the transfer of energy to an external object. Its polar opposite is an archetypal **patient,** an inanimate object that absorbs the energy transmitted via externally initiated physical contact and thereby undergoes an internal change of state.

A final, and in our view critical aspect of Langacker's formulation of cognitive grammar is the recognition it gives to the deep connections between visual perception, event cognition, and language. This is embodied in another model, the *stage model.*

A second basic model pertains to perceptual experience. Let us call it the **stage model,** for the role of perceiver is in many ways analogous to that of someone watching a play. An observer's gaze is generally directed outward, toward other objects. At any moment his field of vision subtends only a limited portion of his surroundings, within which his attention is focused on a particular region, just as a theater-goer focuses his attention on the stage . . . There is further organization along the temporal axis, where clusters of contiguous interactions (particularly those involving the same participants) are perceived as forming discrete **events.** (Langacker, 1991: 284)

These models can be combined and summarized as a *canonical event model* (Figure 2.3). We see here fertile ground for the origins of language in the visually observable movements of interacting, internally complex objects. We submit that the canonical event is deeply connected to a homologous, *canonical gestural event* consisting of visible, manual gestures (Figure 2.4).

2.9 VISIBLE GESTURES: SEEING LANGUAGE

Early in this chapter, we suggested that a question posed to researchers who argue for gestural origins of language, namely, "If language began as gesture, why did it not stay that way?" is

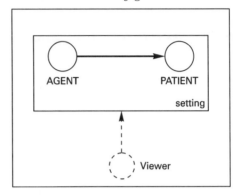

Figure 2.3 Canonical Event Model

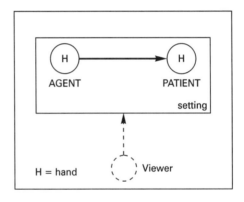

Figure 2.4 Canonical Gestural Event

the wrong question. All language, in the words of Ulrich Neisser (1976), is "articulatory gesturing."

We are not proposing that language began as gesture and became vocal. Language has been and always will be gestural (at least until we evolve a reliable and universal capacity of mental telepathy). We would suggest that a more productive question is, "Since articulatory gesturing can result in both acoustic and optical signals, which type is more likely to have been implicated in the ontogenesis of the human language capacity?" We believe there is solid evidence in favor of *visible* gestures.

The importance of vision, and the connection between visual perception and motor production in the emergence of our cognitive abilities, is a central theme in the work of Edelman, as we have seen above. For example, we pointed out that Edelman places great emphasis on the basal ganglia in the emergence of presyntax. This emphasis on the basal ganglia is especially significant because of the connection of brain structure to visible gestures. There is ample research suggesting that the basal ganglia are involved in the planning and coordination of motor acts (DeLong et al., 1984; Mitchell et al., 1987). In addition, Edelman (1989: 137) suggests that "the basal ganglia may provide a major coupling between sensory responses and motor responses, particularly those involving identity of visual cues for planned action."

The role of vision, as well as the rich intermodal organization of language, is explicit in the work of Deane (1993). As we learned in section 2.1.2, Deane's linguistic theory is built on the Spatialization of Form Hypothesis, which claims that grammatical knowledge is grounded in conceptual metaphor. In turn, conceptual metaphor operates by projecting image schemata onto other cognitive domains. We also learned that image schemata are embodied, they are representations of recurrent, structured patterns which emerge from bodily experience.

Image schemata, according to Deane, are the very stuff out of which cognition and language are built. Some basic image schemata include (Johnson, 1987: 126): CONTAINER, ENABLEMENT, LINK, NEAR-FAR, MERGING, CENTER-PERIPHERY, COMPULSION, and PART-WHOLE.

Embodied image schemata clearly reflect the intermodal nature of language. Image schemata rest on the full range of perceptual grounding, including visual, auditory, and motoric-kinesthetic.

All of this leads Deane to propose a controversial yet bold hypothesis: "grammatical competence is critically represented in a brain region (or regions) whose primary function is to represent the BODY schema and other high-level image schemata. This region should be situated in an area of the brain where information from visual, auditory, kinesthetic, and other sensory modes converge and may therefore be integrated" (Deane 1993: 278). This leads to a strong prediction about brain function: the seat of grammatical competence is the inferior parietal lobe. As evidence for this hypothesis, which he calls the Parietal Hypothesis, Deane offers the following:

(1) the inferior parietal lobe (IPL) is the seat of bodily awareness and orientation to extrapersonal space. Patients with parietal brain damage display such bodily awareness disorders as postural disorders; phantom limbs; failure to recognize a limb, often a hand, as one's own; loss of awareness of fingers; and difficulties with certain abilities strongly connected to the use of the hands and fingers (handwriting, distinguishing left from right). In fact, some researchers have described the hand as "largely the organ of the parietal lobe" (Critchley, 1953: 210).

(2) the IPL is the seat of the capacity to represent and manipulate complex spatial relationships, including the capacity to recognize complex objects by the nature of the arrangement of their parts.

(3) the IPL appears critically necessary for the construction of sequential action plans, that is, for the manipulation of action sequences as mental wholes.

(4) parietal damage can cause a variety of language disorders including global aphasia, aggramaticism, reading disorders, and logicogrammatical disorders.

(5) the IPL is concerned with integrating bodily sensation with sensory perception, particularly visual perception. The IPL is at the intersection of the visual, auditory, and tactile regions of the cerebral cortex. Damage to the parietal lobe can cause loss of vision in one half of the visual field; one-sided visual neglect; and visual disorientation involving the inability to use visual information to guide bodily movements.

Whether or not Deane's theory proves correct in all details, it certainly points the way to the integration of cognitive, perceptual, and motoric capacities in the service of linguistic competence. It also strongly suggests that visual gesturing was important in the origin of language.

More evidence for the deep connections among visible gestures, semantic archetypes, event perception, and language comes from the work of Perrett and his associates (Perrett, Mistlin, & Chitty, 1987; Perrett et al., 1989). Recall that semantic phonology invites us to look at the manual, visible gesture in semantic terms as agent-action, or often as action-object interactional constructions. Perrett has discovered cerebral cortical cells in the superior temporal sulcus of macaque monkeys that respond to visual displays of goal-centered activities of the type where human subjects would attribute causal and intentional relationships. For example, some cells respond quite selectively when macaques view seven different actions: reach for, retrieve, manipulate, pick, tear, present, and hold. Other cells clearly differentiate between the agent of the action. For these cells, a clear sensitivity was found for hand-object interactions (watching a hand approach food) compared to object-object interactions (watching a control bar of similar size to an arm and hand approach food).

Perrett demonstrated that cell responses were dependent on the interrelationship of hand and object movements. In this portion of the study, monkeys observed four action sequences: (1) a hand manipulating an object (a large piece of fur), (2) hand movement (no object visible), (3) the object deforming (no hand visible), and (4) a hand "manipulating" and an object deforming, but both are spatially separated by 3-4 centimeters. The response of the cells to the sight of a hand manipulating an object was significantly greater than to other conditions or spontaneous activity.

Perrett's experimental results also demonstrate the notion of a gesture as a functional unit, an equivalence class of coordinated movements that achieve some end. Perrett (1989: 109) writes that "actions can be achieved by a variety of means. In a trivial sense the act of reaching for a target can be achieved from a variety of starting positions using the same type of arm movement, though aimed in different directions. In a more fundamental sense, entirely different body movements can achieve the same goal." In another experiment using visual stimuli presented to macaques, Perrett demonstrates single cell sensitivity to viewing achievement of goals by different means (Perrett et al., 1989: 109–110):

This cell responded to hand movements which carry an object contained in the hand towards the mouth. Hand movements directed to other parts of the body were less effective – and movement of an empty hand to the mouth was also ineffective. The act of bringing an object and the mouth together can also be achieved by leaving the hand static and moving the whole body and head so that the mouth moves closer to the object. Such movements were also effective in activating the cell . . . Furthermore, the action could be completed with the entire body remaining stationary and the object moved towards the mouth by a second individual. Again, such movements activated this cell.

Perrett's conclusions are instructive for our arguments (Perrett et al., 1989: 111): "The finding of cells in the monkey brain that are selective for the sight of actions and which are unaffected by auditory cues associated with actions indicates the extent to which meaningful relationships can be derived purely within the visual modality, without the reliance on the capacity for language."

The role of vision in the origin of language has been a central theme in the work of Alexander Marshack (1984, 1992). Marshack believes that language is a mode of referencing objects, processes, and relations which is ultimately dependent on the human visual system and its capacity for differentiating types of objects, categories, processes, and relations (Marshack, 1992).

Marshack draws his evidence from the large body of human symbolic imagery which coincides with the appearance in Europe of anatomically modern humans c. 35,000 BP. These imaging systems integrate capacities involving the use of vision and the hands. Marshack does not argue for separate, modular capacities for "art" or "language" but rather for "a long slow process of mosaic evolution involving the development and integration . . . of the full set of cognitive capacities that would support and mediate both the visual and linguistic referential and productive modes" (Marshack, 1992: 421). Although we treat hypotheses for the recent emergence of language critically in Chapter 8, we agree with Marshack's proposals concerning gradual, mosaic evolution.

Marshack also posits a central role for bipedality in the emergence of language, which he claims resulted in a neurological restructuring involving the "asymmetric hemispheric specialization required for the developing two-handed, vision-mediated problem solving capacity of a bipedal hominid" (Marshack, 1992: 423). The hands, according to Marshack, can be used not only for climbing, problem-solving, and food-gathering, but also for affective forms of communication and relation, "forms that are always, once again, mediated and evaluated by vision. The protohominid neurology was there apparently already predisposed and structured at a number of levels for affective and referential forms of meaningful communication by both vocalization and a use of the hands" (Marshack, 1992: 428). These arguments are again central to the scenarios for language evolution that we develop later in this book.

Marshack (1992: 429) proposes that "the true 'deep structure' of language . . . is provided by our perception, abstraction and categorization of the objects and processes of the visual world." What more salient objects and processes existed in our common ancestral visual world than our hands and the gestures they make?

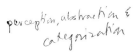

CHAPTER 3

Are signed and spoken languages differently organized?

The fact that signed languages use as articulators the hands, face, and body rather than the vocal tract suggests that spoken and signed languages might be vastly different from one another and that signed languages might lack some of the properties shared by grammars of spoken languages . . . However, despite the differences in resources provided by the two forms of communication, signed languages have been demonstrated to be highly constrained, following general restrictions on structure and organization comparable to those proposed for spoken languages.

H. Poizner, E.S. Klima, and U. Bellugi,
What the hands reveal about the brain

3.1 LANGUAGE FROM A DIFFERENT PART OF THE BODY

Shortly after a signed language used by deaf people was first studied as a language and not as a speech surrogate or secondary code (Stokoe, 1960), it became obvious that information about non-vocal languages might shed light on the nature of language in general. Questions about the possible origin and development of language, whether it evolved from general cognitive capacities or without need of them, whether it resulted from unique and identical neural structures in every brain – these and other questions might well be reexamined in the light of information about language without speech. Many studies of ASL, however, have been based on the untested assumption that language structure is everywhere the same – the same no matter where in the world, the same now as when language began, the same in every brain, the same whether expressed vocally or visibly. Whatever the outcome may be of debates about language theory, differences between signed languages and spoken languages merit careful consideration, for they may help to answer the question of innateness, and whether language evolved or happened all at once.

The trouble is that serious consideration of signed languages as languages has to overcome a further assumption: that only spoken languages are really languages. Thus, in his *Language and linguistics: an introduction*, John Lyons suggests that, "'sign language', 'body language' or 'the language of the bees' would be considered by most people as a metaphorical use of the word 'language'" (1981: 2).

He also dismisses "the language of the deaf and dumb" and bases his entire description of language and language structure on "The sounds of language" (title of his Chapter 3). This is puzzling, because in a lecture "What is language?" at Christ's College, Cambridge, in 1977, Lyons said that words of a language could be made from visual/gestural as well as vocal material. Perhaps he was there considering as words only one kind of visible gesture – those treated like words by speakers and often called "emblems" (Efron, 1941; Ekman & Friesen, 1978). In his 1981 introduction, however, Lyons implies that only vocal material can be the basis of natural languages.

This confusion of sign languages, on the one hand, with phenomena like the language of bees (termed languages only metaphorically), and on the other hand with body language, kinesics, gesticulation, and other behaviors closely associated with language use, is understandable: the boundaries and the nature of language, communication, and interaction are studied by several disciplines, and these disciplines are themselves in dispute over boundaries.

In a monumental study of Aboriginal Australian sign languages, Adam Kendon distinguishes between two kinds of sign language, both of which serve, as all language does, to mediate general and special interaction:

"*primary sign languages*" are languages used by deaf people as their first or only language; "*alternate sign languages* are systems . . . typically developed for use as an alternative to speech in circumstances where, for whatever reason, speech is not used". Both these, of course, differ from *"manually coded language* . . . developed by educators as a means of conveying spoken languages to the deaf by manual actions." (Kendon, 1989: 2–5)

Counter to the widespread belief that the words of languages must be composed of vocal material, the material composing words in the primary sign languages of deaf populations is visual. The observer of a single unfamiliar action could not be sure whether it was a "gesture" (as that term is generally understood) or a "word" of a sign language. We take the position here that the *organization* of primary sign languages is different from the organization of spoken languages, and that the differences do indeed shed light on the physiological, structural, and symbolic nature of language in general – and its evolution (Chapters 7 and 8). However, as we argued in the previous chapter, language in general, whether signed or spoken, shares a common *cognitive* substrate, based on the embodiment of grammatical processing, and a common purpose – to enable communication, and thus human social life.

The dismissal of "the language of the deaf and dumb" in the Lyons textbook is not exceptional: a great many treatments of language and linguistics are still based on the unexamined assumption that language is inseparable from speech. Thus, Calbris, after examining French gestures, concludes with the following short paragraph (note that her use of the adjective *verbal* implies that only the vocal is language, not what is "intended to replace" it):

While they are intimately linked, gestural and verbal signs differ in the way they operate. This difference is flagrant if one compares the operation of a complex, coverbal gesture with that of a compound gesture in sign language, which is intended to replace verbal language. (1990: 208f)

But, of course, a primary sign language does not and was not intended to replace spoken language; it is intended, on the contrary, to perform for a community of persons who cannot hear and may not be able to speak, all the functions that spoken languages perform for those who can.

In a similar misunderstanding, Feyereisen and de Lannoy, begin the third chapter of their *Gestures and speech: psychological investigation* with this statement: "Gestures may substitute for words, as demonstrated by the creation of sign languages . . ." (1991: 49). Further into the book, they note: "Deaf-mutes, like hearing children, use gestures in their engagement with persons and objects" (p. 114).

These statements are true but they stop short of complete truth (see also Stokoe, 1992: 185–190). Hearing and deaf persons may indeed use sign language signs (words) to stand for spoken words, but that does not mean that primary sign languages are created by substituting visible actions for spoken or written words. Interpreters and translators as well as linguists are well aware that, for rendering discourse, a word-for-word matching between two languages can never be exact, even when the two are as closely related as are English and German. An attempt at sign-for-word matching of a primary sign language with a language spoken in the same region (e.g. ASL with American English) shows even greater incongruity: often one ASL word needs a string of English words to translate it accurately, and the polysemy of a single English word may require choosing among several different words of ASL.[1] While it is true that visible gestures, especially those called emblems, may substitute for words, deaf adults (and deaf children in deaf families), "in their engagement with persons and objects," not only use these gestures, as these are commonly understood, but they also use sign language words, which have developed out of visual gestures. In searching for the organizing principles of language it is necessary to distinguish among signed languages, systems of visible gestures, kinesics, and gesticulation; nor is it furthered by the belief that deaf people's sign languages were created, by them or by hearing people, solely to provide them with access to language through word substitutes or speech surrogates.

---

[1] Kendon (1989) shows that an *alternative* sign language, that used by the Walpiri people, does indeed match in a great many respects the language that the Walpiri speak.

Although language is a medium of social interaction and has a symbolic function, some linguists continue to maintain that its constituents at the level of physical expression can be nothing but vocally produced sound. This is also only part truth: the primary sign languages of deaf people are built from and expressed by different kinds of constituents. Deaf people's languages were excluded from linguistic inquiry for a very long time because deaf people, the institutions in which they were educated, and general knowledge about them were intentionally closed off as the private territory of "experts on deafness."

In the first half of the twentieth century, a period of intense linguistic inquiry, linguists dismissed sign languages from their field of study because the self-styled experts in deafness and "the psychology of the deaf" whom they consulted unanimously maintained that sign languages were not languages but were vague and incomplete visual substitutes for speech. Taking their lead from the medical profession, most psychologists and educators of the deaf have long considered deafness as pathology. To them deaf persons were not linguistically and culturally different but sick and in need of the "oralist" treatment – treatment that only they, "the experts," were able to provide. After the World Congress of Educators of the Deaf in Milan, 1880, the treatment was everywhere understood to be teaching deaf children to read speech visually from a speaker's face (i.e. to read lips) and to produce artificial speech monitored not by themselves but by speech therapists who kept them trying until the therapists pronounced it intelligible (Lane, 1984).

Early twentieth-century linguists (e.g. Bloomfield, 1933), if they considered signing at all or recognized its difference from fingerspelling, turned to these "experts" and, without further consideration, accepted the testimony of interested witnesses, whose professional careers depended on repressing sign language use and describing it as a vague, imperfect, and broken code. Linguists at that time wanted to study the language of "the normal," and the professionals they consulted about sign language described deaf people as abnormal.

Once it became possible to bring to the attention of scholars the fact that deaf persons indeed have natural languages – languages

with words made from visible actions, it seemed that new information about the nature of language might come to light (Carroll,
1961; Lunde, 1956; Stokoe, 1960). But by this time, linguists'
attention was shifting from the careful study of languages as
people use them to theories that all languages are generated by
a universal system of rules innate in the human brain. As a result
much recent writing on sign languages has been in support of that
formalist theory.

3.2 DESCRIBING SIGNED LANGUAGE

Here it will be useful to review briefly some of the short history of
modern linguistic description of signed languages. The earliest
(Stokoe, 1960) proposed to treat the sublexical components of
signs, as aspects, i.e. what appears when something is looked at
in a particular way. When signs of a signed language are looked at
not as fitting preconceived rules but in their different aspects, the
action of a sign is looked at as motion, irrespective of what is
moving; the hand configuration is looked at as if it were at rest
(the only way its details may be fully discerned); and the location
where the activity is concentrated is looked at as a place no matter
what activity happens there. "The sign morpheme . . . unlike the
word, is seen to be not sequentially but simultaneously produced.
Analysis of the sign cannot be segmented in time order but must
be aspectual" (Stokoe, 1960: 39f)

Three simultaneous aspects of the sign morpheme were at first
considered: location (where the action takes place), the configuration of the hand or hands acting, and the action or
motion. Later, analysts complicated instead of simplifying sign
description; they proposed that such things as orientation, (the
hand's) facing, its contacting part, and the point of contact be
seen as something more categorical than aspects. Of all this
Kendon observes:

Other writers on sign language have introduced other terms. Thus,
Klima and Bellugi (1979) proposed *parameter* for what is here called
the aspect of a sign, and *prime* for particular organizations within an
aspect, such as a particular handshape, location, or movement. I have

avoided using these terms . . . They are borrowings from mathematics, and do not seem to be appropriate. (1988: 9)

Like the identification of aspects, the question "simultaneity or sequentiality?" is central. Liddell (1984) identified brief moments of time in which no motion is seen and more numerous moments in which the hands move, but this discrimination has been difficult to replicate. There is indeed a time element, but only myographic or even more invasive neurological investigation can detect it with precision; for what happens in signing is very similar physiologically to what happens in speaking: many larger and smaller muscles and muscle groups are put into play with extremely subtle differences in timing. Moreover, any skilled activity whatsoever requires the appropriate sequencing of movements.

An instant before the salient action or motion of a manual sign is effected by the muscles of the arm and hand, those muscles or others must have acted to produce the sign's handshape. The rapid succession of signs in actual sign language conversation is produced by actions of muscles, both to configure the acting hand or hands and to produce the distinctive motions. These (large and small) muscle actions occur with such rapidity that normal visual observation can hardly distinguish which of them are sequential, which simultaneous, and which overlap in time. Liddell, of course, used the technique of slow motion viewing of signs produced in isolation and recorded on videotape to distinguish movement from (relative) motionlessness, but in something as complex as language behavior, the timing of muscle action (in speaking or in signing) may be too swift and complex for direct observation to reveal very much about it.

The analysis of the components of single words, or of single signs produced in isolation yields quite different results from analysis of stretches of rapid signed or spoken discourse. The vocal gestures for vowel production in speech are influenced by preceding or following consonants, and vowels can similarly change the usual way of producing consonants. Signing is likewise subject to coarticulation; this similar or analogous motor activity does not change the fact that signing and speaking are detected by different perceptual systems and consequently involve quite different neurological substrates.

3.3 SEEKING ORGANIZATIONAL SIMILARITY AT THE SUBLEXICAL LEVEL

A recent work by Liddell and Johnson (1989) illustrates many of the difficulties inherent in the application of structural/formalist linguistics to the phonology of signed languages. In their monograph entitled,"American Sign Language: the phonological base," they undertake "the ambitious goal of outlining the phonological structures and processes we have analyzed in [ASL]." Their abstract continues (emphasis added):

In section 1 we detail the types of sequential phenomena found in the production of individual signs, allowing us to argue that ASL signs are composed of sequences of phonological segments, *just as are words in spoken languages*. Section 2 provides the details of a segmental phonetic transcription. Section 3 briefly discusses both paradigmatic and syntagmatic contrast in ASL signs. Section 4 deals with the various types of phonological processes at work in the language, processes remarkable in their similarity to phonological processes found in spoken languages. . . (1989: 195)

The central theme of their essay in ASL phonology is that two kinds of feature bundles combine sequentially to form ASL words – the two differing dynamically: in the first bundle, the hand or hands are in motion; in the other hands are (relatively) stationary. Called "move" and "hold," these are analogous to vowels and consonants in spoken morphemes and words:

The segment is the central element in our view of the structure of signs . . . Segments in sign languages are composed of two major components. One describes the *posture* of the hand; the other describes its *activity*. A description of the posture of the hand is concerned with where it is, how it is oriented, how its own movable parts are configured and so on. The features that describe these details are collectively called articulatory features. We refer to combinations of articulatory features needed to specify a given posture of the hand as an "articulatory bundle". . . . [which] contains four major clusters of features . . . *hand configuration, point of contact, facing,* and *orientation* . . . (209)

The features that specify the activity of the hand during the production of the segment are grouped into a separate segmental feature bundle. They describe whether or not the hand is moving, and, if so, in what manner. The elemental work of this class of features is to distinguish movements from holds. *Movements* are defined as periods of time during which some aspect of the articulation is in transition. *Holds* are defined as periods of time during which all aspects of the articulation bundle are in a steady state (1989: 208ff).

Speaking of the major clusters of features, Liddell and Johnson say, "We have found more than 150 HCs (hand configurations) in ASL lexical signs. Many more occur in the surface forms of running sign" (p. 223). On the score of complication, it is interesting to compare this count of 150+ HCs in ASL with 15 (Stokoe, 1960) and 19 (Stokoe, Croneberg, and Casterline, 1965) in earlier descriptive systems. The early inventories were clearly undercounted; e.g., the 1960 "fist" handshape (symbolized 'A') was lumped together with the fist with thumb extended and the fist with thumb opposed (later symbolized respectively 'Å' and 'S'), which do make contrasting pairs of signs. However, the ongoing muscular activity used to produce the lexical units of signed languages not only composes the hand into a distinctive appearance for a sign but also changes that appearance for the next sign in the sequence. Furthermore, it changes the direction that some or all parts of the hand are facing or pointing. It is not clear whether Liddell and Johnson consider their 150 hand configurations all to be "target" forms fully realized in recorded data, or as hypothetical constructions that come from considering signs in isolation. The phenomenon of coarticulation throws considerable doubt on the accuracy, and the possibility of achieving accuracy, in any attempt to describe as stationary a hand or hands constantly changing both configuration and location, as happens in signed language use.

This brings up another general problem in sign phonology, that of sign "orientation." Liddell and Johnson maintain that:

The orientation of the hand is important in ASL signs, for both lexical contrast and morphological functioning. It appears that signs make use of two dimensions functioning together to orient the hand. The first of these is *facing*, which "points" a part of the hand at a location. The second is *orientation* proper which usually indicates which part of the hand is pointing toward the ground. (1989: 234)

We maintain that it is not abstract space but human anatomy that orients a gesture. A hand or two hands (HCs) having exactly the same configuration of fingers and thumb can be used in contrasting signs otherwise identical; e.g. striking the palm of one hand repeatedly with (a) the palm, (b) the back, or (c) the ulnar edge of the other hand signifies, respectively, in ASL: 'school,' 'money,' and 'stopping.' Presumably the palm in the first is "facing" the other palm; in the second, facing away from the hand's target; and in the third, facing neither way. Liddell and Johnson's "*orientation* proper" would specify that the palm, the back, and the edge, respectively, "point" to the ground. If astronauts in space were to communicate in ASL, "orientation proper" would become a major problem. Again, it is not abstract space, but human physiology that "orients" a gesture.

A sign language phonology that looks through the outward appearance to find the physical causes of that appearance discovers at once that in all such contrasts, indeed in all manual signs of sign languages – as well as in gesticulation, and in what are *generally* understood by use of the term *gestures* – the spatial "dimensions" of "facing" and "orientation" of the hand are impositions from without. What, in fact, produces the differences between visible gestures is muscle action on arm, hand, and finger bones. It should be noted, however, that in a primary sign language, signs identical in arm-hand action may be made "different" by head or face action or both. In the examples above, the major muscle action that causes one hand to strike the other is identical (extension of forearm); the difference comes from the muscles acting an instant earlier that rotated the bones of the forearm, turning the hand, respectively, in pronation and supination and holding it unrotated. Still, significantly, we are left with *body parts acting.*

It is not necessary to accept unquestioningly the Whorfian idea that the language one acquires shapes the universe one perceives to realize that early deafness – a non-functioning auditory system from birth or infancy – forces acquisition of language as well as socialization by eye instead of by ear and thus may directly affect neuronal development (see Neville, 1977). While observers of sign language behavior may make use of the coordinates of Euclidean space in their descriptions, deaf signers respond to sign actions as visible instantiation of actions they also perform, with their own musculature, for the same purposes. Of course, in normal circumstances, it is the meaning of the sign words and sign sentences that signers take in; but they can reproduce what they have seen instantly without resorting to abstract geometry. This makes it likely that they have acquired language as a cognitive system closely linked in the brain with vision and motor behavior. Being without the ability to hear language sound, they cannot have developed language from hearing it spoken. Because of the necessarily different global mappings – visual centers instead of auditory centers – in deaf persons' language and thinking, the organization of signed languages can provide new information on the question of how language is recognized as well as how it developed. It is interesting to note here that the motor theory of speech communication proposed by R. H. Stetson is being developed anew by such scientists as Browman and Fowler (see Chapter 2).

As we have seen, descriptions of sign language phonology that resemble very closely descriptions of spoken language phonology can be proposed – though both seem to us to err on the side of positing far more logical categories, features, bundles, components, tiers, autosegments, and other sublexical entities than are strictly necessary. With their phonological base organized in segments, Liddell and Johnson find eight processes in ASL to be homologous with phonological processes in spoken languages: epenthesis, deletion, metathesis, gemination, assimilation, reduction, perseveration, and anticipation. They also find three morphological processes common to signed and spoken languages: insertion of features in roots, reduplication, and affixation (1989: 237–268).

It is unnecessary to examine all of these processes here, but we will consider the first two of the phonological processes claimed to be parallel in sign and speech: first, *epenthesis*, "the insertion of an excrescent phoneme into a word; e.g. *fillum for film" (*American Heritage Dictionary*). The example Liddell and Johnson (1989) give is the insertion of a MOVE segment between the ASL noun sign **MOTHER** and the verb sign **MULLING-(IT)-OVER** (Figure 3.1 and Figure 3.2). Both have a single HOLD segment; their notation of the feature bundles of the segments for each sign takes up half a page, but the signs are also described and illustrated in drawings. The first uses the spread hand with thumb held on the chin, the fingers wiggling. For the second, the pursed fingers make a circular motion at or on the forehead. The epenthetic MOVE is shown as an insertion between the two HOLD segments; i.e. between the two signs. But to consider this as an example of epenthesis one must bend the dictionary definition; surely it is not insertion of something within one word but instead the movement needed to make the transition between two signed words. To make the case for homology one must also suppress the obvious: producing a sign in which a hand touches the chin and immediately afterward a second sign in which the hand touches or approaches the forehead *requires* the hand to be moved upward. No elaborate theory for inserting excrescent elements is needed. Some of these

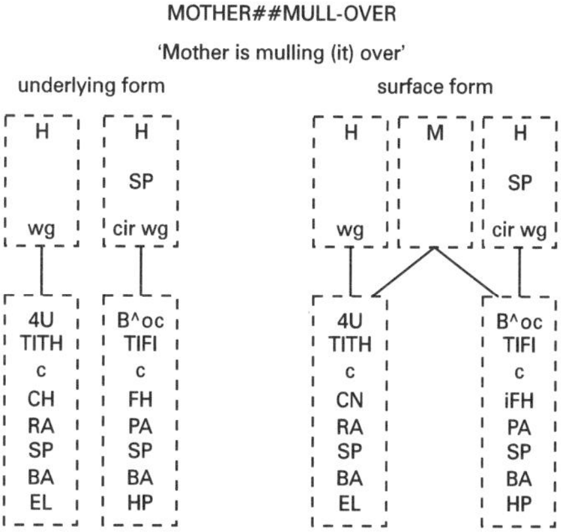

Figure 3.1 Effect of movement epenthesis

Figure 3.2 Signs in isolation and in phrase

objections Liddell and Johnson acknowledge, but they use them to introduce another process, deletion:

> Although it may seem to be unnecessary to propose a rule describing a process so predictable, pervasive, and physically motivated, the M [move] segment introduced into strings by the M-epenthesis rule functions as a critical part of the environment that feeds another phonological process. (1989: 239)

That process, "Hold deletion," is exemplified by the signed phrase **GOOD IDEA** (Figure 3.3). "Because the sign **GOOD** ends with a segment articulated in a different way from the initial segment of **IDEA**, the M Epenthesis Rule will insert a segmental bundle, specified as M, between the two signs" (1989: 240).

Each sign is shown as beginning and ending with a hold, and having a move between, then shown as joined with apparent M-epenthesis (of course the hand had to be moved from out in front of the chin at the end of **GOOD** to the forehead to begin

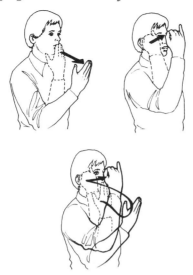

Figure 3.3 Signs GOOD, IDEA and string GOOD IDEA

IDEA). But there is still another change in deep time: instead of holding the end of **GOOD** and the beginning of **IDEA**, under their "H-deletion rule," a MOVE segment appears between the shortened forms of the adjective and noun, and now with a MOVE on either side of the two holds, they are deleted.

Judging from what happens to handshapes in rapid finger-spelling (Chapters 2 and 4), the claimed epenthesis and deletion in ASL appear to be the inevitable results of rapid, coarticulated muscular action rather than the result of a complex series of abstract phonological processes. One can find parallels in the phonologies of signed and spoken languages, but such analysis is far from proving that signed and spoken languages are identically organized at the sublexical level. In fact it is the very thoroughness of Liddell and Johnson's application of formal linguistic principles in their monograph that reveals the deficiencies of the entire formalist approach. It is unlikely that anyone could apply it better.

Wilbur, in *American Sign Language and sign systems*, takes seriously the need to find parallels:

The descriptions of signs presented [i.e. Stokoe, 1960; Stokoe et al., 1965] so far are referred to as the "traditional" descriptions, in that they have not specifically considered possible ways that the descriptions of signs might be *consistent with, and described in terms of, spoken languages.* (1979: 38; emphasis added)

She reviews the descriptions of several researchers (e.g. Woodward, 1973; Lane, Boyes-Braem & Bellugi, 1976; Kegl & Wilbur, 1976), but concludes:

[O]nly Kegl and Wilbur explicitly attempt to organize the handshapes in terms of shared features as suggestions for natural classes [thus identifying the organization, as many linguists do, in the description not the phenomena] . . . However, none of the frameworks for features has yet been carried to the next logical step, which is to attempt to characterize handshape variants as a function of their conditioning environments with the use of features in phonological rules. (1979: 54)

The final sentence expresses clearly her assumption that phonological rules will completely and accurately describe the phonology of signed languages as well as of spoken languages. We argue here, however, that signed languages do not need the whole apparatus of spoken language phonology to describe them: muscular actions produced to be seen as signals differ in an important way from muscular actions that shape air acoustically into sounds to be heard as signals. A visible gesture is perceived as a whole; the effect of a single vocal gesture is not sufficient, in most cases, to provide a meaning-bearing sign. One segment is by definition all that can be produced at one moment by the voice; it must have other segments immediately before or after it, or an intonation pattern over or around it to become a morpheme, the minimal meaning-bearing unit of (spoken) language. Although, as we indicated in Chapter 2, it is no longer tenable to argue that these segments are precisely demarcated. A sign language word, being a visible gesture – or, more accurately, a construction of many coordinated and coarticulated gestures – can in itself signify and communicate.

A different application of phonological theory to sign language description is "autosegmental phonology" (Sandler, 1986). Put forward for tone languages by Goldsmith (1976), autosegmental phonology "states that all vowels are associated with at least one tone; all tones are associated with at least one vowel . . ." (Sandler, 1986: 4): "in the Igbo language . . . the low tone of the verb spreads rightward to the toneless suffixes . . . thus no rule need be stated."

One might assume that such a correlation of segments with suprasegmentals (tone, pitch, stress, etc.) would remind sign linguists that both manual and nonmanual activity occur in sign languages. Sandler, however, shows that the handshape "spreads" rightward to the other segments of a sign (described as Liddell and Johnson describe them). In other words, the handshape is maintained while the sign is moving as well as when it is held – the holding occurring either at the beginning or the end of the sign action. Sandler seems to assume that signed and spoken languages must be structurally related, as they would need to be to support a universal theory of structural generation. She concludes:

The suggestion that sequential units are less central in sign languages than in spoken languages has been offered by researchers (Bellugi, 1980; Studdert-Kennedy & Lane, 1980). The development of formal models of sign language that propose both sequential and "simultaneous" elements (as autosegmental phonology does) will provide a firmer basis for discussion of the structural relationship between signed and spoken languages. (1986: 26)

The earlier researchers are correct: sequential units are necessary to a descriptive system *when they refer to vocal sounds*, the vocalic and consonantal segments of spoken languages. A sequence of such units is necessary to form a meaning-bearing unit of a spoken language.[2] As we have seen, however, visible gestures are perceived as meaning-bearing units directly, whether they

---

[2] Note that although sequentiality is surely necessary in signed and spoken languages, and that segments have been the traditional formal mechanism for describing sequentiality in spoken language, we are not necessarily conceding the neurological reality of segments even in spoken languages (see Chapter 1). What is at issue here is the necessity for or the utility of well-defined segments as elements in a formal, descriptive, phonological system.

are the signs of a primary sign language, the displays commonly understood in a certain social group, or the gesturing
that accompanies spoken interaction. The attempt fails: the
actions producing signed language signs are neither exact
analogues nor homologues of sequential vocal units, whether
they are called segments or autosegments. It fails because it
substitutes an elaborate explanation for something that is in
essence simple. More seriously, it ignores the fundamental
difference between hearing and vision as perceptual systems.
A firm basis for "discussion of the structural relationship
between signed and spoken languages" is of course much to
be desired. A firm basis, however, may require more natural
history, more objective observation, before "the development
of formal models." Observers need to look more closely at
signed language phenomena before they can force onto them
the patterns of (spoken language) linguistic logic: "the pro-
crustean bed of structural linguistics," as Armstrong (1984)
has put it.

3.4 LOOKING AT DIFFERENCES

By letting go the conviction that the basis for understanding
language is through the study of speech and by looking to vision
as the major primate and human perceptual system (Gibson,
1966; Neisser, 1967; Edelman, 1987, 1989; Clark, 1963), we
may escape the error of mistaking the acoustic manifestation of
language for language itself. If language evolved, and did not
result from a macro-mutation of neuron-generating genes, it
can only have developed as a special way of interacting socially.
As we have stated previously, visible actions, and not just actions
in the vocal tract that shape sound waves, need to be looked at for
their role in the evolution of the capacity for language. Social
interaction within mammalian species generally involves signals
of several kinds perceived by several sensory systems, but in the
larger mammals, and in the primate line especially, what individuals see others doing plays a major role in the management of
social life. (The importance of social behavior to language is
explored in Chapter 6.)

The elements of primary sign languages are brain-controlled, muscle-actuated movements of a body part or parts; these are intended and perceived to be more than the movements themselves; in short, they are semiotic signs. Such actions in the vocal apparatus produce sounds, but only certain combinations of the different sounds so produced constitute the words of a spoken language. Sequences of the sounds need to be composed into higher order units. Visible actions, however, can signify in various ways. They can reinforce and duplicate and even substitute for vocal messages; they can stand in the absence of speech for the meanings of unspoken words, as do emblems and other deictic, iconic, and metaphoric gestures;[3] they can accompany speech and help to mark its prosody and regulate its flow; they can express emotion, either intentionally communicating or serving, out of awareness, to furnish unmistakable symptoms of internal states.

But visible actions, physically identical to those mentioned above, can also be the parts of a signed language; they can constitute complete words and enclitics, prosodic signals, word class markers, and syntactic signals. Virtually all the signed language research of the last thirty years attests to the general truth of the foregoing statement, but this is not evidence that signed languages and spoken languages are organized in exactly the same way.

When visible actions and actions producing speech sounds are looked at as phenomena and not as the end products of complicated generative and transformational rule systems (or of computations performed in brain modules), the reason for different organization becomes apparent. Differences between the system for perceiving sound and the system for perceiving light stem from major differences in neural structure, not just in end organs. Signs must be seen; speech must be heard. Speech is invisible (except for some changes of the lower face that make "lip reading" possible but inaccurate). Alphabetical writing, invented long after language began to be spoken, produces the illusion that vocal gestures (actually the acoustic effects they produce, represented in alphabetical writing or phonetic transcription) can reveal the

---

[3] This feature of language and neural functioning underlying language will be discussed more fully in Chapter 8. See also Givón, 1984; Lakoff, 1987.

whole structure of language. Reasoning backward from the organization of *vocal sound* only, linguists, aided by phonetic notation,
have made inferences about the organization of *language*, and these
inferences have been developed into competing theories.

Different organization of spoken languages and signed languages is inevitable, given the differences in the two perceptual
systems. The human auditory system can detect more than
changes in the intensity, frequency, and duration of sounds in
sequence and the relative complexity of their wave shapes. It
can also detect very minute differences, such as those between
[l] and [r], or between a normal and a retroflexed [r], but only
if the particular contrast has been conditioned, early in life, in the
environment of a spoken language that uses these different sounds
distinctively (Kuhl et al., 1992).

Sound to us is abstract; what a sound or a combination of
sounds "means" has to be learned. Relatively little in the sounds
themselves suggests their meaning, though a hearing person learns
soon what has produced the familiar sounds in the environment.[4]
In fact, as primates, we are so visually oriented that it is difficult
for most of us to conceive of the perceptual powers that other
animals may have in different perceptual media. For example,
some mammals, such as dolphins and bats, are able to detect
features of objects acoustically, through echolocation. "Our language is shot through with expressions that point to our visual
primacy: when we need to discover the facts about a crime we
seek an eyewitness, not an earwitness. If we were dogs we would
probably sniff out a nosewitness, but since we are primates and
not carnivores we look for someone who *saw* it done"(Armstrong,
1987: 28).

Vision detects whatever alters the pattern of light reaching the
eye, and the change in what is visible may be as subtle as another's slightly raised brows or as salient as clenched fists and a
threatening posture. But – and this is the effect of the perceptual
difference – what is seen is actual change in the change-produc-
ing organism itself, not a change that must be inferred from
perceived changes in sound. The visual system, then, operates

---

[4] But see Wescott (1976).

on physical, social reality and not on changes in an abstract medium. Moreover, the visual system has a structure that is not greatly different from a central structure of language.

There are two kinds of receptor cells in the retina, the end organ of vision: one adapted for seeing fine detail, the other for seeing something quite different – movement (Clark, 1963: 274). Inanimate objects of common experience are motionless until some potent agency imparts motion to them. When motionless their appearance can be examined in detail by focusing their structure on the eye's center spot, the fovea. We know them, know what they are and what they are like, by "looking them over," by looking at them from different vantage points as we peer at them or move about them. And of course we know many of them by handling and otherwise acting on them as well.

What we see, however, when an object (for instance, a stone) is thrown, is a trajectory. Seeing it in flight, we are unlikely to know that it is a stone; such information comes from our examination of it after it comes to rest, or an earlier glimpse at the moment the thrower reached to pick it up. Our peripheral vision tells us with iconic and indexic accuracy its direction, speed, and the beginning and end of its path; but it tells us little or nothing about the thing itself. For that we must rely on the other kind of vision.[5]

Here, then, in the visual system is an organization that maps into a simple grammar: *something* (seen by foveal vision) *moves* (seen by the rod cells in the retina). Thus, we see subject-cum-predicate, or (in more recent notation: "NP + VP"); i.e. the structure permitted as a rewriting of the prime symbol of trans-formational-generative grammar, "S." This pattern congruity between visible gesture and syntax is examined at length in Chapter 7.

Suppose, however, what is seen is not a stone someone throws but someone's arm and hand in motion. If the hand is flat and vertical, the palm presented at the viewer's face, and if the motion is a sharp thrust forward (i.e. toward or even into the viewer's personal space), then the something moving is of more than casual

---

[5] Swisher (1990; Swisher et al., 1989) has begun investigating the use of peripheral vision by signers of ASL. See also Siple, 1978.

interest: almost anywhere on earth it communicates a message
that may translate variously: 'Danger! Keep back'; 'Get out of
here!' 'Wait a minute; go slow!' But the meaning varies only
within certain limits; this gesture, which mimes thrusting something away, cannot mean anything like 'come here at once';
millions of years of social interaction militate against that.

Behind the gesture may be strong emotion (hostility or apprehension); this and many other gestures are powerful operators
in social interactions. The structure of such gestures – a hand or
hands and the action performed – is the structure of many of the
signs (words) of a signed language; but, being a language, and so
more complexly organized than other gesture systems,[6] a primary
sign language also incorporates nonmanual actions as well; e.g.
facial expressions, head movement, trunk movement, and changes
of stance.

Despite their differences in manner of production and perception, speech, sign language signs, and visible and vocal gestures of all kinds are physical phenomena. They do share a kind of
neurological organization – the fine control of many muscles.
Both visible and vocal activity used for signaling require precise
timing, sequencing, and regulation of the degree of muscle con-
traction. The left anterior cortex of the cerebrum provides this
kind of control for both vocal and manual activity (Kimura, 1981;
Poizner, Klima, & Bellugi, 1987). As facilitators of social interaction, manual gestures and speech also show similarity: spoken
language, signed language, voluntary gestures, and out of awareness "gesticulation" accompanying speech – all these help to
manage social intercourse. In semiotic terms, they function as
sign vehicles, individuals interpret them, they signify and communicate.

For connecting controlled actions of certain muscles in the
individual organism with the world of social interaction, systems
of vocal symbols and systems of visible symbols function and are

---

[6] Visual gestural systems, the actions themselves paired with what they mean in a particular culture, may be more or less extensive; but they are not used to talk about
everything the members of the culture talk about. Sign languages, both primary and
alternate, are so used and thus need and have more complex organization.

organized in very different ways. This is true whether the visible symbols are used "nonverbally" and "coverbally" or are actually the primary symbols of languages, which Hall (1959) terms the major interactional system of face-to-face interaction. To take the simple but satisfying general definition of language offered by John Lyons (in the 1977 Cambridge lecture referred to above), a language consists of a system for making words, a system for making sentences of the words, and a system for reconciling conflicts between the first two.

Words and their constituents, when they are made of vocal gestures, may be considered either acoustically or linguistically. Acoustically, words consist of a syllable or syllables; i.e., pronounceable products of muscular actions in the vocal tract. Syllables are composed of certain sounds with certain acoustic features, imparted by certain actions of the vocal tract, acting simultaneously and sequentially to produce the sound, which consists of one or more segments that can be put into different sequences and emitted with the suprasegmental features of intonation. Linguistically, however, words must be built up out of morphemes if they are to have meaning. For example, in some grammars, the word *conduct* is considered a single morpheme of English, and *conducts* two, the first plus the marker -*s*, (sensitive to tense and number). In other grammars *conduct* is considered two words, each one composed of the same segmental morpheme with one of two suprasegmental morphemes superimposed; the latter, represented as stress patterns on, or "over," the former, yield the words con. **duct,** *v.*, and **con.** duct, *n.*

Words of a signed language made of visible actions can also be considered physically or linguistically. Physically the change is caused by movement of muscles under voluntary control. It can be a change as large as or larger than bowing at the waist or a change as small as winking one eye. Signed language words can be composed of both manual activity and other visual changes. What we call a smile results from actions of several sets of facial muscles acting at the same time on different parts of the face (Ekman & Friesen, 1978). Similarly, a signed language word may use more than one set of muscles; it may have a manual (actually brachial-manual; see Stokoe, 1980) component and a facial component (Baker & Padden, 1978; Liddell, 1980). But in this case, no invisible code is needed, no "abstract systematic patternings." The signer's face and its changes as well as the signer's hands and arms and trunk are all equally visible to the person or persons the signer addresses.

Facial and body changes accompanying ASL signs have been called "modulations" (Klima & Bellugi, 1979) to distinguish them from what are called modifiers in spoken languages. They change the meaning of the manual gesture they accompany, but they are neither prefixes nor suffixes (as in *misconduct*, and *conducting*), nor are they internal changes (as in *brought*). They are simultaneous additions to what is in the visual field of the person addressed by signing.

The organization of a signed language is directly imposed by its need to be perceived by vision and produced by motor action of the upper limbs, head, and face. Simultaneous manual and nonmanual actions in a sign language may function as do the sequential concatenation of a verb and adverb in spoken language; but in speaking, one word must be spoken before the other; in ASL and other sign languages, what may be referred to, with considerable latitude, as "the manual verb" and "the nonmanual adverb" are visible at the same time. Like spoken verbs and adverbs, they can be separated, but separation must be a spatial, not a temporal, operation.

This abstract grammatical similarity, however, is just that, abstract. Spoken languages are organized as they are because of the nature of sound, time, and the perceptual and neurological limitations of humans with respect to the analysis of sounds. Signed languages are organized as they are because of the nature of sight and bodies and time. The latter can build "modulation" into the manual actions themselves without involving the face (Reilly, McIntire & Seago, 1992). A speaker can answer a question by saying: "It is decided," with a decisive intonation or with a delivery that signifies indecision. Changes in voice quality, voice qualifiers, and kinesics can give many different "readings." A signer of ASL can answer the same question with the same or even greater variation in meaning by various changes in the muscle actions that produce the basic movement of the sign DECIDE, as well as by changes in the upper body. Grammar and rhetoric are closer physically, literally closer together, in signed than in spoken languages.

A member of the speaker's culture and subculture will read both the lexical-syntactic and the paralinguistic message of 'It is decided' correctly. The difference in grammatical organization, however, is that the spoken words must be discrete: the speaker to be understood must, within limits, produce the words as others do. Vocal and kinesic changes in delivery that change the meaning are not permitted to destroy the integrity of the words' segments (although /ay haev diysaydid/ may be contracted to /ayv diysaydid/), no matter what suprasegmental ploys are used.

A signer of the same sentence, however, can change the action of the sign itself to change the meaning. In ASL, the sign DECIDE uses both forearms somewhat raised and unrotated with the hands pointing forward, thumbs and forefingers making a ring; the action is movement downward (simultaneous extension at both elbows). If the answer to the question is definite or authoritative, the movement will be abrupt, strong, and may be strongly checked so that the hands may move down only a few inches. If the meaning to be expressed is, 'Well . . . it's more or less decided,' the signer may start the sign with hands near head level and bring them down slowly, smoothly, or in small increments of movement, perhaps even slowing the downward motion as it nears its end point or letting the arms move in small alternations. An exaggerated lengthening and slowing of the arm extension might mean that the decision has been long delayed. Or the question may be answered by a tiny shake of the hands without other movement: 'Yes; it's been decided; big deal!' (carrying the additional message that the signer was not at all pleased with the decision).

There are two main implications of these differences. Because so much of the animal and human expression of emotion is gestural, as Darwin made clear long ago, the carry over of emotion from involuntary displays to such tasks as asking and answering questions has often been treated as nonverbal. To many linguists, language to be language must be fully abstracted from emotion, its words fully symbolic, "unmotivated" as they say. But there is another way of viewing this involvement of emotion in language.

The work of Darwin cannot help but convince us that in the matter of experiencing and expressing emotions there is not a great deal of difference between humans and other animals. The big difference − language as the expression of much besides emotions − must have evolved from something, and emotion with its displays is as likely a candidate as any. Visible expressions of emotion (e.g. surprise, fear, antipathy to, or desire for, something, etc.) in bipedal animals naturally bring the upper limbs into play. Sarles (1974) has noted that linguists and callists each tend "to presume much more about the subject and results of the other than appears to be warranted." A direct evolutionary link between animal calls (avian, mammalian, or primate) and spoken language has been questioned (e.g. Burling, 1993), but when the human potential for fully developed language − with nouns and verbs, adjectives and adverbs, and ways to embed sentences within sentences − in primary sign languages is examined, it becomes evident that there may have been evolutionary steps from animal to human emotion displays, to iconic and symbolic visual gesturing, to fully developed gestural language that involved primarily the visual channel. This topic is treated at much greater length in Chapters 7 and 8.

3.5 SUMMARY

Sign languages and speech languages *are* differently organized. Language structure, according to most linguistic theories, consists of (or includes) phonology, morphology, and syntax. To make words out of vocal sound the kind of organization called phonology is necessary. Phonology is the system that selects certain speech sounds from all possible speech sounds and presents them as phonemes, the segments composing words. Phonemes selected and combined are put into morphemes (words and word classes) in another subsystem of language organization, morphology. Morphology provides the elements that syntax puts together into phrases and sentences. This organization may be viewed as beginning with sound and ending with sentences; or, as Transformational-Generative theory sees it, as beginning with sentences (S → NP + VP), and moving to lexical selection, then realized in language sounds. Viewed either way, the organization of language appears to be linear and hierarchical – but only if viewed from the vantage point of spoken language.

Sign languages use visible actions, not sounds, to make words. Visible actions signify and communicate directly; they do not need to be selected and combined to compose meaningful signals. The organization of visible gestures, which are kinetically and visibly indistinguishable from the words of a sign language, is quite different from the organization of spoken words. The phonology of sign language words is essentially "semantic phonology." That is to say, a sign language word can be analyzed. But when a sign language word is analyzed as what it is and not as a homologue of a spoken word, two components appear: *what is active* (a hand or hands or other body part) and *what it does* (the motion or action of that part). So described, the sign language word has the structure of a miniature sentence: *what is active* is the agent or subject or "S," and *what it does* is the action or verb or "V." Moreover, in many sign language words (those using a hand or hands as agent), the action is transitive – it ends by touching, grazing, grasping, or striking another body part (the patient or object or "O").

Instead of a linear, hierarchical organization, then, signed language signs have a circular or reentrant organization. Edelman (1987) uses the term "reentrant mapping" to describe the neural activity involved in consciousness and spoken language; but it fits just as well the organization of a language organized to be seen. The sentence structure embedded in the gesture is mapped in the word structure, and the word structure is mapped in the sentence structure. There is no need to use external criteria nor categories imposed by speech and hearing to analyze the composition of a sign word. *What is active* is the result of motor actions controlled in part by neural structures of the left cerebral hemisphere but also by the global mappings required for perceptual categories, memory, conceptualization, and consciousness. What the active body part *does* is controlled in exactly the same manner, but at a usually imperceptibly later instant.

Signed languages, of course, also have hierarchical syntactic structure built up from these elementary units.

Another way that sign language organization differs from speech language organization is in its utilization of simultaneous but separate signals.[7] For instance, the direction of the motion and starting and ending locations in an ASL verb can make further expression of the agent and patient or beneficiary of the action redundant. (Verb inflection in many languages can specify closely a verb's subject, but the visual nature of sign language makes it possible to indicate both the subject and the verb complement in the performance of the verb itself.)

It is also possible to incorporate other syntactic information in a verb of ASL. Simultaneous nonmanual activity visible at the same time as the verb's formation-movement can signal that a question is being asked or responded to. For example, to sign the verb meaning 'remember' the closed hand with thumb extended is brought down in an arc from forehead height until the ball of the thumb presses on the opposite thumbnail. When a signer of ASL uses this sign to ask, 'Do you remember . . . ?' the question sentence is expressed by looking questioningly (direct eye contact) at another person while making the sign as described, and then holding the thumbs in contact a little longer than would be done if the sign were simply performed in isolation. If the one so questioned responds, 'I remember . . .' the manual sign is repeated, but the responding signer nods the head forward and lowers the gaze, perhaps even focuses on the hands.[8]

This fundamental difference in organization provides useful information about language. Bateson (1979: 67) asks, "What bonus or increment of knowing follows from combining information from two or more sources?" We have been concerned in this chapter with just this question. If the phonology and other grammatical systems of spoken languages and signed languages are just

---

[7] These are of course available to speakers through "tone of voice" and other, sometimes visible, "paralinguistic" systems, but these – at least in most linguistic thinking – are not considered to be built into grammar proper. We will argue later that, perhaps, they should be.

[8] Stokoe, 1960. See also Baker-Shenk, 1976; Klima & Bellugi, 1979, chapters 11,12; Liddell, 1980.

alike and part of a deep universal linguistic identity, there is no information to combine – no increment whatever. But the difference described here does indeed bestow a bonus, an increment of knowing, which will be fully explored in Chapter 7 where we discuss the origin of syntax.

In suggesting that there are differences in organization at the phonological level between signed and spoken languages, we are not suggesting that there is no cognitive unity underlying language in general. The differences we have been interested in here result from differences in the sensory and perceptual systems used in the production and reception of signals, not of the cognitive substrates discussed in Chapter 2. So our position remains: the underlying unity will be found by considering all of language as systems for organizing gestures.

The assertion that signed and spoken languages have different organizing principles at the phonological level also leads us to question the assertion that language could have a modular organization in the brain. We take up this topic in Chapter 4.

CHAPTER 4

Is language modular?

Faculty psychology is getting to be respectable again after
centuries of hanging around with phrenologists and other
dubious types.

Jerry Fodor, *The modularity of mind*

4.1 MODULAR VERSUS ASSOCIATIONIST THEORIES OF LANGUAGE

There is a recent version of the nativist theory of language that
makes use of the modern concept of modularity, a concept
derived from the construction of electronic devices, especially
computers. According to modular theories, the brain can be
understood as a processing device that contains a number of
innately differentiated components, modules, each of which is
responsible for a separate subroutine or type of computing activity. Modular theories are in contrast with associationist theories,
which assume that the brain is relatively homogeneous and its
interconnections are relatively unconstrained but become differentiated primarily through the organism's interactions with the
environment. Modular theorists ordinarily cite regularities in
human behavior, especially language, as evidence for innately
determined mechanisms; while associationists have traditionally
cited the great diversity of human languages and cultures as
evidence for plasticity.

Precursors of modular as well as associationist theories of the
causation of human behavior have very long histories in Western
thought. Modular theories have been associated with the idealist
tradition in philosophy (largely French), and associationist theories

have been linked with the empiricist tradition (largely English). The fundamental issue is the opposition of the notion that all ideas (concepts) must be pre-programmed or built in, as against the observable plasticity and flexibility of the organism. Because this antinomy has so long a tradition in Western philosophy, we will consider briefly its history and its various current manifestations. At the outset it is important to note that the possibility of languages existing in modes other than speech (i.e. signed languages) has been used in support of both modular and associationist theories. We will argue here that gestural theory points in the direction of plasticity and thus makes it likely that associationist approaches to language should prove more fruitful.

The notion that humans might possess innately determined thought patterns (ideas) can be traced back at least to Plato, but we will take up the history of the antinomy in Western thought at the time when it develops into theories recognizably like those current today, namely in post-Renaissance Europe. Several modern modularists trace their ideas to those of the French mathematician and idealist philosopher, René Descartes. Noam Chomsky (1966: 4) quotes a passage from Descartes' *Discourse on Method* (1637) that sets forth the argument for innate brain mechanisms underlying language in terms that are very familiar today:

[I]t is a very remarkable fact that there are none so depraved and stupid, without even excepting idiots, that they cannot arrange different words together, forming of them a statement by which they make known their thoughts; while, on the other hand, there is no other animal, however perfect and fortunately circumstanced it may be, which can do the same . . . It is not the want of organs that brings this to pass, for it is evident that magpies and parrots are able to utter words just like ourselves, and yet they cannot speak as we do, that is, so as to give evidence that they think of what they say. On the other hand, men who, being born deaf and dumb, are in the same degree, or even more than the brutes, destitute of the organs which serve the others for talking, and are in the habit of themselves inventing certain signs by which they make themselves understood.

Along with Descartes' famous speculations that specific brain
structures are associated with specific human characteristics (e.g.
the pineal gland as the seat of the soul), this remarkable passage
foreshadows most of the arguments that are currently adduced in
support of the modularity of language. For example, as we will see
later on, modularists have in recent years spent a good deal of
time developing experiments and arguments to show that "signing
apes" are not, in fact, using language (e.g. Terrace et al., 1979;
Premack, 1986).

4.2 MODULARITY AND CEREBRAL LOCALIZATION

The idea of modularity or "locationism" received an empirical
basis with the discovery in the mid-nineteenth century by the
French anatomist and anthropologist Paul Broca that a region
in the brain, ordinarily located in the left frontal cortex of the
cerebrum, seemed to play an inordinately important role in the
production of speech. Broca's discovery and most of the location-
ist discoveries that were to follow resulted from observations of
people with various sorts of brain injuries and diseases, coupled
with dissection of their brains following death. A panoply of
specialized behavioral programs and correlated brain structures
was thus isolated. Some brain insults have been found to result in
truly bizarre and exotic behavioral syndromes that have attracted
much popular attention (e.g. Sacks, 1985). Disruptions of language have been generically termed aphasias, and those affecting
other identifiable behavioral patterns have been termed apraxias
(see, e.g. Denny Brown, 1958; Corballis, 1991; Kimura, 1993).
Broadly speaking, lesions resulting in disruptions of seemingly
compartmentalized behavioral programs (e.g. language disorders, manual apraxias) appeared primarily in the left cerebral
hemisphere.

Until the 1960s, little attention had been given to the possible
functions of the right cerebral hemisphere. It is not our intention
here to discuss in depth the great expansion in knowledge about
cerebral lateralization that followed the initial work of Roger
Sperry and his associates (a recent extended account can be
found in Corballis, 1991), but a modest introduction is necessary

to an understanding of the issues that we will raise in the course of discussing modularity. This more recent research, based on "split brain" patients (i.e. those with sectioned cerebral commissures), has identified major cognitive functions for which the right hemisphere is specialized (Sperry, Gazzaniga & Bogen, 1969). According to this and subsequent research, the right hemisphere appears to be critically involved in the comprehension of complex spatial relations, as well as certain related but more specialized abilities, such as the recognition of faces. Here then, seemingly, is strong support for the idea of modularity – not only do we find areas of the brain that appear to be specialized for language, but there are other areas that appear to specialized for quite different functions.

4.3 PLASTICITY AND ASSOCIATIONISM

The idea that the human brain is remarkably plastic, and hence that innately determined mechanisms are unnecessary, also has an ancient history. As was noted above, this position is usually taken up by those impressed with the variety and diversity of human behavior instead of with its regularities. This idea in its purest form is traditionally traced to the *tabula rasa* of John Locke.[1] The title of the second chapter of his *Essay concerning human understanding* (1690) puts it most succinctly: "No innate principles in the mind." Specifically with respect to the capacity of the mind to *associate* ideas and connect them to *names* (words of a language), Locke remarks:

But if we attentively consider these ideas I call mixed modes we are now speaking of, we shall find their original quite different. The mind often exercises an *active* power in making these several combinations. For, it being once furnished with simple ideas, it can put them together in several compositions, and so make variety of complex ideas, without examining whether they exist so together in nature . . . This shows us how it comes to pass that there are in every language many particular words which cannot be rendered by any one single word of another. For the several fashions, customs, and manners of one nation, making

---

[1] The term *tabula rasa* was not actually coined by Locke but is frequently attributed to him.

several combinations of ideas familiar and necessary in one, which another people have had never any occasion to make, or perhaps so much as take notice of, names come of course to be annexed to them . . . (Locke, 1971: 180–182 [Woozley ed.]))

It is not our intention here to trace the intellectual connection between the ideas of Locke and those of the behavioral psychologists and neurologists of twentieth-century North America – others have done so effectively in recent accounts (e.g. Gardner, 1985; Corballis, 1991). Our concern will be to show how research concerning signed languages has been and can be usefully applied to the fundamental underlying philosophical split between associationism and idealism (modularity).

What many took as the final confrontation between behaviorism and modularism took place in 1959, when Noam Chomsky wrote a devastating review of B. F. Skinner's *Verbal behavior.* Prior to this confrontation, behaviorism–associationism had been the dominant psychological approach to language study, and this dominance of associationism extended into the neurological study of language. The first part of the twentieth century had seen a general abandonment of the notion of localization of function toward a view of the brain as holistic and plastic in its development. The Chomskyan attack on associationism and behaviorism contained a number of elements, but those most relevant to this discussion may be summarized as follows:

- Language is separate from and more complicated than other kinds of cognitive systems; languages are so complicated that it is impossible for people to infer all of the rules of sentence production simply by being exposed to samples of grammatical sentences.
- Languages differ in their surface forms of expression but all share fundamental organizational properties at a deeper level that must be rooted in human brain structure.
- The foregoing suggest that there must be some sort of innate process of unfolding of brain structure and function that enables a child to learn his or her native language; it is specifically not possible for the child to learn the language

strictly under the classical behaviorist (stimulus-response-reinforcement) paradigm.

Coupled with the renewed interest in cerebral laterality and locationism (especially the "connectionism" of Geschwind, 1970) Chomsky's attack was so devastating that many assumed a complete victory over empiricism had been won (e.g. A. Neisser, 1983). As we will see, however, doubts that the issue is settled continue to arise.

4.4 LINGUISTIC MODALITY AND MODULARITY

Radical modular theories of mind and brain were reintroduced by Jerry Fodor and Howard Gardner in 1983. Gardner's theory is presented in terms of a fairly limited number of independent "intelligences," including one governing language; while Fodor's is presented in the more traditional terms of "faculty psychology" – again the key faculty is the faculty for language as conceived by Chomsky. Gardner's more general theory presents the possibility of quantitative assessment of individual differences, always a problem for more formal, radical modular theories, such as Fodor's.

Michael Gazzaniga, long a student of the lateralized human brain and proponent of the modular position, puts it in these terms:

The modular organization of the human brain is now fairly well accepted. The functioning modules do have some physical instantiation, but the brain sciences are not yet able to specify the nature of the actual neural networks involved for most of them. It is clear that they operate largely outside the realm of awareness and announce their computational products to various executive systems that produce behavior or cognitive states. (Gazzaniga, 1992: 124)

Lieberman (1991: 11) develops a critique of modular theories, pointing out that scientific models of brain function tend to mimic the operation of the most advanced machines available at the time the theories are developed. According to modern modular theory, he writes, the brain consists of "hypothetical modules [that] are functionally similar to the 'plug-in' components that are often used to assemble complex electronic devices" (*ibid.*, 13).

A particular behavioral system such as language might, in fact, be supported by a number of modules controlling a number of diverse functions. The literature concerning victims of brain trauma seems to support that notion, at least in part. A variety of aphasias, affecting quite specific aspects of linguistic ability, and associated with injury to specific areas of the left cerebral hemisphere, have been identified. For example, injury to the area originally identified by Broca is supposed to be associated with deficits in speech production and grammatical processing; while injury to the area on the temporal lobe known as Wernicke's area is associated with difficulties in receptive ability and lexical selection/word retrieval (but see Kimura, 1993 for a critique of this received wisdom). Criticisms of radical modularity have focused on the problems that a prewired system would have in explaining the full diversity of human languages – much as presaged by the quotation above from Locke.

Lieberman presents a telling critique based on the logical extension of radical modularity and the observation that there is natural variability in all genetically based systems. If it were true that all aspects of language were genetically programmed, then: "Some 'general principle' or some component of the 'markedness system' *would necessarily be absent in some children because it is genetically transmitted*" (Lieberman, 1991: 131).

In fact, language in general is quite unlike this – human beings are remarkably uniform in their ability to learn at least the rudiments of any language if exposed to it early enough in life. Paradoxically, this was one of the principal supports of the general modularity theory of Descartes quoted above. Nevertheless, Pinker (1991) cites recent evidence suggestive of inherited defects in specific aspects of grammatical processing. We develop a further critique of Pinker's argument in Chapter 6, but we believe that the observation in the opening sentence of this paragraph continues to hold. The ability to learn language is powerfully protected, even after early brain trauma (see, e.g., Levy, 1969; Satz, 1973), and regions of the brain not generally associated with language may come into use following early insult. This level of plasticity in the brain may be lost progressively as the individual grows to adulthood.

If there is genetic programming specific to language, then, it probably operates at a relatively general level, and the literature on aphasias would seem to support this. In most people, there is something corresponding to Broca's area, generally in the same location, injury to which generally leads to similar deficits. But like fingerprints and faces, brains cannot be exactly alike in detail (Edelman, 1989: ch. 3). The evidence would seem to suggest some combination of genetic predisposition with variation – the latter based on physical differences and the different experiences of individuals and social groups – i.e. some combination of modularism and associationism.

What might the nature of general genetic programming be? Visible gesture and signed languages provide a substantial clue, but first we will take a detour into the related realm of the apraxias. Would it not seem to strain the capacity of the genome if we have to explain every conceivable behavioral subprogram as having separate, genetically controlled causation? The course of human evolution has been away from separate genetically controlled behavioral causation and toward plasticity, flexibility, and intentionality. These certainly are (at least some of) the major functions of the enlarged and elaborated neocortex – especially its frontal areas, the areas of vast enlargement in humans. However, there appears to be little question that lateralization of cognitive functions between the two cerebral hemispheres is under fairly tight genetic control (e.g. Corballis, 1991). Study of the apraxias leads to the conclusion that all of the behavioral systems having left hemisphere associations, including language, are united in having an underlying reliance on assembling complex sequences of actions. This basic left hemisphere capacity has been termed *praxis* or *praxic skill* (Corballis, 1991: 197; Kimura, 1993). The right hemisphere is then seen as being specialized for dealing with simultaneity, or spatial analysis.

Nevertheless, there are several recent and powerful arguments in favor of a more specific modularism for language that grow out of research on signed languages. Poizner, Klima, and Bellugi

(1987) develop a strong argument for a "grammar module," based on research on the linguistic abilities of deaf signers who have suffered strokes to various regions of their right and left cerebral hemispheres. ASL has been described as having processes for specifying syntactic relations that rely only on the spatial arrangements of the lexical elements and not upon their order of presentation (Bellugi & Klima, 1982). If that interpretation is correct, and if it could be shown that damage to left hemisphere language centers resulted in impairments in "spatial" syntax, sequential processing arguments for left hemisphere location of the language centers would be undermined. Following is a discussion of "spatial" syntax.

4.5 "SPATIAL" SYNTAX AND THE LEFT BRAIN

For the purpose of establishing pronomial or nominal reference, ASL employs a complex system of indexing, in which the signer establishes the identity of the referent and then "places" it in space by pointing to a location in front of him/her. The noun or pronoun thus placed may be referred to again, as a conversation proceeds, whenever the signer simply points to or initiates action from the appropriate location. As Poizner, Klima and Bellugi (1987: 18) point out, this is an example of signers taking advantage of the (visual) medium of transmission. The ASL sentence below illustrates the concept of spatial syntax. The ASL may be translated into English as follows:

GIRL INDEX$_a$, BOY INDEX$_b$, $_a$HIT$_b$
'The girl hit the boy.'

It is pointed out (*ibid*: 53) that the only thing distinguishing this sentence from another sentence, 'The boy hit the girl,' is the place of origin of the action of the verb HIT. If this spatial analysis is true it has profound implications for a neurological finding presented by Poizner, Klima and Bellugi. What they have found in their examination of six brain-damaged deaf signers is that deaf signers appear to suffer impairments (aphasias) in their signing very similar to the impairments suffered by hearing people with injuries in the same cortical locations. The subjects included three with left hemisphere lesions and three with right hemisphere lesions. In particular, two subjects with injuries to Broca's area and adjacent left hemisphere cortical and subcortical structures had special difficulty with sentences similar to the example given above, difficulties with "spatial" syntax. One of the signers had particularly significant deficits, including problems with spatial syntax, but not with syntax dependent on sign order. The three subjects with right hemisphere lesions showed no significant grammatical deficits, although there was evidence of problems with sign recognition.

The authors conclude from this that there must be a grammar module in the left brain which is independent of the general ordering, sequential processing functions of the left hemisphere. There are, however, several problems with this interpretation. First, the conclusion depends principally upon assessments of the signing of only two deaf individuals, identified as Paul D. and Karen L. Paul D. was the subject who suffered an impairment in spatial but not sequential syntax and Karen L. was the signer who suffered an overall loss of syntactic ability, both spatialized and sequentially based. A third signer, Gail D., suffered massive damage to her left hemisphere that led to an almost complete breakdown in grammatical ability. It is readily apparent that the key test case is provided by Paul D. In the other two cases the impairments were so global that it would be impossible to tease out a specific module. Although the case of Karen L. could be taken as evidence of a generalized grammar module, Kimura (1988) points out that both Karen L. and Gail D. also gave clear indications of *apraxias* that could only with great difficulty be separated from sign language *aphasias*, a separation required for establishing a grammar module.

There are considerable difficulties however with the stated interpretation of Paul D.'s case. Paul D. is a well-known elder of the deaf community in North America, who suffered his first stroke some twenty years ago, about ten years before being tested by Poizner, Klima and Bellugi. Kimura (1988) points out that although Poizner, Klima and Bellugi found no evidence of apraxia at the time they tested Paul D., he *was* apraxic when *she* had tested him some years earlier. She suggests that either he had recovered or he was, after repeated testing, "showing learning effects."

There is, in addition, a more general question concerning the status of "spatialized" syntax. Were Paul D.'s deficits really in spatial grammar? Or is the underlying process here really ordering/sequencing in ASL also? Consider the ASL example presented above: 'The girl hit the boy.' In ASL the pronominal reference must be established first through indexing. Then the action must proceed from the location of the person doing the hitting to the location of the person being hit. It cannot proceed in the opposite order, from the person being hit to the hitter, which in effect would be a passive. Here, then, is our old friend the SVO sentence, albeit in somewhat exotic guise.

In fact, for this example, ASL may be more rigidly ordered in sequence than English, because ASL appears not to have a passive. It is also possible to create an English sentence with exactly the same structure, including the spatial indexing (pointing): "The girl was here (points to the left). The boy was there (points to the right). She hit him." We suggest that the spatialization really operates here at the semantic/lexical level, that is, by establishing pronominal reference, not at the syntactic level. With respect to this example, then, ASL may be just as sequential as spoken language at the syntactic level. This point becomes especially important when we consider Paul D.'s symptomatology in greater detail. Paul D., in fact, based on his post-stroke writing and signing, is a classic Wernicke's aphasic. That is, his most obvious impairment is in appropriate lexical selection or sign/word retrieval, while his word ordering abilities appear to be intact, fitting precisely with our interpretation of his difficulties with spatialization.

4.6 SIMULTANEITY AND SEQUENTIALITY: MODULES AND ISOMORPHS

At the outset of linguistic research on signed languages, it was apparent that in order to put this research on the same footing as the linguistics of spoken languages the primary problem to be overcome was the problem of simultaneity (i.e. "spatialization") in the presentation of the elements of signs. This problem is due, of course, to the construction of signs in the three dimensions of space and their perception and apprehension by the powerful visuospatial processing apparatus that humans, as primates, possess. Stokoe describes how the problem was solved at the phonological level:

Signs cannot be performed one aspect at a time, as speakers can utter one segment of sound at a time. Signers can of course display hand-shapes of manual signs *ad libitum*, but they cannot demonstrate any significant sign action without using something to make that action somewhere. By an act of the imagination, however, it is possible to "look at" a sign *as if* one could see its action only or its active element only or its location only. In this way *three aspects* of a manual sign of sign language are distinguished, not by segmentation, it must be reemphasized, but by imagination . . . (Stokoe, 1980: 369)

Although we are critical of the notion that there is a grammar module that includes a "spatialized syntactic" module, we do assent to the idea that grammatical competence in ASL as well as in spoken language involves spatial as well as sequential processes. As we indicated in Chapter 2, we support a theory of grammatical competence that posits a metaphoric or image-schematic level of grammatical processing (Deane, 1991):

(i)   According to the hypothesis, the acquisition of grammatical competence occurs when linguistic information is routed to and processed by spatial centers in the brain.
(ii) Specifically, it is claimed that linguistic expressions are processed as if they were objects with internal structural configurations. That is, they are processed in terms of certain basic image schemas, namely part-whole and linkage schemas critical to the recognition of the configurations which define complex physical objects.
(iii) But as Johnson (1987) argues at length, image schemas are basically embodied schemas, high-level schemas which function as cognitive models of the body and its interaction with the environment.

We have previously shown the relationship of this model to Semantic Phonology. Here we will explore its implications for the neurological bases of language.

Armstrong and Katz (1981) reviewed the extensive literature on right brain involvement in signed and spoken languages, and suggested that the role of simultaneity and associated right hemisphere involvement had been underestimated in the neurological study of *spoken* languages. They proposed that semantic processes classified roughly as "connotational" or metaphoric can be shown to have a right hemispheric basis. Although Poizner, Klima and Bellugi deny right hemisphere involvement in ASL (1987: 133–159), they identify impairments in right-brain-damaged signers, including hemispatial neglect and failure to complete signs, defects that they classify as extralinguistic. If we posit an underlying connectionism in language use, none of this should be surprising.

There is recent neurological evidence for the importance of whole-brain interaction in verbal fluency. It has been known for some time that males and females differ in average abilities associated respectively with the right and left cerebral hemispheres (Kimura, 1992). For example, males generally score higher on tasks involving spatial relations; while females generally score higher on tests of verbal fluency (see e.g. Maccoby & Jacklin, 1978). There is also evidence that females are less "lateralized" for language than are males; e.g. during ordinary language processing tasks they exhibit more involvement of the right hemisphere. With this in mind a team using magnetic resonance imaging (Hines et al., 1992) has found that the splenium, a structure in the corpus callosum, is larger in females who score higher on verbal fluency tests than in other females.

The corpus callosum is a bundle of fibers that connect the two cerebral hemispheres. Here then is direct evidence for the involvement of the right hemisphere, the spatial imaging hemisphere, in the production of language. We believe that the involvement of the right hemisphere in language processing supports the theory that spatialization/object recognition underlies linguistic ability.

As we indicated in Chapter 2, Deane (1992) also implicates the inferior parietal lobe of the *left* hemisphere in this spatialization process underlying language use. Several other authors have called attention to the importance of this cortical area to the cognitive processes underlying language (e.g. Geschwind, 1965; Laughlin & D'Aquili, 1974; Armstrong, 1983). In particular Geschwind proposes this area as a "cross-modal" association area, in which sensory input from several modalities, including vision, hearing, and somatosensory systems, is integrated. Because in humans cross-modal sensory input is integrated here without mediation by the limbic system, this area may be seen as vital to conceptualization (Laughlin & D'Acquili, 1974). Deane sees this area as mediating the spatialization processes underlying grammar and as having a role in the development of body image. We argue that body image plays a vital part in the evolution of language through gesture. There is recent evidence that chimpanzees may be capable of cross-modal association as well (Hopkins & Morris, 1992; Savage-Rumbaugh et al., 1988).

The characterization of language, both signed and spoken, as gestural and as having underlying processes that are both linear and three-dimensional, along with the involvement of brain centers that subserve these processing functions, challenges the notion that language could be modular in a very simplistic way. If there is modularity, it must be complex, involving a large number of interconnected brain parts that are tuned by environmental stimuli and that can be reallocated following trauma. A philosophical question emerges: in what sense could such a complex and modifiable *system* be considered modular? We will consider this question further near the end of this chapter.

We propose further, that a gestural as opposed to a formalist approach to the study of language can help us to overcome some of the conceptual difficulties that continue to retard study of the nature of language. As we argued in Chapters 2 and 3, formalist doctrine, as well as limitations on the human capacity to process acoustic input, has misled us into believing that the stream of manual gestures produced in the three-dimensional space in front of a signer is somehow "thicker" than the stream of vocal gestures produced in the three-dimensional space inside the supralaryngeal tube of a speaker. A gestural approach, coupled with the more powerful analytic devices now at our disposal, gives us a better way of "seeing" that, although they are perceived by human beings in fundamentally different ways, the two streams share fundamental characteristics: for both speaking and signing, a fundamental problem is to get the right gestures into the right order as they are produced rapidly. A gestural approach can be applied to a specific problem, that of coarticulation.

4.7 COARTICULATION IN SPEECH AND SIGN

There is another recent argument for modularization, based upon the supposed absence of coarticulation in signed languages and its presence in spoken languages. Coarticulation can be defined as a blending of one phonetic element into the next, so that the "elementary" form is altered slightly. Each element, thus, is influenced by its phonetic surroundings:

> the relationship between gesture and signal is not straightforward . . . [T]he movements for gestures implied by a single [phonetic] symbol are typically not simultaneous, and the movements implied by successive symbols often overlap extensively. This coarticulation means that the changing shape of the vocal tract, and hence the resulting signal, is influenced by several gestures at the same time. Thus, the relation between gesture and signal, though certainly systematic, is systematic in a way that is peculiar to speech. (Liberman & Mattingly, 1985)

Liberman and Mattingly argue that this coded relationship between gesture and signal requires a special module for phonetic perception, beyond what is required for general acoustic perception (see also Lieberman, 1991). Liberman suggests that signed languages are quite different: " [Signed language] phonetics is transparent and . . . nothing special is required to process it . . . In these visually based instances, the phonetics is perfectly transparent, permitting immediate recourse to the phonologic system."

Klima notes that while signed languages certainly require the structural notion of phonemes, perception of signing requires nothing more than vision:

It has always seemed sort of an interesting tactic to say that Sign has no phonetics, though the intention is really to say that there is no perceptual necessity for signers to have a sign module. The necessity for a special psychological mechanism for decoding the phonetics of the signal and the necessity for a linguistic description to admit phonetic phenomena are utterly different issues. American Sign Language certainly has a phonetics and certainly has phonetic determination of categories, which we would call phonemes. It has all those linguistic characteristics, but I quite agree that there is nothing to require special perceptual mechanisms . . . A lot of evidence has been presented here that the perception of speech is very different from the perception of other acoustic phenomena. I am convinced that for speech, a module is required for phonetics . . . A module for visual phonetics, specifically for Sign, is probably not necessary (though it may be). (Klima, 1991: 189)

The arguments that Klima mentions are based on the coded nature of speech – the fact that, as we saw in Chapter 2, invariants for speech segments are extremely difficult to identify. But if a visual phonetic module is not required, this surely means that the same type of evidence which supports such a module for speech cannot be found for signed or visual languages. If such evidence can be found – if we can locate a highly coded relationship between gesture and signal in a visual language – then the argument that a visual phonetic module is necessary is lost.

Of course, this does not mean that such evidence requires us to accept the existence of visual and speech phonetic modules. It could be that the evidence of coarticulation supports neither a speech nor a visual phonetic module. Perhaps a more general cognitive capacity allows us to decode highly coded signals.

As we saw in Chapter 2, it would seem that a reasonable working hypothesis would be that there is little difference between the visual and the speech realms in this regard. For example, Zeki (1992: 69) notes that:

The visual stimuli available to the brain do not offer a stable code of information. The wavelengths of light reflected from surfaces change along with alterations in the illumination, yet the brain is able to assign a constant color to them. The retinal image produced by the hand of a gesticulating speaker is never the same from moment to moment, yet the brain must consistently categorize it as a hand . . . The brain's task, then, is to extract the constant, invariant features of objects from the perpetually changing flood of information it receives from them.

Fingerspelling represents a special case of manual signing that permits us to test whether visible gesturing may be coarticulated just as spoken language is. Fingerspelling is a system ancillary to ASL (in North America) that permits the manual representation of written English words. For each letter of the English alphabet, there is a corresponding handshape (or handshape with movement in the case of the letters J and Z). The production and reception of fingerspelling have generally been thought of as consisting of the achievement and perception of a series of static targets, with transitions in between. Wilcox (1992) challenges this notion and shows that in fingerspelling, as in speech, the articulators are in almost constant motion. In addition, it is possible to show, through video and photographic analysis, that the "targets" themselves, that is the canonical forms of the letter-representing handshapes, are almost never achieved. Fingerspelled letters, thus, are coarticulated, as are spoken "phonemes." The person receiving the fingerspelled message, therefore, must be performing an analytic process similar to that involved in the reception of speech. What is being perceived and apprehended is the gestured message itself, not static target end states of the articulators.

4.7.1 Is there evidence for coarticulation in visual languages?

The presence of coarticulation in signed languages thus provides evidence in two ways. First, if coarticulation can be shown to exist, it calls into question the claim that visual phonetics is transparent and lacks the coded relationship between gesture and signal described by Liberman and Mattingly. Second, if it does exist, it also calls into question the need for a special module to decode the relation between acoustic phonetic signal and vocal gesture. This second question is especially important because, if coarticulation can be found in fingerspelling, it would seem to suggest the need for a special visual phonetic module to decode the relation between optical signal and gesture *in fingerspelling* – surely an unlikely conclusion, given the fact that fingerspelling is a relatively recent (in evolutionary terms) invention.

The clues needed to begin the search for coarticulation in fingerspelling are to be found in the paragraph cited above by Liberman and Mattingly (1985). Coarticulation in spoken languages results from two phenomena:

(i) Movements for gestures implied by a single [phonetic] symbol are typically not simultaneous;
(ii) Movements implied by successive symbols overlap extensively.

So, to begin our search for coarticulation in fingerspelling, we must not only adapt these two principles to fingerspelling. We must determine whether:

(i) Movements for gestures implied by a single [fingerspelled] symbol are typically simultaneous or not
(ii) Movements implied by successive [fingerspelled] symbols overlap extensively.

The data presented in table 1 address primarily the second point. That is, they suggest that the movements of successive fingerspelled symbols show the existence of extensive overlap.

The pictures in table 1 provide a preliminary look at both anticipatory and carry-over coarticulation effects in fingerspelling. Most of the pictures depict fingerspelling "targets" – periods during which the hand articulates a canonical handshape. Pictures 4 and 5 depict fingerspelling "transitions" – periods between the canonical targets.

Pictures 1-3 show the three Es in the fingerspelled word ADVERTISEMENT. The most interesting is picture 1; we will save discussion of this picture for last. Picture 2 shows E_2 between S and M; picture 3 shows E_3 between M and N. The two are almost

Table 1: Coarticulation in fingerspelling

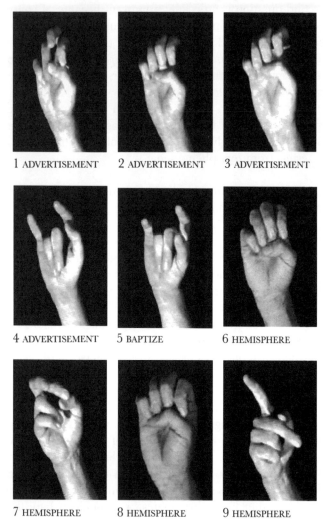

1 ADVERTISEMENT 2 ADVERTISEMENT 3 ADVERTISEMENT

4 ADVERTISEMENT 5 BAPTIZE 6 HEMISPHERE

7 HEMISPHERE 8 HEMISPHERE 9 HEMISPHERE

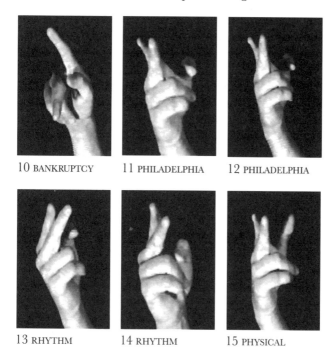

10 BANKRUPTCY   11 PHILADELPHIA   12 PHILADELPHIA

13 RHYTHM   14 RHYTHM   15 PHYSICAL

identical. The only difference is that E_2 is more fully formed (fully uses three fingers), perhaps indicative of the fact that both s and m are also three-fingered.

Picture 1 is the first E (E_1) in the word, occurring between v and R. Note that both v and R are two-fingered. This feature has spread to E_1. Also note that E_1 has a distinctly raised middle finger, atypical of the canonical letter E. This same feature appears in picture 7, E_2 in the word HEMISPHERE. Like ADVERTISEMENT'S E_1, E_2 in HEMISPHERE occurs before an R. It thus seems that the raised-middle-finger allophone of E is a variant that occurs before Rs for this particular signer.

Pictures 4 and 5 depict two transitions: TI in ADVERTISEMENT, and IZ in BAPTIZE. The point of these images is that two different sequences – TI and IZ – provide virtually identical optical arrays.

It may seem inappropriate to treat such transitions as "targets," on a par with normal fingerspelling targets. We believe the comparison is entirely appropriate, however. Wilcox (1992) demonstrates that in terms of raw amount of time, transitions predominate over targets in the optical signal. Thus, these two transitions very likely are as perceptually salient as the Es depicted in pictures 1–3, possibly more so. Second, even though pictures 4 and 5 depict the core of the transitions, that point at which their resemblance is most similar, the same is true for the targets. Pictures 1–3 are the best instances of their respective targets. Moving in either direction temporally from pictures 1–3 will result in optical signals which bear even less resemblance to each other.

Pictures 6–9 are from the word HEMISPHERE. Again, the most interesting is picture 7, which was described in part above. Pictures 6 and 8 depict E_1 – which occurs between H and M – and E_3 which occurs word final, after an R.

Notice that picture 7, E_2, also has a partially supinated orientation, different from any of the Es seen so far. This is the result of carry-over coarticulation from the preceding H, which has a supinated orientation. This feature in fact spreads to the following letter P, depicted in picture 9. Note that the P in HEMISPHERE is quite different from the P in BANKRUPTCY (picture 10). In BANKRUPTCY, the P occurs between U and T, both of which have fully pronated orientations.

Finally, pictures 11-15 depict a series of HS. The most interesting are pictures 14 and 15. In picture 14 we see the first H in the word RHYTHM. Note that the thumb is tucked in. Picture 15 depicts the first H in the word PHYSICAL. Note that here the thumb is opened out. Considering only picture 15, we might suppose that open thumb (which is not typical for a true canonical H) is the result of the following Y, which does have the thumb open. However, in RHYTHM the first H is also followed by a Y, yet the thumb is tucked. In the preceding letters, R and P, the thumb is in approximately the same position – slightly touching the ring finger for R and slightly touching the middle finger for P. Given this limited set of data, it is impossible to say definitively what is causing the difference in thumb positions. However, we might note several facts. First, R is two-fingered, a feature which may spread to the following H. H is also typically two-fingered. P does not have the feature two-fingered. Second, note that the articulator energy required to oppose the thumb to touch the ring finger (R) is greater than to touch the middle finger (P). It is only in the H following the R that the thumb remains opposed (or tucked in).

Figure 4.1 below gives a rough description of the time course of coarticulation (or coproduction) in the fingerspelled word HEMISPHERE. The horizontal bars indicate the beginning, end, and duration of individual letters in the word. The beginnings were identified by noting when the first feature unique to the

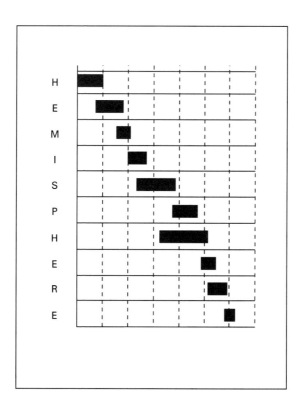

Figure 4.1 Time course of coarticulation

letter appeared; the ends mark when the last feature unique to the letter was visible. Thus, note that during the first third of the production of the first occurrence of E, the H was being co-produced. During the first half of the production of M, the preceding E was still being produced. Note also that features for the H appear halfway through the preceding s, and in fact before the immediately preceding P is begun (or tucked in).

4.7.2 How can we understand this evidence?

How can we interpret coarticulation in speech, sign, and hand-writing? Could there be a separate visual phonetic module for fingerspelling? Fingerspelling is not a natural language system and its "phonetic" elements can be presented singly without coarticu-lation of the elements. No signed language would develop a subsystem like fingerspelling in the absence of alphabetic writ-ing, although there is evidence that some signs of Chinese Sign Language mimic logographs (Fok et al., 1991).

It is impossible for us to believe that a separate "fingerspelling" decoding module could have evolved in the absence of the beha-vior. Manual codes for alphabets are ancient, but rapid finger-spelling of words dates only from the eighteenth century when classes of deaf people instead of exceptional individuals began to be educated. Neither, as we pointed out above, is fingerspelling a feature of natural signed languages (see Chapter 3).

Although he dismisses the notion of language modules, Lieberman nevertheless maintains that there is a need for a special evolutionary argument to explain the speed of production that humans can attain in speech and in the comprehension of spoken utterances (1991: 83). We suggest that our analysis of rapid transmission in fingerspelling calls into question the need for such a special explanation related to speech alone. Again, if the latter were true, it would be necessary to invoke a special evolutionary argument also for fingerspelling, a patently artificial and recently invented language system. In addition, Lieberman seems to imply that grammar is heavily tied to the motor program needed to drive the speech organs (1991: 86–87). We would agree with this argument if it were extended to include signing. In this regard we feel that a gestural approach is particularly critical in explaining the origin of syntax, and we develop an evolutionary argument based on this approach in Chapter 7.

4.8 MODULARISM VERSUS ASSOCIATIONISM

Corballis (1991: 33) points out that, at the genetic level, human beings are remarkably undifferentiated from the African apes. Differences between chimpanzees and humans, in terms of DNA base pair replacements, may be less than 2 percent. There are few anatomical structures in humans that are not also present in chimpanzees (Broca's area is arguably one). The anatomical differences between chimps and humans are matters of degree – based upon differential rates of development of the structural members. What all of this suggests is that whatever is uniquely human is most likely expressed *quantitatively and developmentally* rather than *qualitatively and structurally*. The general trend we should be searching for in hominid evolution is most likely to be toward the introduction of general organizing principles rather than specially evolved structures or modules.

The issue of regular neurological features such as Broca's area remains, however. A parsimonious non-modular argument invokes a genetically based, general functional asymmetry between the two cerebral hemispheres, coupled with topological or "field" effects (see Falk, 1980). The functional split between the hemispheres was described above as "right = simultaneous and spatial vs. left = timebound and sequential." Ten Houten (1976) points out that there is also a caudal–rostral functional axis in the brain that could be roughly described as concrete– abstract. The most immediately noticeable feature of hominid brain evolution is the great expansion of the anterior portion of the cerebrum, especially the frontal lobes, which can most conveniently be described as the seat of abstract reasoning and planning. The ability to construct a complex plan is perhaps the most basic ability needed to produce a complex sentence (Lieberman, 1991). As we will show in Chapter 7, there is a great deal more to the syntax of human language than simply arranging actions in the right order. However, the ability to manipulate complex strings of gestures is a prerequisite to syntactic capacity (Calvin, 1990).

The so-called language centers (Broca's and Wernicke's areas) are located in or near the left anterior quadrant of the cerebral cortex, adjacent to the sensory and motor processing centers associated with hearing and motor control of the organs of speech. This seems to us a sufficient explanation for the regular placement of the speech centers at this location. The caudal–rostral axis and the location of the primary sensory and motor areas are common to the primates and need no special evolutionary explanation for the hominids. The expansion of the anterior portions of the brain is a fairly continuous quantitative feature of hominid, mammalian and indeed vertebrate evolution. That would leave the right–left functional asymmetry as the single neurological feature underlying language that needs a special evolutionary explanation (see Chapter 8), and neurological and behavioral asymmetries are not uncommon among the vertebrates (Bradshaw & Rogers, 1993).

In addition, parietal and occipital areas of the brain, especially the inferior parietal lobule, have been implicated in the evolution of language. These regions of the brain have also undergone significant expansion during the course of hominid evolution.

Does this leave a raw, *tabula rasa* sort of associationism as the only remaining neurological principle needed to explain the origin and diversification of languages? Not necessarily, according to Lieberman (1991) and others. More powerful and sophisticated associationist models have been proposed in recent years, the most promising being distributed neural networks.

Some will object to the classification of neural network theory, particularly Edelman's Theory of Neuronal Group Selection (TNGS) as associationist. It could be argued (and has been by Piattelli-Palmarini, 1989) that this theory is precisely non-associationist. In this respect, it is important to define some terms. Edelman has referred to his theory as "neural Darwinism" because it proposes, as a mechanism for ontogenetic change in brain structure, a process that is, broadly speaking, *selective* rather than *instructive*. These two theoretical mechanisms are extraordinarily important in the history of biological thought, and to understand them fully we need to start by contrasting the evolutionary theories of Darwin and Lamarck.

It is popularly but incorrectly believed that Darwin was the first naturalist to propose a comprehensive theory of evolutionary change in organisms based on adaptive responses to changes in the environment. In fact, others had proposed this sort of change before him. The best-known and perhaps best-reasoned of these pre-Darwinian theories was that of the Chevalier de Lamarck, a French naturalist, who preceded Darwin by a generation. It has been Lamarck's fate, in the history of Western thought, that he is best remembered not as a major contributor to the development of evolutionary theory but for a discredited mechanism of genetic change. Lamarck proposed, as did Darwin later, that organisms changed gradually, over many generations, in response to factors in the environments in which they lived. The mechanism that he proposed for this change is commonly known as "the inheritance of acquired characteristics." According to this theory, animals in each generation make slight alterations in their behavior, or in their structural features, that better suit them to their environments. The most vivid, most frequently satirized, example of such an evolutionary scenario is that of the giraffe. Each generation of giraffes is seen as stretching its neck a little further to get at slightly higher branches. If these small changes could be passed on to each new generation of giraffes, there would be a cumulative effect over a long period of time, in which the giraffe changed from an animal resembling a horse to the ungainly, long-necked creature of today. Lamarck pointed out that the fossil record was full of evidence for this sort of gradual change.

It is not too difficult to see why this mechanism for change has been called *instructive*. In effect, the environment acts directly on the organism by calling forth exertion. This exertion then influences the genetic material, the mode of action of which is unknown. The environment, then, has "instructed" the organism to change its behavior and its anatomical structure by directly influencing its genetic potential.

Darwin's great insight was not to propose that organisms gradually changed into new forms through time, in fact, he accepted the inheritance of acquired characteristics as a major evolutionary force; but he proposed, in addition, a radically different mechanism for the way change came to be recorded in the genetic material. Darwin's insight was based on two principal observations about the biological world. First was the observation, credited to the economist Thomas Malthus, that populations tend to increase geometrically; thereby creating competition for natural resources. Second was Darwin's original observation that there is great variety in the surface expression of traits – what we would now call phenotypes – within species of organisms. To the extent that there are intraspecific differences, then, some organisms would be better suited, better adapted, to survive in the particular environment in which the population found itself. Following competition for resources with conspecifics, these better adapted organisms would leave more offspring in the next generation than those less well adapted. The former were termed more "fit" by Darwin. To the extent that their superior traits were determined by their genetic material, that genetic material would tend to predominate, and there would be a shift in the overall genetic makeup of the population through time. This mechanism was called "natural selection" by Darwin.

This view of how evolution occurs differs fundamentally from earlier "instructive" theories, not with respect to the end result but with respect to the process by which it happens. The environment directs change, but only indirectly, by selecting preexisting traits in greater proportion in each generation. Darwin's intellectual Achilles heel was that he lacked a plausible mechanism for particulate genetic transmission. Like most other naturalists of his day, Darwin believed that, in sexual reproduction, the genetic material of the two parents was mixed or "blended." It was pointed out that this process would tend to obviate natural selection if the benefit accruing to a trait possessed by one parent could be offset if not possessed by the other. Darwin also believed that some acquired traits could be inherited directly, as Lamarck had proposed.

The lack of a mechanism of genetic transmission threatened Darwin's theory for approximately the first fifty years of its existence. The problem was solved by the recognition of Mendel's particulate theory of inheritance, ironically developed at roughly the time of the publication of *The origin of species*, but not generally understood or recognized until the turn of the twentieth century. What Mendel proposed, and proved, in effect, was that there was no blending of the genetic material in sexual reproduction. The contributions of each parent remained separate in the offspring, and could be transmitted separately to the next generation. Concurrently, it was recognized that the genetic material must be carried by the chromosomes in the nuclei of cells, that the latter reproduced themselves in a manner consistent with Mendel's theory, and that it must be carried on the chromosomes in linear sequences called genes. Finally, at the middle of the twentieth century, the structure of the genetic material itself, the molecule deoxyribonucleic acid (DNA), was worked out.

Central to all of this is the notion that the genetic material is buffered, protected against structural change that the surrounding environment might cause. It is known that DNA can be modified by external factors such as radiation, a process called mutation, but that this modification is random. It is random mutation, in fact, that must be the source of the variation in phenotypic expression called for in Darwin's theory. The relative imperviousness of DNA to environmental effects and its general tendency to self-replicate without error has been called the "central dogma" of molecular genetics (Watson, 1976: 281–282).

Edelman won the Nobel Prize for showing that selective, as opposed to instructive, mechanisms could be invoked to explain changes that occur in ontogeny as well as phylogeny, specifically in the ontogeny of the immune system. The dominant theory, prior to Edelman's work in the 1960s, had held that the ability of an individual's immune system to respond to a variety of infectious agents was the result of an instructive process. It was believed that a stock of relatively undifferentiated precursors of antibodies changed in surface form in response to antigens that they came into contact with. Edelman showed, on the contrary, that all of the varieties of antibodies that the individual will produce are already present when an infectious agent is introduced:

When a foreign molecule (say on a virus or bacterium) is introduced into the body, it encounters a *population* of cells, each with a *different* antibody on its surface. It binds to those cells in the repertoire having antibodies whose combining sites happen to be more or less complementary to it. When a portion of an antigen binds to an antibody with a sufficiently close fit, it stimulates the cell (called a lymphocyte) bearing that antibody to divide repeatedly. This results in many more "progeny" cells having antibodies of the same shape and binding specificity. (Edelman, 1992: 77)

Underlying immunological responses, then, is a selection process. Selection, operating upon variation within a population, produces a shift in the proportional makeup of the population, in this case a population of antibodies. Our reason for discussing this is that Edelman has proposed that selection processes that he terms neural Darwinism underlie neurological development as well. We have previously mentioned Edelman's neurological theory and will discuss it in more detail in the next several chapters, but will outline briefly here its impact on the notion of modularity.

It can be argued (and has been) that Edelman's theory supports both the associationist and the modular positions. In effect, it provides an intellectual basis for resolving this ancient antinomy by incorporating elements of both. By postulating a vast and variable number of elementary preexisting neural structures, it appeals to modular theorists. However, by postulating that the development of the brain depends upon the strengthening or weakening of linkages among those elementary structures, it suggests that behavior is not predetermined in large degree and that its ramification is fundamentally associationist.

In closing we note that biological processes are built upon stochastic foundations. At their most basic level, they are probabilistic and statistical, like all other known processes in the natural world – they are not absolute and Cartesian. Their outcomes cannot be predicted from knowledge, no matter how detailed, of initial conditions. This is the great lesson that Darwin taught us.

CHAPTER 5

Do we have a genetically programmed drive to acquire language?

Men are created, not with a God-given language, but with a God-given capacity to make signs and sounds, and by the use of these to form a language. No child comes into the world with a language; that is an acquisition, and the child always acquires the language of its parents, or of those by whom it is surrounded.

Amos Kendall, *Introductory address at the inauguration of the College for the Deaf and Dumb*

It is apparent that the question in the title of this chapter is closely related to the question of linguistic modularity, and it is also apparent that in its most general sense the answer to it, as was apparent to Amos Kendall, must be yes, since all children under normal circumstances do, more or less, acquire the language of their community. The principal problem for modularists is to show how an innate program could lead to such a variety of languages, now known to include signed languages. More particularly, how, if language were genetically programmed, is it that an infant from any social group can easily learn the language of any other social group? Is there a general program that operates from global rules, or a series of modules related to specific aspects of language? Or, as associationists would insist, is the brain extremely plastic and languages based entirely upon negotiated conventions within social groups?

As is true of so many other fundamental issues in the study of language, the groundwork for much recent study of children's acquisition of language was laid by Chomsky, most especially in his 1959 review of B. F. Skinner's *Verbal behavior*. Chomsky's solution to the problems raised above was essentially twofold – he posited a Language Acquisition Device (LAD) and a Universal Grammar (UG). According to Chomsky, the UG

> may be regarded as a characterization of the genetically determined language faculty. One may think of this faculty as a "language acquisition device," an innate component of the human mind that yields a particular language through interaction with presented experience. (Chomsky, 1986: 3 and see Lieberman, 1991: 128)

5.1 UNIVERSAL GRAMMAR

The fundamental problem with a "universal grammar" can be stated most simply as a hoary anthropological conundrum: "How many ways are there to make an oar?" Are the similarities among languages due to an innate, genetically determined "grammar organ," or, as we would propose, are they due to natural constraints imposed by human perceptual, cognitive and motor limitations and the need for language to "work"?

What is the *work* that a language must do? Most fundamentally, a language must be able to encode a sender's *propositions*, concerning the perceptible world, the sender's internal state, nonexistent objects, etc., in gestures that can be perceived and apprehended by the receiver's sensory and cognitive systems. A few examples will help us to illustrate the problem of separating linguistic mechanisms that might be innately determined by the human genome, *per se*, from those that might be existentially directed.

Human beings everywhere are attentive to the flight of time's arrow. In American Sign Language, "the future" is represented by the space in front of the signer and the past by the space behind (in a signed language where the future is not in front of the speaker, it could be behind – metaphoric explanation of the nature of time could accompany this arrangement). This, of course, can be translated into the "grammar" of locomotion. The space in front of the signer is where he or she will be in the future and the space behind is where he or she was in the past. Similarly, in most spoken and signed languages, the sequence of signals typically falls into an agent/action or subject/predicate pattern – the order of events in the world as human beings perceive them.

Consideration of some of the evidence adduced in support of a LAD, or in support of more general innateness will allow us to explore the application of gestural theory to this issue.

5.2 ARE THERE GENETICALLY DETERMINED MILESTONES IN LANGUAGE DEVELOPMENT?

Again in its most general form, this question must be answered in the affirmative. There is a general sequence of developmental stages that virtually all children pass through during the acquisition of language. This sequence may now, in general, be said to apply to the acquisition of signed languages by deaf children, as well as the acquisition of spoken languages by hearing children (Volterra & Erting, 1990: 302–303):

> To summarize, *the fundamental stages of sign language and spoken language acquisition are the same.* In addition, *the timing of the achievement of milestones in sign language acquisition corresponds fairly well to the achievement of their counterparts in spoken language acquisition.*

Recent research has suggested, for example, that deaf infants acquiring ASL go through a babbling stage, in which they manipulate the sublexical elements of signs, much like the babbling stage of hearing infants (Petitto & Marentette, 1991).

In their discussion of recent research, Volterra and Erting (1990: 299) point to the difficulty many researchers encounter in attempting to distinguish among "gestures," "signs," and "words." This suggests a problem that undermines the entire argument for genetically preprogrammed stages. The problem may lie in the conceptual insufficiency of the terms.

The underlying problem is easy to state in terms of the Aristotelian concept of efficient and final explanations. The strong argument for genetic causation in language acquisition posits a special genetic program as *the* efficient explanation of the unfolding behavioral sequence. The weak argument, which we assented to above, posits genetic causation as *part* of a final explanation.

The genetic program is seen as determining the target end state, an adult capable of using a language, and the unfolding behavioral sequence is seen as a necessary consequence of basic mammalian developmental processes, involving myelinization and dendritic proliferation of nerves and growth and development of the limbs and structures of the vocal apparatus coupled with appropriate social interaction. Moreover, as we argued previously, language itself is seen as part of a more general behavioral and cognitive complex.

The nature of this argument may be illustrated by consideration of another basic human adaptation – arguably *the* basic human adaptation – bipedal locomotion (see Chapter 8). During the "acquisition" of walking, the human infant follows a developmental sequence that is not dissimilar from the sequence followed in language acquisition, with respect to the regularity of stages and the timing of milestones. Yet we don't hear that there must, as a result, be a genetically preprogrammed "locomotion acquisition device." Most of us are satisfied with the argument presented above. Namely that the regularity of this sequence is due to more basic underlying bio-behavioral forces, and that the genetic causation is for the end state behavior, upright walking, not the developmental sequence itself.

The counterargument of the modularists invokes the complexity of language compared to any other human behavioral system, such as locomotion. John Morton (1970: 86) responds as follows:

> But how complex a job, for example, is it for a child to learn how to walk? This achievement involves not just muscular coordination but also requires the development of a body image, and coordination with visual and other information. Is this more or less complex than learning how to speak?

As we suggested above, it may be the creation of an artificial distinction between gestures and linguistic categories that misleads us into this intellectual trap. There are several defining characteristics that are taken as separating linguistic signs or words from gestures, including: identifiable sublexical structure and decontextualization.

As we have seen, the problem of separating gestural from linguistic behaviors is especially difficult in the study of language acquisition. Deuchar (1985: 242) presents a way out of this dilemma, along the lines that we are advocating in this book:

It may therefore be appropriate to redefine Saussure's principle [that language is arbitrary or can be decontextualized] as one of conventionality. Language would then be characterized as a system based on convention, or shared knowledge, among its users.

This would also suggest that the proper arena of study is not inside the head of the linguist but in the real world among real speakers or signers. It is the necessity for naturalistic study in the domains of language acquisition and signed language use that has made obvious the problems described above. Deuchar's conceptual solution also grows out of this variety of naturalistic study.

The notion of conventionality also relates in another way to the question of modularity. One formulation of the modular assumption can be stated as the autonomy thesis (Langacker, 1991a: 515):

Grammar constitutes a separate, irreducible level of linguistic structure (one with its own constructs, representations, primitives, etc.) that is properly described without essential reference to meaning.

It is commonly assumed that the autonomy thesis is proven if any aspect of grammatical structure is less than fully predictable from meaning or other independent factors. But, as we know, language is conventional. Some parts of it are certainly predictable, others are less so. Grammar is not absolutely predictable on semantic grounds. However, as Langacker points out, we cannot proceed from this fact to the conclusion that it is autonomous. Doing so constitutes the **type/predictability fallacy** (Langacker, 1991a: 517): "it confuses the distinct issues of (1) what *kinds* of structures there are, and (2) the *predictability* of their behavior."

5.3 WHAT MUST BE MASTERED? STRUCTURE AND PLASTICITY

In the previous chapter, we discussed some of the questions surrounding the hypothesis that language can be explained as a modular phenomenon. There is a related question that is, perhaps, even more slippery. This concerns the biological status and ontogeny of behavioral structures in general. Any theory of language acquisition must take account of human behavioral plasticity, that is the ability of any human infant to learn any human language, and it must be able to account for the development of structure. In this respect we will have to define what we mean by structure, even whether it is any longer a relevant term.

We begin by citing William James (1961: 2) on the question of the interrelationship of structure and plasticity:

> Plasticity, then, in the wide sense of the word means the possession of structure weak enough to yield to an influence, but strong enough not to yield all at once. Each relatively stable phase of equilibrium in such a structure is marked by what we may call a new set of habits. Organic matter, especially nervous tissue, seems endowed with a very extraordinary degree of plasticity of this sort . . .

This notion of a "structural equilibrium" giving way to a period of change followed by the establishment of a new equilibrium fits well with subsequent structural theories of intellectual development, especially a theory that Piaget (1970) calls "genetic epistemology."

It should be noted here that Piaget's theory is interactionist in that it postulates the genetic structures underlying mental development as resulting in *predisposition* to form cognitive structures which could not be fully realized in the absence of appropriate environmental, especially social, conditions:

> Mental growth is inseparable from physical growth: the maturation of nervous and endocrine systems, in particular, continues until the age of sixteen. From a theoretical point of view, it . . . implies that child psychology must be regarded as the study of one aspect of embryogenesis, the embryogenesis of organic as well as mental growth, up to the

beginning of the state of relative equilibrium which is the adult level.

Organically as well as mentally, however, environmental influences assume increasing importance after birth. Child psychology in its search for factors of development cannot be limited to a study of biological maturation. Other, equally important factors are to be considered – exercise of acquired experience as well as social life in general. (Piaget & Inhelder, 1969: vii-viii)

This general postulate fits well with notions that we will develop concerning the role of social life in the ontogeny and phylogeny of language (Chapter 7).

5.4 THE CRITICAL PERIOD FOR ACQUISITION AND SPECIES SPECIFICITY

In support of the separate genetic control of language acquisition, a "critical period" for the acquisition of language has been proposed (Lenneberg, 1967). Does the neurological plasticity required for language acquisition shut off at some critical point, say the end of puberty? There is a body of research concerning language-deprived children that should have a bearing on this issue. These include children supposedly raised in language-free environments, including so-called "wild" children, raised without human contact or in forced isolation, and deaf children raised in the absence of a visual language. A related question concerns the language learning capabilities of animals closely related, phylogenetically, to humans, namely the African apes. For the past twenty years, research in this area has focused on the alleged ability of these primates to learn at least aspects of ASL. If language acquisition is separately controlled genetically, then non-human primates should be unable to learn important aspects of human language. As we will show, interpretation of the results of this research depends critically on how one defines human language.

It is hard to imagine a field of "research" which has produced more controversial results than that concerning "wild" children. Western folklore is rife with mythological heroes who were abandoned by their parents and raised by wild animals. The most famous of these is Romulus, mythical eponymous founder of Rome, raised, with his twin brother Remus, by a she-wolf. A function of such founder myths is to emphasize the uniqueness of the people so established, including the uniqueness of their language, which had to be invented, or reinvented, by the founder and his/her descendants.

What real-life "wild" children actually represent has been much more difficult to interpret. The most famous is probably Victor, the "enfant sauvage de l'Aveyron," subject of numerous literary, theatrical and film interpretations. Victor is the classic wild child – he was discovered, at about age twelve, roaming naked through the forests of central France, apparently subsisting on nuts and roots (Lane, 1976). The case of Victor illustrates many of the problems associated with the study of feral children – nothing was known of his background. How long had he been roaming alone? What were his circumstances and treatment before his abandonment?

When he was discovered he was virtually mute – at first it was assumed that he was deaf. Subsequent study suggested otherwise, but he failed to acquire much speech or other outward signs of language development after years of "treatment" by Jean-Marc Itard, an educator of the deaf. Was his lack of language development confirmation of a critical period, or might he have been autistic (to use current jargon), or an idiot (to use somewhat older jargon)? Might he have been abandoned for such a reason? Lane (1976: 164–165) gives the following assessment of Victor and those who have speculated about what his case reveals:

The pivotal question seems to be, why didn't Victor progress further in his intellectual development and, in particular, why didn't he acquire spoken language? The answer you receive to this question tells a lot about your respondent's conception of man. If he is impressed by the plasticity of human behavior, by the environment to determine the human condition, as Itard was, he is liable to answer "Itard's technique left much to be desired"; or, if he has a higher opinion of Itard's methods, "the asocial habits Victor acquired in the wild were practically irreversible". Besides the "poor technique" and "refractory habit" explanations, there is a third, allied interpretation, namely childhood autism: "early and prolonged mistreatment left Victor with a profound emotional disorder." If your respondent is more impressed, on the other hand, with givens in the human condition, if he sees human growth in terms of biological unfolding, he is liable to answer that Victor had passed the critical period for language learning . . .

A similarly complex case is presented by a modern wild child from California, Genie. Genie's case has been used to support the notion of a critical period, especially for the acquisition of syntax. Genie's case is important as much for what it reveals about the methods of behavioral science as about the issue of critical periods. An excellent recent account of the Genie affair is given in a set of articles in the *New Yorker* magazine (Rymer, 1992a; 1992b). Genie was the victim of horrific abuse, having been confined to a single room almost from birth to the age of thirteen. She had very limited contact with other human beings and when discovered was capable of uttering and understanding a very limited number of words. Rymer recounts the entire sad history of Genie, including the almost ghoulish attention that she received from psychologists and linguists. Her age at discovery is very significant, as it coincides with the onset of puberty in normal girls, an hypothesized endpoint of the critical period for language acquisition. Although Genie received extensive training and evaluation and acquired a substantial vocabulary, she apparently never fully mastered the syntax of the English language. In this level of attainment, she seems to fit into an emerging picture of what may be critical about the "critical period."

A similar framework for "natural experimentation," but in a contrariwise fashion, is thought to be provided by deaf children reared in an all-oral environment, or in a completely "language free" environment. Whereas wild children are usually seen as the victims of aggravated abuse, oral deaf children, in this view, are seen as the victims of a stifling benevolence (e.g. Lane, 1992). In the most extreme situations, they may be cut off from normal language development by being forced to attempt to acquire a language that is largely inaccessible to their operating senses. Two complementary sets of findings concerning oral deaf children are thought to bear on the question of a critical period and genetic programming for language. First, is the finding that the brains of

deaf children, not exposed to sign language early in life, tend to be
incompletely lateralized (Neville, 1977), while deaf children who
are exposed to sign language early tend to have brains that are
organized similarly to those of hearing children. Second, there is
evidence that deaf children cut off from a sign language tend to
invent sign languages of their own (sometimes called "home sign")
(Goldin-Meadow & Feldman, 1977; Washabaugh,1986; Neisser,
1983). However, oral deaf children cannot be said to live in
"language-free" environments, they necessarily interact with
other humans through visible gesture, etc. Our conclusion
about this category of evidence, therefore, is that it is inconclu-
sive, because its generation cannot be controlled.[1]

Third is the case of apes, especially chimpanzees, who have
been taught ASL or some other visual language surrogate
(Gardner et al., 1989; Premack, 1986). The extent to which
they have been able to learn aspects of language remains a
bone of considerable contention. We will discuss this evidence
in somewhat greater detail in the final chapter of this book, but
a brief summary will suffice here. First, trainers have had more
success teaching chimpanzees manual signs than spoken words.
However, this requires considerable qualification – the hands of
chimpanzees are very different from those of humans.

---

[1] A related case is that of Simon, recently reported in a newspaper article (New York
Times, September 1, 1992). The research was conducted by Elissa Newport and Jenny
Singleton. Simon is a deaf child of oral parents, and his parents learned sign language
only as adults. Although they sign to Simon, his parents apparently do not use ASL;
rather, they use English-based signing, referred to variously as sign English, Pidgin Sign
English, and Simultaneous Communication. It is alleged in the newspaper report that
Simon was thus exposed only to "imperfect" or "incorrect" versions of ASL, but that he
learned to use some of the grammatical structures of ASL, apparently on his own.
Chomsky is paraphrased in the article as seeing this as evidence "that children can
extract more from language than they are ever explicitly shown." Since we have not
seen this material we are unable to evaluate it. However, it raises several questions. First,
there is previous evidence (Supalla & Newport, 1978) that deaf children inherently make
use of space in their signing in predictable ways when they are presented only linear,
English-like signing. We would be more inclined to explain this along the lines of
universal constraints on perception and production, as we are arguing in this chapter.
Second, it seems unlikely that Simon could have had no experience with deaf signers
who in fact used ASL, although this claim is made in the newspaper article. Third, we do
not know if this research differs from results previously published by Singleton and
Newport (1989). As discussed by Lieberman (1991), this research could be interpreted
as the child making probabilistic inferences from its parents' "imperfect" signing.

Chimpanzees have only semi-opposable thumbs and their fingers are long and curved. Consequently, they can only form approximations to many ASL handshapes. It is also apparent that it is easy for trainers to mold the hands of chimpanzees into desired shapes, while the vocal apparatus is not easily molded in this way. The techniques of modern speech pathology have apparently never been tried with chimpanzees (fortunately for them), so in fact little is actually known about the *capacity* of chimpanzees to acquire speech under training. Second, it is clear that chimpanzees have well-developed capabilities to learn and use signs (symbols, icons, indices) to communicate with humans and with other chimpanzees. Third, although they can form these signs into short strings, they appear not to be capable of complex syntactic abilities (e.g. Terrace et al., 1979; Premack, 1986), although there are recent claims of "proto-grammar" in pygmy chimps (Greenfield & Savage-Rumbaugh, 1991). Among the primates, realization of full-blown syntax appears to be a uniquely human trait.

The problem with all of these "natural" experiments is that they represent only partially the conditions that would be needed to test the major hypotheses that they are said to test. Wild children are necessarily the victims of serious abuse. Oral deaf children cannot be said to have lived in language-free environments. Chimpanzees are not primitive humans (although we will argue below that they may be used to model the capabilities of early hominids). They are members of a separately evolved species that shares many attributes with humans. Their ability or inability to learn human language will tell us little about the details of any genetic program for acquisition that might exist, since it would have to have evolved after the phylogenetic split between ancestral chimpanzees and humans. Two conclusions are suggested, however. First, there is certainly a critical period for full acquisition of a first language. Whether this is evidence for a separate and distinct language module or simply a natural feature of central nervous system development – indeed, whether any and all examples of cortical self-organization are ipso facto examples of modules – remains in question. Consider, for example, visual development (Abeles, 1991): "in the normal newborn monkey, the

segregation between left-eye and right-eye dominance zones was
very poor. These zones develop during the first few weeks of life.
They found that if during that period the lids of one eye were
sutured, the ocular dominance zones of the other eye expanded at
the expense of the zones of the sutured eye. But if the eyelids were
sutured at the age of six weeks or later, the normal segregation of
the terminals from the two eyes was not affected." Second, the
acquisition of fully realized syntax appears to pose a special
problem (e.g. Lord Zuckerman, 1992). We will discuss this problem more fully in Chapter 7.

5.5 A GRAMMAR GENE?

Recent work by Gopnick (1990) and Tomblin (1989) suggests
genetic determination specific to grammatical processing, which
has been taken as indicative of genetic control of language acquisition (Pinker, 1991). The genetic syndrome in question is Specific
Language Impairment (SLI). According to published reports,
victims of the syndrome have problems with syntactic and grammatical relations, being unable, for example, to form simple past
tenses. Transmission of the deficit appears to follow simple
Mendelian rules as a dominant trait, and the reported deficits
are consistent with aphasias following destruction of parts of
Broca's area.

The name that has been given to this syndrome suggests a
theoretical orientation and points to some questions about just
how specific it is. First, are there other subtle behavioral deficits
that have not yet been identified? For example, right hemisphere
damage to normally lateralized hearing/speaking people is frequently said not to result in language impairment. However,
reviews of the literature by Armstrong and Katz (1981) and
Armstrong (1983; 1987) suggest a host of language deficits,
mostly subtle, associated with right hemisphere trauma. Second,
how would such a simple genetic mechanism operate? Frequently,
in the announcement of genetic causation, there is little consideration given to what specific genes actually determine. DNA
sequences specify the arrangement of peptide chains into complex protein molecules. How would a simple dominant specify

syntactic deep structure through the assembly of a single protein molecule? What is that molecule and what is its action? These questions would need answers before we could accept such a simple genetic hypothesis, and the authors of the studies themselves give only qualified genetic interpretations.

Nevertheless, the existence of a specific genetic mechanism, for example, for the operation of Broca's area, would not be inconsistent with arguments from topology that we developed in the previous chapter, or with Edelman's notions of distributed neuronal circuits and neural Darwinism that we discuss in the next two sections.

5.6 PAST TENSE AND SEMIMODULARITY

According to Lieberman (1991: 180), the "MIT school of linguists" has recently begun to argue that the UG determines "only the 'core' of a language's syntactic rules." The remainder, the "periphery" is determined by other cognitive or associationist mechanisms. As Lieberman points out, this obviates the modular argument altogether, because it becomes unfalsifiable. If something doesn't fit, it can simply be placed in the "periphery." An argument intended to overcome this difficulty has recently been proposed by Pinker (1991).

It has long been recognized that acquisition of the simple past tense in English poses an interesting problem in language acquisition (e.g. Rosenfield, 1988:153–155), because it involves elements both of rote memorization and rule generalization and because it involves a series of easily recognizable stages. In the first stage, the child correctly learns the past tenses of common irregular verbs (e.g. go-went). In the second stage, the child learns the regular past tense rule – add -*ed* to the stem of any verb, and in this stage the child incorrectly regularizes irregular verbs for which he or she had previously used the correct irregular form. In the final stage, the child sorts out the irregular verbs from the regulars and again forms their past tenses correctly.

Pinker argues that acquisition of this simple past tense, with its combination of regular and irregular forms, poses a special problem for both modular and associationist theories. Pinker points out that there are essentially three types of past tense formations in English: regular forms in which the verb stem takes the -ed suffix, irregular forms in which the stem is supplanted by a phonologically unrelated form (e.g. *go, went*), and irregulars that are partly regular in that the past tense is related phonologically to the stem (e.g. *spring, sprang*). In Pinker's view, a rule-based or modular system would be invoked to explain the regulars and a rote or associationist system would explain the first type of irregulars (suppletions). In other words, no rule we could conceive of would explain these irregulars, they could only be learned by rote memorization.

It is the third category of irregulars that Pinker finds most problematic, those that appear to be at least partly determined by rules. For example, we might propose a rule that would generate *spring, sprang, sprung*, and *sing, sang, sung*; but it would also generate *bring, brang, brung*, as in fact it sometimes does – but the latter paradigm is generally considered incorrect. Pinker suggests that some combination of rule and rote, or modular and association processes must be at work.

Examples are also provided of the strength of the regular past tense rule, in the case of neologisms, by overcoming sound patterns that are closely related to irregular forms, in cases of verbs derived from nouns or adjectives. Pinker (1991: 533) gives the following examples of this problem: "one says *grandstanded* not *grandstood*; *flied out* in baseball [from a fly (ball)] not *flew out*; *high-sticked* in hockey, not *high-stuck*." Pinker's explanation for this phenomenon of regularization is that because these are nominal forms there can be no irregular (learned) past tense lodged in the mental lexicon, and, therefore, the speaker has no choice but to apply the regular rule.

Finally, Pinker cites evidence of aphasic and genetic developmental disorders that lead to selective impairment of regular verb usage and not irregulars as evidence of the neurological reality of a regular past tense generating module.

We propose that there are several problems with Pinker's analysis. First the bifurcation between irregular and regular forms is subject to historical analysis. As Pinker (1991: 532) points out, irregular verbs tend to be more frequently used than regulars – in fact, the thirteen most commonly used verbs in English are all irregular. These verbs are all also part of the core vocabulary of the language, derived from the Germanic languages of post-Roman England. In fact, the vast majority of irregular verbs in English come from these languages. If we were positing an associationist explanation for irregulars and regulars in English, we might propose that *regularization* is simply a practical response to growth in the size of the lexicon. At some point in the growth of the language, it may have become too taxing to the memory to continue adding irregulars (in this regard, see Hymes, 1971). At which point, new verbs tended to be added as regulars. One might even consider the possibility of conscious engineering in this historical process. This partially explains also the regularization of *neologisms*. We do not accept the implication that use of a regular rule requires a hard-wired module. Humans generalize rules of all kinds as part of their general cognitive endowment, and we will consider below a general, non-modular explanation for language acquisition (Bybee, 1988) that allows for this.

With respect to Pinker's list of neologisms, we are also not sure that he has got it quite right. For example, after some introspection, we submitted the verb *grandstand* to our mini-usage panel of three English-speaking Ph.D.s (actually the authors of this book). We agreed (3-0) with Pinker that, if forced to choose between *grandstanded* and *grandstood*, we would opt for *grandstanded*. However, we also find *grandstanded* to be awkward and voted unanimously for the past progressive, *was grandstanding*, as our preferred method for forming the past tense of that verb. We note in addition, that the past progressive *rule* will get us around just about any potentially awkward past tense of a durational verb.

We must also cite an example that might at first glance appear to affirm Pinker's rule. This example also comes from sports, in this case American football. The word in question is "fair catch," which like "fly out" may be either a noun or a verb. For those not familiar with the sport, it is an option for a player receiving a punt who wishes to avoid being tackled. The player indicates that he wishes to make a fair catch by raising one of his arms. One of us heard an announcer for the American Broadcasting Corporation make the following statement: "He fair caught the ball." This might affirm Pinker's rule because "catch" begins as a verb. However, although our mini-usage panel did not like "fair catched" at all, we still felt somewhat uncomfortable with "fair caught." We agreed unanimously on the usual way that forming this simple past tense is avoided, by using "fair catch" in its nominal form, e.g.: "He made a fair catch." All of this suggests that what we are dealing with here are phenomena much more amenable to analysis in terms of fuzzy-logical prototypes than traditional, dichotomous categories.

The case of *fly out* is similarly problematic. In fact, at least one of us has heard the form *flew out* used by a major league baseball announcer. Of course, use of *flew out* introduces a potential semantic problem, as in "the batter flew out to center field," which could be misconstrued as the unlikely possibility that the batter had taken flight to the farthest reaches of the ballpark (perhaps with the aid of a jetpack, perhaps without, in the case of the Orioles, Blue Jays and Cardinals). So, we could hypothesize that *flied out* comes into play to avoid the possibility of semantic ambiguity. As long as baseball is the subject, we note with pleasure the (perhaps apocryphal) past tense of *slide* introduced by "Dizzy" Dean, the great St. Louis Cardinals pitcher and radio announcer – *slud*, as in "the runner slud into second."

Finally, we may have to grant Pinker *high-sticked*. Although we also find that form awkward, it might become necessary to put it into a non-progressive past tense. But, here again, there are several ways one *could* avoid using *high-sticked*. For example, "he was penalized for high-sticking the Bruins' center," as opposed to "he high-sticked the Bruins' center." We find the latter quite difficult to digest.

Bybee (1988) has proposed a general explanation for neural processing and language acquisition that avoids the need for rules of this kind altogether. Bybee notes that most theories of language processing involve "rules" and "representations." This is clearly the model that Pinker and other generative grammarians operate from (Chomsky, 1980). According to rule and representation theories there is a mental lexicon that includes stored items, usually conceived of as that sample of the morphemes of the language known to the speaker, and a set of rules for assembling them into words. Thus, in the case of the English past tense, there would be stems, to which would be added the suffixes or upon which would operate the rules for internal inflection needed to get the appropriate forms. In the case of the most notoriously irregular verbs (e.g. to be, the paradigm for which is derived from three distinct Old English verbs) there would be no rules, only representations.

Like Pinker, Bybee is concerned with the anomalies that pop out of what is obviously an incomplete *system*. Unlike Pinker, Bybee is willing to acknowledge the possibility that children acquiring language make probabilistic inferences. In fact, the unwillingness to admit probability into the acquisition process is a major defect of modular systems. According to these models, rules are rules. But in real life, people don't act that way. When Dizzy Dean said *slud* on the radio he was applying neither a rule (there is no irregular paradigm we are aware of that contains that vowel alteration), nor was he retrieving a learned representation from his mental lexicon. We can hypothesize about the process that Dean actually used, and suggest how that could relate to language acquisition in general, according to the associative model proposed by Bybee.

Dean had very little formal education, but he had undoubtedly observed that educated people frequently used verb forms that were different from those he had learned in the Ozarks. We can assume that Dean grew up using *slid* as the past tense of *slide*. However, confronted with the necessity of forming the past tense of *slide* in a formal situation, he apparently assumed that the version of it he had learned was "incorrect." Not having a clue what the "correct" form might be, he hypothesized, because *slide* belonged to a class of phonologically related verbs having a high probability of being irregular, that the "correct" form would involve a vowel alteration. It is also possible that Dean, who enjoyed being colorful, was simply pulling everyone's leg.

Bybee gives us a framework for understanding phenomena such as this. She proposes a storage system in which all of the lexical items are stored – in the case of English verbs, the forms of the present tense as well as the past tense are represented fully. She adds that there is no neural analog of stem plus rules for transformation. To explain the interrelationships that we discussed above, she proposes a network of semantic and phonological linkages among the lexical entries. These, then would be interpreted in linguistic analysis as "rules." The linkages might be more or less strong given the *lexical strength* of the entries, lexical strength being a measure of the frequency of occurrence of the word or sign. The great advantage of a model such as this is that it matches what little is known about how the brain actually develops and functions. It also has the advantage of acknowledging the importance of inferential reasoning on the basis of probability. It can readily be seen that this sort of reasoning would have been highly adaptive for a mobile hunter-gatherer, as we must assume that hominids have been from the australopithecines on.

The neurological underpinnings of a general learning theory that is neither modular nor associationist, as usually conceived, have begun to emerge during the past few decades. It was originally proposed by Hebb (1949) that learning might be recorded in the brain by the establishment of neural circuits. Hebb proposed that the circuits could be established by the strengthening of synaptic connections through use, providing a probabilistic/ statistical basis for the underlying neurophysiological process. "Learning" could be seen as the facilitation of neural transmission among interconnected neurons, in the manner of distributed electrical networks. In effect, according to this theory, the networks of neurons so established, would act as information storage devices. It is also easy to see how this general theory could dovetail with the connectionist theory of Geschwind (1970). The general model has been supported by two kinds of evidence: physical evidence from experiments that have detected increased production of certain kinds of neural transmitters during learning (Edelman) and computer simulations involving distributed electronic networks (see Lieberman, 1991). The language learning model proposed by Bybee has been similarly supported by distributed neural network simulations (Rumelhart & McClelland, 1986), although Pinker (1991) is critical of these.

5.7 DISTRIBUTED NEURONAL CIRCUITS AND NEURAL DARWINISM

A major question in neurobiology concerns just how such circuits might be established. The most general theoretical approach, following Hebb, is that they would be built up by use, that synaptic connections between neurons would be strengthened as activity takes place at the synapse. This would provide a neurophysiological basis for associative learning. Because transmission at the synapse depends upon chemical transmitters, the search for an associative mechanism has focused upon chemicals that might act as facilitators for activation of one neuron by another. Alternatively, circuits might be produced by chemicals that cause particular cells to associate with other cells during development. In fact, such molecules, called cell adhesion molecules or CAMs, have been shown to exist by Edelman.

To account for the function of distributed circuits, Edelman has produced a theory to explain associative processes based not upon *learning* but upon *selection* (see Chapter 2). In order to understand Edelman's theory, it is important to understand the difference, therefore, between learning and selection (see Chapter 4). In a classic associative learning paradigm, the establishment of a particular circuit would "grow" out of relatively undifferentiated neural material based upon particular sensory input. According to Edelman's selectionist approach, a particular stimulus would *select* a particular preexisting circuit and strengthen its ability to respond to that class of stimuli. The key here is the idea that there would be selection among an extremely large number of preexisting circuits or "neuronal groups," not by the building up of circuits, de novo.

Elementary groups, built during development by CAMs, could also be formed into larger, or secondary groups. The nature of memory, then, would resemble a program that could be activated by specific input, rather than as a permanent trace, as in older associationist doctrine. The relationship of this neuronal development theory to gestural approaches to language acquisition has been made explicit by Israel Rosenfield (1988). Gestural theory supports the notion that the neurological underpinnings of language should comprise motor programs and the perceptual and cognitive apparatus for decoding them. Traditional structuralist theory predicts that there should be permanently stored "rules and representations," as we suggested above. It should be clear that Edelman's selectionist theory, with its emphasis on dynamic interaction among neuronal groups and activation of motor programs, more readily accommodates a gestural approach to language acquisition than it does a formalist approach (Rosenfield, 1988).

This latter assertion does not go unchallenged, however. In a major defense of Chomskyan theory, Piattelli-Palmarini (1989) argues precisely the opposite, that selectionist theory supports Chomsky's nativism. Piattelli's argument vis-a-vis language acquisition is somewhat complicated by the fact that it is embedded in a larger non-adaptationist (specifically "exaptationist") argument for language evolution (see Chapter 4), but we can outline the main points here. The argument as stated is for the existence of the UG, which Piattelli sees as compatible with the preexisting, later to be selected, neuronal groups of Edelman. In Piattelli's view, the UG can be conceived as a set of preexisting parameters (read neuronal groups) that are set by exposure to a particular language. In our view, if one accepts a general selectionist theory, this is a plausible argument. However, the exact nature of the preexisting circuits remains to be specified, and we suspect that Piattelli may be a bit premature in trumpeting the demise of learning in the development of human cognition. As we have seen, a neural Darwinian, selectionist theory may be employed to support either a gestural or a traditional structuralist approach to language acquisition.

5.8 THE NATURE OF A GESTURAL ACQUISITION THEORY

What would the stages be like in a gestural acquisition theory? We will draw here on a recent exposition by Rosenfield (1988), because it fits well with our presentation of gestural theory, and because it also dovetails with evolutionary arguments that we introduced in Chapter 1 and develop further in Chapter 8.

There are at least two aspects of language acquisition on which gestural theory could shed some light. First, to what extent is spoken language acquired by children in response to the visible gestures that accompany the articulations of their interlocutors? There is evidence that children's own attempts at vocal articulation are governed to some extent by their visual observations of articulation patterns of others (e.g. Studdert-Kennedy, 1987). "Apparently the child recognizes speech sounds as *patterns of gestures* and, in attempting to reproduce them, often fails to produce the correct sound because of an error in timing" (Rosenfield, 1988: 101).

Second, there is evidence that the developing child's first entree into language comprehension is facilitated by intonational patterns of speech less than by its phonemic structure, that is by prosodic features: "A child's entry into language is mediated by meaning; and meaning cannot be conveyed by isolated features or phonemes. The child's earliest unit of meaning is probably the prosodic contour: the rising pitch of question and surprise, the falling pitch of declaration, and so on, often observed in stretches of 'jargon' or intonated babble. The earliest *segmental* unit of meaning is the word (or formulaic phrase)" (Studdert-Kennedy, 1987: 76, cited in Rosenfield, 1988: 101–102).

However, there is also recent evidence that infants extract the particular phonemes used in the language of their environment, *before* they can extract meaning (Kuhl et al., 1992). This suggests that recognition of formal categories at an early age also plays a significant role in language learning. However, contrary to a modular hypothesis, this extractive role can be seen as part of the development of more general cognitive capabilities:

The results show that the initial appearance of a language specific pattern of phonetic perception does not depend on the emergence of contrastive phonology and an understanding of word meaning. Rather, infants' language-specific phonetic categories may initially emerge from an underlying cognitive capacity and proclivity to store in memory biologically important stimuli and from the ability to represent information in the form of a prototype. (Kuhl et al., 1992: 608)

We would amend this statement somewhat to reflect our orientation to the role of social interaction and gesture in the

acquisition of language by suggesting that the biologically significant stimuli are so because they are *socially* important, and
their acquisition prepares the infant to interact in socially effective ways.

This is true of all aspects of human "cultural" behavior, not just
language. If we are to propose a LAD, we will also have to
propose a CAD (Culture Acquisition Device). Human infants
are extraordinarily attentive to socially important behaviors of
all kinds, behaviors that signify gender, position in the social
hierarchy, affection, rejection, etc. All of these behaviors must
be understood and acquired rapidly if the infant is to function
effectively as a human being. These behaviors are complexly
patterned and differ in their "surface" forms from culture to
culture. Underlying all of them, including language, is communication through gesture.

CHAPTER 6

Language from the body politic

Language is a part of social behavior. What is the
mechanism whereby the social process goes on? It is the
mechanism of gesture . . .

George Herbert Mead, *Mind, self, and society*

6.1 LANGUAGE FROM A SPECIAL PART OF THE UNIVERSE

If nothing else, language acquisition studies show that language
does not develop through an individual's interaction with the
natural environment. It emerges only out of social interaction,
but social interaction within constrained limits. We would not
know what a word means if we had not heard or seen it used
by someone else *in a context that made the relation between word and
meaning reasonably unambiguous.* Once language is acquired at a
sufficient level, of course, its possessor is able to use language
and the aids to thought that language provides to determine the
meaning of an unfamiliar word by inference from its context. But
the statement still holds. Without the introduction to words and
the seminal idea that words symbolize – without the initial acquisition process, which is social – we would have no equipment with
which to make linguistic inferences.

It may seem that the condition emphasized above is crucial; the
association of a word with meaning makes both conversing and
verbal thinking possible; but verbal thinking needs language, and
language needs the interaction of at least two human beings.
Consciously to make signs that signify reliably – if only to oneself – requires, if not language, most of the neural prerequisites

for language. To make signs that communicate as well requires at least one other than the maker of the sign.

Edelman's biological theory of mind (1987, 1988, 1989, 1992) credits higher animals with brain processes that can categorize perceptions, remember, form concepts, and be at least vaguely conscious of self but insists that a species in which primary consciousness has evolved must also acquire language to achieve higher-order consciousness. A brain able to correlate information coming from outside with information obtained from inside the organism does not need language or higher-order consciousness to generate certain kinds of global mappings; these, if we could put them into language are mappings that mean, for example: 'This thing, or action, is good for me.' 'That's something I'd better avoid or else . . .' But to acquire language in the first place, a creature with a brain capable of the functions just described needs something more than knowing from inside that all is well (or that trouble is coming) and knowing from perception a great deal about the outside world. That creature needs to be able to recognize a category midway between self and everything else, a new category neither self nor nonself but a special part of nonself that contains others very like self – others with whom one's life and well being are linked.

The brain and brain functions of all animals can only have evolved from those of earlier species. Possessing a brain evolved until it is capable of primary consciousness, however, does not ensure that a species will develop language. Individuals of a species with primary consciousness as one characteristic may be very successful in the struggle for survival and so promote the survival of their kind. Each such individual will have extensive and complex neural networks well adjusted to its habitat and life style. Chimpanzees have fairly sophisticated means of communicating with others but have not developed these into language. And creatures closely related to chimpanzees, the earliest hominids, also had complex brains. It must have been their *more differentiated social life*, however, that provided the kind of behavioral milieu language and higher-order consciousness need to evolve from. For it is the life of the group, not lives of individuals alone, that adapts a social species to its environment; or, from another viewpoint, for the individual, the group is the (most significant portion of the) environment. The group and group behavior may even be said to be the individual's world.

Adam Kendon suggests that a radical difference between chimpanzee and hominid social structure might have been the occasion for visible and vocal gestures, of the kind chimpanzees use, to become true language symbols, with the feature of displacement:

> Chimpanzees, then, seem on the verge of developing a language, yet they have not done so. What is missing? What holds them back? . . . Chimpanzees have not developed a system of language-like communication because they do not need to. The kind of social life they lead is one that does not require it. Chimpanzees lead a social life in which cooperation, involving a complementary relationship between the behavior of two or more individuals, is largely absent . . . [The social life of the hominid line] probably began with the emergence of a differentiation between the sexes in how food is obtained, combined with a tendency for food to be shared . . . [With division of labor between the sexes, there was also] prolongation of infant dependency, the development of sustained consort relationships, and of continuous female sexual receptivity associated with this. (Kendon, 1991: 212)

During the millions of years of hominid evolution the gradual or sudden differentiation of roles – males as hunters, females as gatherers – would have led to repeated separations and rejoinings. Such a life style would make useful, even vital, the ability to use signs referring to things and events not present but at other times, in other places, or present to one but not the other. Emergence of such signs would not only reinforce the existing social structure but would enable it to diversify further, with the consequent enlargement of the brain and its sign system, now possessing crucial features of language (see Chapter 8).

The "population thinking" that informs Darwin's theory of biological selection and Edelman's theory of neural group selection applies also to the behavior of social groups. Edelman says: "The main *level* at which [biological] selection occurs is the individual and his behavior" (1992: 43f). When the individual's behavior is to some extent dependent, however, on the behavior of other individuals in a social group, the group's behavior as well as individual behavior becomes a selective factor. Stephen Jay Gould adds that Darwinian selection is now seen to operate on "genes 'below' organisms [individuals], and species 'above'" (1992: 18). The concept of "individual," has been influenced as Gould points out by our human perception, but while biologists now can consider genes and species and neural groups as individuals in a Darwinian context, the "evolution" of human groups and cultures cannot be demonstrated by microbiology.

G. H. Mead, who gave psychology at the turn of the century a social and biological dimension it had lacked, wrote: "Language is a part of social behavior" (1970: 13). Mead also looked for the beginning of language in social behavior. There is no contradiction here: social behavior (or as it may be termed, the culture) of pre-linguistic hominid groups was the behavior that became language; and language as it emerged naturally transformed that social behavior. Despite lack of physical evidence, it is safe to say that language and society coevolved.

Yet this primary function of language – the facilitation of social life – has been ignored in many attempts to explain language as an abstract, formal, recursive system. When the social function of language is considered, however, it becomes obvious that social behavior is involved in everything about language from its original emergence and its acquisition by infants to its inevitable evolution as people used it. Once biology is taken into consideration, the conclusion that language must be embodied in the individual human brain is inescapable. The mind is embodied in the brain, and language to operate must, in a certain sense, be *in* the individual mind. But this focus on the individual, the phenotype, should not lead to disregard of social behavior.

Edelman argues that a brain capable of primary consciousness is necessary for language and language is necessary for higher-order consciousness. In this formulation, the neurological description of higher-order consciousness as a prerequisite of language keeps the relation from complete circularity, but there is still the suggestion that "bootstrapping" is needed: consciousness is necessary for language, and language is necessary for (full) consciousness.

Even if language and consciousness do not rephrase the "hen or egg" priority question, it should be worthwhile to look for the mechanism by which each generates the other. We believe that two clues must be explored more diligently in order to discover the mechanism: one is the information to be gained from looking at visible gestures and primary sign languages instead of exclusively at spoken languages; that clue, the central theme of this book, is explored more fully in Chapter 7. The other is the social basis of language. If Edelman and others are right and the mind is embodied in the brain, language must also be in the brain; but language can never be more than partly in an *individual* brain.

We must make it clear that we are not using the term *language* here in the abstract sense of "competence" as defined by generative-transformational linguists and psycholinguists, but in the everyday sense of a system of communication that a person uses and understands when others use it. Language in this sense is the language of a particular community, and knowing it entails much more than knowing its phonology, morphology, and syntax — that is, knowing how to formulate its sentences grammatically and select and pronounce its words correctly. Knowing a language means knowing the meanings of individual words as others use them *and* being able to use the words and sentences that will be meaningful to other members of the language community — in short, knowing the culture.

Obviously there will be utterances and writings by some individuals — at least in large, stratified societies — that not everyone in the community will understand. The specific knowledge symbolized by these instances of language use is therefore in the brains of some individuals but not of all. Thus, like the locus of mathematical reality (White, 1979: 283–302), the locus of language can be neither the individual brain nor the ideal universe as Plato and some contemporary linguists have imagined it. The locus of mathematics and language is diffuse; both reside in a specific culture, a body of knowledge shared by the community that possesses them — but any individual member of that community may possess a larger or smaller share of that knowledge, and none, perhaps, can possess the totality of that cultural store.

Thus defined, language is a social as well as a physiological *system*. Just as language can be described as a major component of higher-order consciousness, and so a function of the individual brain, it can be seen also as a major component of human society. Language makes human society possible, but we are taking Mead's view that social interaction and association were necessary to make language possible. That language and society evolved together seems evident; Kendon's theory suggests how a change in social structure could have provided the condition for pre-language gestures of primates to evolve into true linguistic symbols.

Testing this coevolutionary hypothesis is not an easy task, because the evidence has to be circumstantial. The case for physical evolution exhibits skeletal remains and artifacts of human manufacture, but there is no material evidence for the role of social life in the evolution of consciousness. That language existed in a particular prehistoric period has to be deduced. Residues of fires and other evidence of long habitation, usually of cave sites, imply social grouping of hominids and early humans, but human possession of language and higher-order consciousness can only be inferred from another inference – the evidence of ashes and middens implying that they lived in communicating groups.

Burial practices have also been inferred from archaeological evidence, which is taken to imply that early societies possessed a human culture and therefore a language. It has been argued that providing grave furnishings for an imagined life after death is hardly possible without the freedom from the here-and-now that language and higher-order consciousness can bestow.

Fossil evidence concerning the shape of the vocal tract has been used to argue that some of the humans who put artifacts in their fellows' graves may have lacked the physiological features needed for fully human speech (Lieberman & Crelin, 1971). Whether or not pre-sapiens hominids spoke is a problem, but it is only a part of the larger problem of how and when primate communication systems became linguistic systems. The problem is complicated by the invisibility of speech – the phenomenal evidence of language as most people ordinarily experience it. Yet there are languages and language communities without speech. In them there is direct evidence that social behavior need not depend on speech: social behavior and language in a silent, non-speaking community can provide clues to the coevolution of social behavior and language. Moreover, hominid visual, motor, and upper limb anatomy had no need to change to make rudimentary gestural language possible.

6.2 MOVEMENT, BRAIN, SOCIETY, LANGUAGE

. . . there is an intimate relation between animal functions (especially movement) and the development of the brain. (Edelman, 1992: 7)

The kind of symbolic communication that consists of movements of arms and hands and faces – that is, visible gestures – not only escapes the cloak of invisibility that cave fires could only partially penetrate; it also constitutes a special kind of brain-controlled movement linking body movements to visual perception, to memory, to concept formation, and in human beings, to self-consciousness and consciousness of others. Other animals, not just chimpanzees, use visible acts that communicate. Thus, visible actions are social behavior *par excellence* on which the evolution of language could operate as brains developed. Visible gestures are also likely candidates for the material out of which were made the words and sentences of the first languages, as we suggested in Chapter 1 and argue more fully in Chapter 7. They may also have provided the means by which groups of hominids were formed, kept together, and enabled to function more efficiently than could isolated individuals in the struggle for survival, long before what would be recognized as language emerged.

Remember we are concerned here with language as a component of mind, and with mind as embodied, especially in the brain and body of early hominids. The first hominid individual to conceive of intending a certain combination of vocal sounds to *mean* something could not have invented language *unless* there was a fellow creature nearby who heard the sound pattern produced and somehow tumbled to the amazing and unprecedented concept that the sound pattern he or she had listened to indeed referred to exactly that object. But even given a preexisting social structure, one which would assure the presence of an indispensable co-inventor or co-inventors of language, the coming together all at once of intention, sign creation and production, sign function, and sign decoding is improbable. (See also this scenario applied to visual gestural communication in Kendon, 1991: 203–205.)

The producer of the sound pattern would have had to create a *novel* acoustic event – strikingly distinct from all the noises already familiar to members of the group; for they would understand those sounds for what they had always been – signs of some inanimate or animate event, like thunder or a fellow creature's cry of pain. The novelty of the acoustic event might be sufficient to command a hearer's attention, but the hearer must then divine what it is supposed to mean, and before that has to have entertained the radically new idea that it has been produced with the intention of meaning something. The hearer would also have to entertain another novel notion: that the originator of the sound had the intention of communicating the meaning *to* her or him. The falling into place of all these necessary conditions requires belief in a remarkable chain of coincidence.

A producer's and a hearer's attachment of meaning to, and perception of meaning in, vocal sound, however, would not be difficult at all for a group in which primate visual gestural communication had already evolved to the level of language – a group making manual, facial, postural words and sentences. Association of different vocal sounds with already known visual gesture-meaning pairs would be a further step easy to take.

Understanding that a vocal production may have meaning and discovering what that meaning might be are still problems today. They are problems that every human infant has to solve and does solve in the first few years of life, but infants do not have to solve them unaided. Blount and Kempton (1976) present evidence that parents, without knowing that they are doing so, change more than three dozen features of their normal speaking style, apparently so that their very young children will pay attention to speech. Then when the children are a little older, the parents (still unconscious that they are doing so) use some of these, and additional vocal strategies, apparently to help the children realize that their own as well as their parents' speech may be meaningful. It is not necessary to go more fully into the details of language acquisition here, or of parental contributions to it (but see Chapter 5), to show that language acquisition is not an entirely individual psychological process. Nor is it a hard-wired computational process; it is instead a social process that requires participation of others besides the infant.

A large body of research[1] shows that visible symbol use, by both deaf and hearing children, is an important part of the process of acquiring language – and acquiring the communicative competence that being enculturated into a particular society demands. Note that the form of the preceding sentence does what grammar makes possible but does not validate: it separates language from culture. Our argument is that to understand language and higher-order consciousness we must see language and culture as a unity, inseparable. Alfred North Whitehead, asked by a student, which was more important, ideas or things, is said to have replied: "Ideas about things." Language is *both physiological*, the function of a highly evolved brain and body, *and social*, a function of a human group. Language itself incorporates into the brain the realization that the conscious self is linked to other conscious selves like the self but distinct from it.

The key to understanding this argument is the notion of *novelty* in the association of a gesture, whether visible or vocal, with a particular object. There is no doubt that chimpanzees and hominids are vocal animals. Anyone who has observed chimpanzees in the wild or in captivity must be very impressed by their volubility. We are, thus, not proposing a "mute" stage in human evolution. The earliest hominids must certainly have been noisy creatures as well, when the occasion dictated. The important points to consider are how such vocal gestures (or "calls") might have been used and how they might have evolved into speech. It is clear from a variety of studies of higher primates in the wild that vocalizations play a large role in threat warnings, in attracting

---

[1] See e.g. Bullowa (1977), Condon (1976), Maestas y Moores (1980), and especially collections of research in Kendon (1980) and Volterra and Erting (1990) .

members of a social group to food sources, and in a variety of other situations in which animals are out of sight of each other or may not be attending to each other visually. What is also clear about these vocal gestures is that, as far as can be determined, although they are symbolic in a semiotic sense, they tend to be tied to particular stimuli in a neurological sense – that is, they tend to be reflexive.

The evolutionary problem in deriving human speech is to loosen these gestures from the bonds of reflex. There has been a fair amount of debate on this issue, starting with the question of just how tightly bound these vocalizations may be neurologically to the stimuli that evoke them (see Myers, 1976; Armstrong, 1983; Steklis, 1985). The scenario we propose involves an evolutionary stage in which visible gestures, for the reasons proposed here, take the lead in respect to flexibility of output and, critically, in the elaboration of syntax. The neural circuitry necessary to support this would then be available for employment in speech as well. In Chapter 8, we consider in greater detail why speech would ultimately come to predominate in human communication.

The sudden emergence of language *as speech*, at least as sketched above and in many theories, seems to us to require too many unprecedented mental events to have happened at once, but the presumed social nature of the hominids provides a clue. Whether in herds, flocks, packs, or troops, social animals give and get important, even vital, visible signs from each other. Darwin concentrated on the similarity of their emotional displays to those of humans, but G. H. Mead sees more than emotion in such displays:

Conversation in gestures between individuals may be very perfect. Dogs approaching each other in hostile attitude carry on such a language of gestures. They walk around each other, growling and snapping, and waiting for the opportunity to attack . . .

If one animal attacks another, or is on the point of attacking, or of taking the bone of another dog, that action calls out violent responses which express the anger of the second dog. There we have a set of attitudes which express the emotional attitude of dogs; and we can carry this analysis into the human expression of emotion. (1970: 13)

Mead makes the significant observation that these expressions – attitudes, gestures – translated into language, express anger, fear, etc., but the animal "conversation" needs and gets no such translation. Instead the animals learn that certain behavior elicits other behavior, and what they learn – to switch to Edelman's terminology – becomes the memory of higher animals, their categorization, and their concept formation. Mead explains the social basis of this kind of language further:

Language is a part of social behavior. What is the mechanism whereby the social process goes on? It is the mechanism of gesture, which makes possible the appropriate responses to one another's behavior of the different individual organisms involved in the social process. Within any given social act, an adjustment is effected, by means of gestures, of the actions of one organism involved to the actions of another; the gestures are movements of the first organism which act as specific stimuli calling forth the (socially) appropriate responses of the second organism. The field of the operation of gestures is the field within which the rise and development of human intelligence has taken place through the process of the symbolization of experience which gestures – especially vocal gestures – have made possible. The specialization of the human animal within this field of the gesture has been responsible, ultimately, for the origin and growth of present human society and knowledge, with all the control over nature and over the human environment which science makes possible. (*ibid.*)

About Mead's bold incorporation of social behavior in psychology, Charles Morris writes:

. . . Mead had studied in Germany. Although he was at Berlin, and not at Leipzig with Wundt, there can be no doubt that the influence of Wundt must be given credit for helping to isolate the concept of the gesture by seeing the social context in which it functions; instead of being simply "expressions of emotions" in the Darwinian sense, gestures were well on the way to being regarded as early stages of the act of one organism responded to by another as indications of the later stages of the social act. Mead specifically thinks of the gesture in social terms, and from such gestures traces the development of genuine language communication . . . .

Mead's endeavor is to show that mind and the self are without residue social emergents; and that language, in the form of vocal gesture, provides the mechanism for their emergence. (1970: xiii)

We agree, but omitting the qualification *vocal* in Morris's last sentence would improve, not injure, this excellent summary of Mead's purpose. Our endeavor throughout this work is to show that *language in the form of visible as well as vocal gesture provides the mechanism for the emergence of mind and self.*

Mead's example of the hostile dogs provides a much better scenario than the bogus one we offered above about the first hominid speaker and the hearer who must guess that speech is meaningful, is intended for others, and has meaning to be guessed. Dogs do not have language, but they have intentions – for example, to dispute territorial rights or seize another's food. Thus, their actions cannot "mean" as language means. Nevertheless, the sequence of actions and their responses do become part of the repertoire of canine behavior. Dogs learn how to behave in such circumstances, and so in a sense the whole sequence has meaning for dogs and is remembered as dogs remember. "Conversation in gestures," though not language, does take place, even among dogs, and it warrants serious consideration as a precursor of language in another species.

The example of the dogs, however, is in some ways inappropriate. First, dogs are special when the point of view is Mead's "social behaviorism." Dogs for a very long time have been socialized in human groups and not in societies of their own. Thus, much or most of their conversation in gestures is not with other dogs (in today's urban and suburban societies) but with their human providers of food, shelter, and (for the fortunate ones) congenial tasks. Better examples of canid "conversation" and of social acts that become meaningful have come from recent description of the behavior of dogs' close relatives, wolves, in the wild. Cooperative hunting by wolves seems more pertinent to early hominid life and communication than do dog encounters with humans. Wolves too have the ability to communicate intention by action and attitude, thus subordinating the individual's intentions to the group's need for success in the hunt. Dogs, however well they cooperate with their masters after training, have little opportunity now to exercise the genetic repertoires inherited from their remote wild ancestors. Second, the dogs in Mead's scenario are very much on their own, though their hostile encounter might later be replaced by less antagonistic behavior should both become "socialized," perhaps as members of a shepherd's working team. Unlike Mead's gesturally conversing dogs, many social species, as modern ethologists describe them, have remarkable success in communicating many intentions besides aggression.

We have already seen that both Mead and Morris call special attention to "vocal gestures." This is understandable; all but about one-thousandth of the human species use vocal gestures as the primary material of language. The fact that the sign languages of deaf social groups are in the full sense of the word *languages*, not secondary or tertiary codes, was unknown when Mead and Morris were writing. It is something that should be known by more recent writers on society, language, and brain, but too often is not; or if known, it is not related to the important understanding of language as social as well as neural. The habit of thinking that language must be spoken to *be* language is strong, as Bacon warned with his caution about the "idol of the cave." It was hard even for those in high civilizations of the past to ascribe full mentality to barbarians – those whose speech sounded like "buh-buh-buh" to Athenian Greeks. It is hard still, unless one has been carefully trained, to feel deep down that on the other side of a language barrier real people exist. Consciousness has been raised to some extent today, lip service is given to the proposition that linguistic and cultural difference is not inferiority, but it is still difficult for linguistically sophisticated speakers to believe implicitly that non-speaking deaf signers understand as much as hearing speakers do.

Understandably too, Mead and Morris and Edelman want to explain language as the vast majority of the species have it and use it now – a system manifested by vocal gestures. One of our goals in this book is to show that what has been discovered about visible signs and their physiological substrate may qualify them for consideration as the basis of *language* in general. The relation of visible signs to social behavior, vision, movement, and brain function can explain one of the most difficult problems in language evolution, the quantum change from naming to language; that is, from words to sentences.

Social animals' visible movements have long been recognized as signifying (cf. Darwin, 1873); not only do heads and faces express emotions, but a grazing herd is alert to detect and respond to a sentinel's movements. All such movements require the correlation of vision and motor action and the adjustment of self to others and the rest of the environment – in short, they directly involve brain functioning. Movements, in some primate species that are highly social, namely African apes, have evolved an increment to this mammalian social model: their forelimbs, evolved for brachiation and knuckle walking, are available, and to some extent are used to signify and communicate. For example, chimpanzees use the horizontal supine forearm for a begging gesture, and the gesture of an arm extended upward (an infant chimp's request for grooming also used by young adults to mean 'stop the rough stuff; this is play'; Kendon, 1991: 211f). These are only a few of countless examples that could be cited of the extensive use social animals make of vision and movement to communicate.

In the hominid line, however, full bipedalism freed forelimbs from support and locomotion so that they could perform both practical acts and signifying acts – that is, gestures. Fully binocular vision (possessed by all higher primates), the new freedom of forelimbs for gesturing, and the hairless face (of females) would have enhanced, not diminished, the visual attention that individuals paid to others in the group. Likewise, the movements would have become more numerous, more complex, and more differentiated. In this way, the social basis of hominid life, as well as the increased involvement of visuomotor actions with perception, proprioception, and the environment, could only have imparted a selective advantage for increased brain complexity.

What seems difficult for many to assent to, however, is that visible movements, gestures, could ever have possessed the unique qualities of language as it is presently realized in speech. Edelman's theory is a complete, biologically-grounded hypothesis for the evolution of consciousness and language, but he too gives only a passing glance at visible gesturing in social groups. We think he looks for the emergence too early of the admittedly remarkable mechanism of speech.

Because Edelman's theory is so complete and its foundation in neuroscience so thoroughly laid, we will examine part of it in detail here to show where, we believe, more information about visible movements and social behavior could strengthen it by solving some of the problems it leaves unresolved. In his *Bright air, brilliant fire: on the matter of the mind,* the twelfth chapter is entitled "Language and higher-order consciousness," a crucial section of which is, "Speech: an epigenetic theory" (1992: 126–131). The quotations that follow are from that section.

> The considerations presented so far suggest that a model for speech acquisition requires primary consciousness. Furthermore, the development of a rich syntax and grammar is highly improbable without the prior evolution of a neural means for concepts . . . .
> I propose that before language evolved, the brain already had the necessary bases for meanings in its capacities to produce and act on concepts. The evolution in primates of rich conceptual memories, and in hominids of phonological capabilities and special brain regions for the production, ordering, and memory of speech sounds, then opened up the possibility of the emergence of higher-order consciousness. (126)

We are in complete agreement with the requirement of primary consciousness, concepts, and conceptual memories, but we will argue that the social creatures with these neural means could have acquired and developed language well before full phonological capabilities evolved. It will be difficult to determine how much of the rich syntax and grammar of present languages developed after basic syntax emerged, but the work of Givón, Langacker, Lakoff, and Haiman (e.g. 1985) reveals the iconicity of grammar, thus making this a matter directly related to "topobiology," the spatial arrangement of cells, and of brain centers, and the title of one of the parts of Edelman's trilogy (1988).

In the first place, it seems indisputable that the rich repertoire of visible signs for regulating social behavior possessed by many species of animals evolved into the far richer gestural repertoire of social primates. Certainly, in the larger brains of fully bipedal, differentially two-handed hominids, this repertoire, so useful for social living, would have evolved still further.

In the general anthropological view, life in the open savannas after departure from the forests selected for the physical differences, especially bipedalism, found in remains of *Australopithecus* and later species (see Chapter 8). Constant vocal noise, so typical of and useful to chimpanzees in dense rain forests, would have been less useful, even counterproductive in some situations in the open; but visual alertness to others' movements, so striking when chimpanzees in groups have others within view, would have been even more useful to a social species living where there were fewer impediments to vision. This is especially true in primate species like baboons, currently living in such open environments (Chance & Jolly, 1970).

Second, the development of rich syntax and grammar in a vocal medium poses problems. Some of these problems are taken up and possible solutions offered in Chapter 7, but the central question is this: how could signs made by phonation to signify *persons* and *objects* and *events* have been combined to signify *relations among such concepts?*

Words and sentences are very different logical types. The primary consciousness of social primates and their capacity for concepts would make the evolution of a vocabulary of signs for *things* an easy step, but the ability to signify *relations* does not automatically follow. Edelman, in the section we are examining, offers this suggestion:

We may reasonably assume that phonology arose in a speech community that used primitive sentences (perhaps resembling present-day pidgin languages) as major units of exchange. In such an early community, utterances correlated nouns with objects and led to the beginnings of semantics . . . Verbs followed. Note that the preexisting capacity for concepts provided a necessary basis for these semantic developments. In early humans, the presyntactical organization of gestures may have allowed a simple ordering of nouns and verbs. (1992: 127)

But what is the nature of these primitive sentences? Where do they come from? Examples from present-day pidgin and creole speakers do not provide unequivocal answers, for example Bickerton (1985: 11); 'tumach mani mi tink kechi do'. Translation: 'I think he earns a lot of money though.' The word 'tink' is clearly a verb in an embedded sentence, 'mi tink'; but there is no way to determine that this or other verb words "followed" the emergence of nouns; moreover, a sentence embedded in a larger complex sentence is not what comes to mind as a characteristic of primitive grammar. If the primitive sentences Edelman postulates were visibly gestured, however – possibly with accompanying vocal noises – the emergence of phonology for producing vocal synonyms for gestural words becomes much more likely.

It is in the last sentence of the quotation that we find an unexplored and promising clue, but the characterization "presyntactical" needs careful explanation. We assume, and leave to readers to find it reasonable or not, that indeed the organization of gestures showed a simple *and natural* ordering of nouns and verbs. An early language community (but not yet a speech community) may have used many gestural nouns – as chimpanzees seem to do but in a limited way, pointing at, touching objects, miming their use or shape, using metaphor and metonymy (Kendon, 1991: 209–212). The members of that community with the conceptual capacity Edelman describes would also have used gestures, particularly the miming of certain movements, to designate actions; that is, they would also have used gestural verbs imitating actions.

Presyntax as we see it does not need to stop there. An arm and its hand being used to designate a person or an object is free to move and even to assume the movement of another manual gesture already used to depict motion. This combination in one action, of gestural noun *plus* gestural verb, performed by motor actions, and seen by keen-eyed creatures, would be a powerful stimulus for new brain connections, and more complex reentrant mappings (n-tuple correlation sets in Edelman's terms, 1989). In that way, the preexisting capacity for concepts expressed in manual gestures would lead to a further capacity, that for correlating conceptual *relationships among concepts* with the natural, visible, motoric combination of noun and verb.

This view of early language has the virtue of fitting Edelman's theory, except for the following explanation of syntax:

Syntax then emerged by connecting preexisting conceptual learning to lexical learning. A similar idea has been proposed by Steven Pinker and others within the framework of a grammar developed by Joan Bresnan, which she calls lexical functional grammar. They call this process semantic bootstrapping. (1992: 129)

The view of early language presented in this chapter also has the virtue of regarding sentences as more than a simple ordering of (vocally expressed) nouns and verbs. It does not require semantic or other "bootstrapping" because it considers visible motor actions (controlled, of course, by complex brains) in which noun function and verb function are combined, and which any member of the social group can see, and can correlate in the brain with correlated concepts.

CHAPTER 7

The origin of syntax: gesture as name and relation

The evidence . . . indicates that language could not have
developed gradually out of protolanguage, and it suggests
that no intermediate form exists. If this is so, then syntax
must have emerged in one piece, at one time – the most
likely cause being some kind of mutation that affected the
organization of the brain. Since mutations are due to
change, and beneficial ones are rare, it is implausible to
hypothesize more than one such mutation.

Derek Bickerton, *Language and species*

7.1 THE SYSTEM OF LANGUAGE

It should be clear by now that we will argue against this hypothesis
by Bickerton, an hypothesis which flows from transformational
linguistic theory; although, in Chapter 8, we will discuss a candidate gene that has recently been proposed as a possible basis for this
brain reorganization, as well as changes in the vocal tract
(Greenhood, 1992). We propose, instead, that there are intermediate stages between non-syntactic communication and fully
syntactic language. The essential vehicle of communication that
must be understood according to our argument is the iconic,
visible gesture. The key problem, according to Bickerton, is getting from nonhierarchical strings of symbols to hierarchical
structures, with embedding of phrases. We have already presented alternatives to the rules and representations system that
this implies (Chapter 5). Here we will argue that the key to
building syntax incrementally is the discovery of *relationships*
within symbols, and that embryo sentences are already inherent
in simple visible gestures. There is a larger scientific question

underlying this issue, and that is the question of how evolution works – whether by gradual change that accumulates through time or by rapid change followed by periods of stability. We will discuss this issue in greater depth in our concluding chapter. Here we indicate that we prefer to think of our position on the origin of syntax as "incremental" rather than gradual.

We address the subject of language evolution with the expectation that new knowledge gained from signed languages may enable us to construct a theory including the biological as well as the social aspects of language. The transformational-generative theory of language, also known as the "standard theory" by linguists, may be construed as anti-evolutionary: it rests on premises that: (a) language performance depends on language competence and (b) language competence is made possible by brain wiring, identical in all humans, that contains and operates on rigorous, abstract, universal, immutable rules that do not have homologues among our primate relatives. Opposing theories are not by any means united, but some propose that primate communication evolved into human communication, which grew into language; while others theorize that the development of more sophisticated anatomy (and coevolving neural mechanisms) for producing and modifying vocal sounds gave rise first to phonology and then to morphology and syntax. Speech-based theories take little account of the meaning and social function of language. On the other hand, communication-based theories cannot point to patterns of social communication in other animals that seem likely to have evolved into language.

The following definition proposed by John Lyons is neutral on the issue of whether language is acquired or innate, evolved or bestowed:

Language is a system with three essential subsystems: one for making words out of vocal *or gestural* material, another for making sentences out of words, and a third for making the necessary adjustments when the operations of the first two result in conflict; e.g., the English word *eat* has to be changed to *eats* when used in a sentence with a singular subject; or the structure of the sentence has to be changed, as when the word *allow* replaces the word *let*. (Lecture, "What is language," by Lyons at Christ's College, Cambridge 1977)

This definition makes explicit the power of language to name things, states, and actions and to represent perceived or imagined relations among them. In the world of phenomena, only language can stably and reliably represent such relations; nevertheless, prior to language, the naming function must have begun as neural processes, some of which Edelman has identified as perceptual categorization, memory, concept formation, and primary consciousness (1987, 1988, 1989, 1992).

Although nonhuman primates do not use language naturally, they have shown the ability to associate fairly long lists of manual gestural signs or movable tokens with persons and objects and actions, and to produce the sign or token when shown the referent (Kendon, 1991). These animals, admittedly, *do not make names* out of the gestures or tokens the experimenters introduce; instead they are taught the signs along with what the signs designate, but it is important to realize that such teaching succeeds precisely because chimpanzees have already learned what bananas and dogs and experimenters are – they have perceptually categorized them. The chimpanzee subjects in these experiments already know also what the various things in their environment are good for or why they should be avoided – they have correlated the things' qualities with their own internal states. In Edelman's terms, they have begun to form concepts (1992: ch. 8).

In the wild, apes and other animals communicate of course, but we have no evidence that in the wild they create names for things and actions and states, as language users do. It does appear, however, that the ability to correlate vocalizations or bodypart movements with perceived categories (neural mapping of what is "out there" in their world) is an attribute of primates and other higher vertebrates (Edelman, 1992; Kendon, 1991); thus, the differences between the primate and the human processes of perceptual categorization and primary consciousness require no extra-evolutionary mechanism, no special language modules.

The changes that distinguish apes from monkeys and hominids from apes are changes in a direction away from a high degree of specialization to the greater behavioral flexibility that increased neural plasticity makes possible. Evolution in the hominids has gone in the direction of greater adaptability to widely varying environments. Empirical evidence of this phylogenetic difference has been found by Jenny Kien and others at the Regensburg Zoological Institute:

Action units in behavior are all organised within a clearly definable, narrow time window or temporal segment. This temporal segmentation appears to represent a basic property of the neuronal mechanisms underlying the integration and organisation of successive events. By comparing the temporal segmentation in primate and human behavior, aspects of the evolution of motor systems are revealed. This supports an evolution of language ability from the motor system.

Although temporal segmentation is generally similar in baboon, chimpanzee, and humans, crucial differences occur. Baboons show no ability to organise the motor units within a temporal sequence; repetitions of movements are achieved by stringing further segments together. In contrast, both chimpanzees and humans can organise the movements *within* a temporal segment [our emphasis]; one repetition of movements is achieved in the same time range as action units without repetition. (Kien, 1992: 19)

Kien with justification calls this temporal organization "presyntax." It is presyntax, not syntax, because the motor action units are simple movements of a limb, not signs in the semiotic sense. It is presyntax also because this neural preplanning of motor action is precisely what true syntax uses to execute an utterance.

Although central nervous system change cannot be as easily detected as gross physical changes, it has to evolve, like them, by selecting from overt behaviors. A species whose members have begun (without human intervention) to associate visible gestures and vocal calls with things perceived, and to perform and make use of more and more such associated pairs, has not yet arrived at, but is on the way to, the word-forming system – one essential component of language. For example, vervet monkeys have different calls for danger from different sources; chimpanzees can communicate more about more detailed information (Cheney & Seyfarth, 1990; see also Kendon, 1991: 204ff).

Communication among early hominids must have become still more highly developed than that of chimpanzees. At some point the hominids' lexicon of vocal or gestural "sign-standing-for-thing (or action)" must have become inordinately large. In addition, users of this lexicon would have gained great selective advantage. Being aware of the benefits or dangers in an object or an action and being able to signify some of that awareness and able to see another's signification of similar awareness by vocal or visible actions would make transmitting knowledge to offspring more efficient than usual "bootstrap" learning and would confer survival advantage on the group as well as the individual.

If early hominids were using mainly vocal actions to signify and communicate, they would have found very useful the ability to recognize not just the vocal signs they and others used for various objects and actions but also the steps to be taken to adjust for inevitable individual variation in the production of vocal signs for the same referent. This is the basis of Lieberman's theory of language evolution; he has pointed out that the "same" vowel produced by a juvenile and an adult (or small and large) speaker can sound quite different. Thus, creatures communicating with vocal signals would need not only to associate a sound pattern with what it signified but at first also to associate this individual's and that individual's different sounding output with a single referent. Lieberman (1985, 1991) has thoroughly investigated the two-chambered supra-laryngeal vocal tract, unique in humans, which makes it possible to calibrate the sense of hearing for formant variation. But speaking and producing and recognizing vowel sounds that can be calibrated for their maker's vocal tract size are not the only behaviors that might be cited to explain the difference in brain size between *Homo erectus* and *Homo sapiens*. When the products of perceptions – duly categorized, recognized, remembered, and assorted into "good for me" or "bad for me" categories – came to be associated regularly with specific vocal *or visible* gestures, a great increase in brain size and complexity would have been needed to take full advantage of the behavioral possibilities.

There is substantial agreement that a creature able to use vocal or visible signs displaced from immediate perceptions would not only have gained selective advantage by strengthened social organization but also would have evolved a more complex and larger brain. Making words, however, is by no means the whole of language. What Lyons has stated succinctly is also generally acknowledged: in addition to a system for making words, a symbol system is not a language unless it includes also a system for making sentences of words. Here the evolutionary trail from vervet monkey to *Homo sapiens* appears to break off abruptly. It is one thing to associate gestures made out in the open where they can be seen (or gestures made in the vocal tract to be heard) with something else that is seen, categorized, and remembered. It is quite another matter to use such gestures to represent more or less complex relations – relations, it is important to note, between different logical types.

Current idealist theories of language hold that the relations represented in sentences are essentially those of abstract syntactic structures generated by a unique neural structure identical (or nearly identical) in every human brain. One such theory supposes further that each brain has an identical set of separate modules and that each module processes a different subsystem or level of grammar. Opposed to this, some associationist theories of language, in the empiricist tradition, maintain that sentences, which language users make out of words, reflect relations in the world outside the individual, relations that are perceived and processed by normal human cognitive operations. Syntax, in that view, is a property of the universe before it is a property of language.

A radically different theory holds that knowledge (named by words) of categories, objects, and events can be neither part of the world "out there" nor hard-wired into human brains, which as biologists know cannot be identical. According to Edelman's theory of neural Darwinism (1987) and his biological theory of consciousness (1989), a selectionist epigenesis (development from fertilized egg to viable individual) controls the unfolding of an individual's neural system as well as the whole phenotype. Genetic instructions guide cell growth, division, and migration; the result reproduces all the characteristics peculiar to the species. But these genetic instructions allow great individual variation as they are carried out. The creature, consequently, is born with a set or repertoire of similar but not identical neural circuits or "populations" of neural cell groups, which compete to receive and recognize and respond to what the perceptual systems import. The most successful (hence adaptive) of these interconnected ("reentrant") neural circuits are selected and amplified; they "survive"; the others are inhibited and their interconnections decay. This process is learning; biologically it is a set of neural connections utilizing existing neural groups and develops through experience. These connections enable successively: recognition, categorization, memory, learning, concept formation, primary consciousness, pre-syntax, and penultimately representation by neuromotor actions – i.e. language – which leads to thinking and higher-order consciousness (Edelman, 1989: ch. 6).

Edelman's theory does not require the assumption that the universe was designed expressly to be recognized by creatures in it nor that the creatures are endowed with a ready-made key to it all; neither does it hold that human beings have been uniquely designed with homunculi (or language modules) inside to make sense of that world (and its languages). Sentences are neither direct reflections of structures in the external universe nor are they made from linguistic structures inherent in the brain. Instead, word making and sentence making – exactly like other cognitive functions: perception, categorization, memory, global mapping, etc. – both produce and are produced by global neural mappings, which have resulted from natural selection of more adaptive "populations" of neural groups in the whole brain.

7.3 LANGUAGE FROM THE WHOLE BRAIN

Edelman's discussion of language, however, relies heavily on descriptions of language made by linguists who believe that the rules of language are universal, innate, and identical in every brain. Such a belief may contradict his Theory of Neural

Group Selection (TNGS). Edelman sees language as a necessary step in the evolution from primary consciousness to higher level consciousness. Yet despite the compelling logic of his whole argument, and the weight of the neurological evidence, his treatment of language has the blind spot found in many studies of language and gesture – a lack of recognition that primary sign languages have all the features of language but do not depend on speech or hearing. He denies an intention "to develop a complete psycholinguistic theory" or to "venture into linguistics proper." But he then admits: "Obviously, despite my disclaimers, this project cannot be completely divorced from current work on linguistics and psycholinguistics" (1989: 173). The difficulty is that much current work in these fields still fails to recognize the difference between language and speech. Between the two passages just quoted, Edelman has written:

I want to show how, in a global brain theory, the evolution and acquisition of *language* may be related to the previous evolution of brain areas for concepts. This will require some consideration of the special apparatus of *speech*, of phonology and syntax, and of semantics and language comprehension. The goal will be to sketch a model for the acquisition of *speech* and *language* based on the extended TNGS. (1989: 173; emphasis added).

Our disagreement with Edelman's theory is a matter of degree only. By relying, as he does, on Lenneberg, Lieberman, Chomsky, and Pinker (to name some of the psycholinguists and linguists he cites), he must attribute a Herculean task to the neural circuits that are illustrated schematically in his Figs. 10.1 and 10.2 (1989) . These figures schematize the way neural networks relate acoustic-motor, phonological, syntactic, semantic, and conceptual functions of language, *as speech*. Getting from speech (acoustic-motor brain patterns) to syntax, however, requires what Edelman terms "bootstrapping." What we will attempt to show below is that hominids could have acquired syntax without the aid of the admittedly complex evolution of vocal-tract structure and even more complex matter of spoken-language phonology.

This is not to deny the possibility that phonology and human vocal physiology may have been evolving more or less contemporaneously with the acquisition of syntax. In plain terms, speech is physiological-physical material; vocal noises are waves of compression in air. Phonology ties speech into language with neural circuitry; so it has both a physical and an abstract side. Syntax, though, is unlike phonology; it is entirely neural. Syntax consists of patterns discernible in language, and it is formed in the brain by global mappings that correlate one kind of concept – "something acting" – with another kind of concept – "does so and so."

Lieberman's experiments in reconstructing the vocal capabilities of human ancestors belongs in, and is a triumph of, the empiricist tradition. But Lieberman, an authority on the evolution of the organs of speech, assumes that after speaking emerged, the sentence-forming subsystem of language needed nothing else:

> Brain mechanisms adapted to handle the complex sequential operations necessary for speech production would have no difficulty in handling the comparatively simple problems of syntax. (Lieberman, 1991: 107)

In an account of language written for laymen, John McCrone offers a guess that syntax (whether simple or complex) comes from luck:

> There are obviously a variety of sources for this structure [syntax]. Some of the orderliness [of subject, verb, and object] is a reflection of the patterns of cause and effect we see in the world around us. And some parts of grammar are an arbitrary point of style adopted by a culture. But the true root of grammar is probably a lucky fluke stemming from the way language has to spill out of our mouths in a steady two-dimensional stream of noises. (McCrone, 1991: 167)

This attribution to luck puts a still lower valuation on syntax, though it includes the assumption that language began with "spilled-out noises."

Language is generally conceded to be the evolutionary change that raised a species, in Edelman's terms, from primary consciousness to higher-order consciousness. Other animals use gestures for pointing out things and calling them to others' attention. Only human brains, so far as we know, can think. A crow "knows" a man with a gun is dangerous but that the same man without the gun is not; a crow can also let other crows know that danger is near; but a crow's cawing is at some remove from language.

Creating words, spoken words, for an ever expanding number of things and constellations of things is indeed a different order of signifying from vervet monkeys' different danger calls in the presence of differing threats. But creating words does not turn vocal systems or gesture systems into languages. Hominids did not have to depend, as monkeys do, on a brain formed in epigenesis to associate certain kinds of perceived danger with certain cries. Hominids could surely learn to associate various actions with various perceptual categories. Human speakers, once they had begun to exploit vocal sounds, may have found that they could assemble the intricately varied effects of vocal gestures into words signifying something and could invent more and more combinations of sounds and associate these with more and more things and events of vital interest to themselves and their fellows.

But words and sentences are different logical types. There is no number of words large enough to turn a lexicon of signs or words into a language. It is true that words without syntax can be used for successful referential communication, especially when the words' referents are all or mostly all in immediate view or in the top layer of their hearers' memories.

Language is a true system: like other systems, it stops working, it breaks down completely, it loses its nature, when either of its major components is missing. Syntax, another way of referring to the system for making sentences out of words, is neither a simple step nor a stroke of luck; it does not just happen because humans speak words one after the other. Syntax is essential to language, and its beginnings and evolution merit just as careful consideration as do the beginnings and evolution of speech.

According to Edelman (1987), words, whether made of vocal or visible gestural material, refer through neural nets to other neural nets that sweep through the brain when still other nets have transformed perception into recognition and recognition into memory. The brain structure needed for such connections and transformations has obviously evolved in the human species. But it is a plastic structure, not hard-wired: actual nerve connections and reconnections (neither abstract nor identical) are being made constantly in the experience of every individual. The first of these myriad connections owe to epigenesis, the development, gene-guided but subject to wide variation, of nerve cells and net-works. Each individual engaged in naming (word-making) whether in the Pleistocene or the present, must *learn* to associate any particular *word* or *sign* (the common term for words in a signed language) with a particular object or event.

Such learning continues to begin in mother-infant interaction. And before such learning begins, the infant engages in pre-liminary learning, correlating actions with perceptions. Petitto and Marentette (1991) have shown that deaf babies in deaf, sign-ing families go through a phase of "tuning" (as McCrone terms it) their word-making machinery; deaf babies "babble" gesturally, just as hearing babies babble vocally.

But learning words does not automatically lead to learning either to understand or to produce sentences. Sentences do not directly connect words made out of vocal or visible gestural ma-terial with things or events that are perceived and recognized and remembered. Words do that. Sentences *imply relations* between things and events, between actors and actions. Sentences refer to the relation of *doer* and *doing* (and, if there are any, who or what the doing is *done to*). Sentences, as grade-school grammar books used to phrase it, "express a complete thought." But where did that thought come from? What is a thought? How does a thought get completed? Edelman's "Biological theory of con-sciousness" shows how brain and neurological science can explain steps in the process by which higher-order consciousness evolves. In his theory, language is necessary for higher-order consciousness but language requires previous evolution of percep-tual categorization, primary consciousness, pre-syntax, and espe-cially conceptualization (a requisite of naming).

Words and the behavior and brain function of naming represent a significant step up from the primate potential for making motor acts that stand for concepts, but what a word stands for may be simple or complex, a very specific thing or a whole cluster of interrelated things, events, causes, and consequences – anything that catches the creature's attention and is represented by gestures, whether of upper body or vocal tract. But the very important cognitive act of deciding whether something is a thing in itself or merely a portion or aspect of something else requires a more sophisticated kind of brain function. Analysis and synthesis require language – word *and* sentence.

Recent research in brain functioning traces the way that words add a new fourth layer to perception and recognition and memory – those three cognitive activities performed by the brains of many animals. The argument is that frequently uttered words become inner words, and inner words become part of brain activity (neural connections), and brain activity of that kind can call up memory and initiate imagination, which is a novel arrangement of neural networks. With language (both word system and sentence system), new arrangements can be made of the many word-thing or word-event elements of thought. With language, thoughts can be completed (Edelman, 1989).

But random arrangements of words do not express a relationship. To do that requires syntax, a system for *making sense*, for putting words into certain relationships. Merely uttering words one after another does not confer syntax, although as we argued in Chapter 4, the ability to process complex strings is a prerequisite for the development of syntax. The question remains: how did hominids add a word-combining (not just word-stringing) system to their word-making system and so invent language?

To Lieberman, engaged as he is with the complexity of the organs of the speech tract and the brain's control over them, syntax may seem to offer "comparatively simple problems." Syntax looks anything but simple, however, to a reader of transformational-generative grammarians. Their pages are filled with rules of many different kinds, supposed to operate at many different levels. These rules do not explain the origin of syntax, however. Instead, the rule writers suppose that syntax is already there – in a single "language organ" or a set of different processing modules in the brain. They adopt the metaphor that the brain is a computer, already stocked with computational programs. Thus Steven Pinker:

A grammar defines a mapping between sounds and meanings, but the mapping is not done in a single step but through a chain of intermediate data structures, each governed by a subsystem. Morphology is the subsystem that computes the forms of words. (1991: 530).

The metaphor of brain as computer does not explain language nor its sentence-forming component, as Edelman makes clear. It simply transfers the problem. Besides, "a description of an ideal speaker-hearer's intrinsic competence" (Chomsky, 1965: 4) is a far more complex task than designing a computer and its subsystems.

The central problem in the origin of syntax is neither as simple as Lieberman would have it nor as complex as Chomsky's theory and "modular" theories derived from it make syntax seem to be. The central problem is this: how did hominids making signed and spoken words – engaging in visible and vocal gesturing (as we suppose) with both symbolic and communicative function – first begin to combine these discrete symbols in ways that caused the combination to mean more than the components could mean separately? Or were the "components" ever entirely discrete?

One solution to the problem as it has just been stated is that words have to be uttered one at a time, while signs can be produced simultaneously. Serious scholars of language origins (e.g. Wescott et al. 1974) have therefore suggested that signs and words may have worked together at first. McCrone's popular account offers this scenario:

> ... a general grunt would have stood for a very broad idea such as "termiting" or "share the food," serving to focus attention on the general topic of conversation. Extra meaning would then be given through the tone of voice or gestures. (1991: 159)

But the very likely possibility that hominids used both vocal and visible gestures to communicate does not in itself explain how doing so could lead to the invention of syntax. Syntax is neither simple nor a lucky fluke, as will be seen when its beginning is looked for in nonvocal gestures. The justification for this line of argument is that while the vocal tracts of modern humans differ from those of early hominids in ways that Lieberman has shown, the eyes, fingers, hands, arms, heads, and faces used by humans for visible gesturing have not changed significantly in perhaps millions of years. Laitman and others have shown a progressive evolution of the vocal tract toward its modern human configuration and that this evolution had begun as early as *Homo erectus* (Laitman, 1985). But visible gestures make use of anatomical structures little changed since the appearance of the hominid line. The gestures of *Homo erectus* would have looked quite like those of today's signers: hands and arms as different in structure as those of chimpanzees and humans can and do make gestures mutually understood, but once a hominid stood and walked in a fully upright posture and had a human, not a pongid, thumb, hand, and arm, its gestures would be physically indistinguishable from those of today (see Chapter 8).

7.4 SIGN LANGUAGES AND MANUAL GESTURES

Modern primary sign languages may differ as much from the earliest visible gestural communication as modern spoken languages differ from the earliest languages using speech;[1] but a close examination of the gestural activity in modern signed languages (as well as visible gestures used coincidentally with spoken languages) can reveal a hitherto overlooked source of syntax.

Lieberman, convinced that speech is a necessary prerequisite for language, does not rule sign language entirely outside the beginnings of language; he says:

[A]lthough scholars such as Gordn [sic] Hewes (1973) are probably correct in claiming that it [gesture] may have played an important role in the earlier stages of hominid evolution, sign language was never the exclusive channel for human language. (1991: 106)

Like other categorical negatives, this "never" is on dangerous ground. If visible gestures were the first and, at least for a time,

---

[1] However, the kinds of variations in speaking that lead to language change come about in the vocal tract where the productive actions are invisible; it is possible that gestures of the visible kind are constrained both by their visibility and by social conservatism to change more slowly (but see Frishberg, 1975).

eeh, both change pretty quickly

the preponderant, if not exclusive, channel for human language, much would be explained. The great increase of brain size and the emergence of those left-hemisphere elaborations that Lieberman sees as the effect of enormously expanded interconnections of vocal musculature, with ear, and brain could equally have resulted from interconnections of eye and brain with skeletal and facial musculature. Neurological research has shown that one of these brain structures, Broca's area may be just as intimately connected with timing and sequencing complex arm and hand and facial activity as with vocal activity (Kimura & Archibald, 1974). If visible gestures were early and for long periods used as words, the same enormously expanded interconnections between perceptual and central processing and motor networks could have – just as much as the use of spoken words – led to increase in brain size and required the evolution of the timing and sequencing functions in Broca's area.

Moreover, existence of an early sign language, whatever the size of its lexicon, would solve a problem that Lieberman's own research poses. His experiments suggest that Neandertal vocal tracts could not have produced all of the sounds required by languages of the kind that *Homo sapiens* uses (particularly [i] and [a]), yet Neandertal burials strongly suggest human culture. Neandertals may have been unable to manage fully a spoken language because of their vocal tract physiology, but if they had a system of visible signs for making words and could also form sentences from them – and there is no evidence that they could not – they would, by definition, have had a language and a culture with genuinely human characteristics.

But this and similar untestable hypotheses are side issues that we discuss in more depth in Chapter 8. Whether visible words alone or audible words alone became the material for sentences, or whether both together served in early populations' languages, the question how sentences might first have been made remains unanswered.

Again, direct proof may be lacking, but in its absence it is all the more important to understand the physical and the cognitive nature of visible gestures. Fortunately, scholars have begun to focus on visible gestures the attention they deserve as one of the possible first media of human language.

7.5 GESTURAL SYNTAX

The visible gestures most familiar to hearing people of many cultures are those that accompany speaking in face-to-face inter-action. Recent research has shown that such gestures are inti-mately connected with the gestures that produce speech and may well equally be the product of central language processing (Bolinger, 1972; Kendon, 1980; McNeill, 1985, 1992; McClave, 1991). The visible gestures deaf people use for language are much less well known for several reasons: deaf people constitute only about one-thousandth of the population; they tend generally to interact with others like themselves; they often suppress the open and full use of their language when they interact with hearing people.

There is another reason that signed languages are treated as less than language: the size of a sign language lexicon seems to the uninitiated observer small compared with that of a world lan-guage. But this apparent disproportion is an illusion. An observer without full competence in a sign language may conclude that one sign is seen again and again, but the signer and sign addressee see subtle differences in the movements that make a similar-appear-ing action into two different words; e.g. the difference between verb and noun (Supalla & Newport, 1978). Changes in facial expression, eye shifts, and head and shoulder movements also directly change the meaning: what seems the same sign repeated in a long passage may be as many as a dozen or more different signs.

Signs of a signed language are for convenience talked and written about as if they were the exact counterparts of words. Of course, they are not. Words and the sound segments compos-ing them must be uttered in sequence. Signs of a sign language can and do vary – within themselves, so to speak – because they are composed of things to be seen at the same time. Those unfamiliar with signed languages may find it hard to credit signed languages with lexicons as large as those of spoken lan-guages, and certainly the *available* lexicon of English vastly exceeds that of ASL (as it does all other spoken languages), but the number of different lexical items in the active vocabulary of a signer of ASL is of the same order as the number of words in a speaker's active vocabulary. Moreover, deaf people share the universal human attribute of inventing new words as the need arises.

Visible gestures of the familiar kind, the gesticulations hearing people make when they talk, have been thought to be less precise in meaning than the strings of words they accompany, but that may be a result of history: ever since writing was invented, speech recorded phonetically has been easier to investigate than visible gesture – for which there is still no satisfactory and generally accepted notational system. When other forms of notation (pictorial, ideographic) were displaced by alphabetic representation, with its focus on the sounds of spoken language, the meanings of words could be explained by other words, and language could be used to explain the structure of strings of words and sentences. The meanings of visible gestures could be explained in spoken and written language; but only words, not these gestures, could be written down for later study and closer analysis.

Although visible gestures often make clear what a speaker intends even though the spoken message is unclear, whether these gestures convey meaning directly, illustrate syntactic and semantic structure, or help maintain the rhythm of language utterance, most linguists have been slow to recognize that exclusion of this nonvocal part of language limits discovery (Birdwhistell, 1970; Kendon, 1975). What is clear from these alternatives is that gestures of this kind are variously related to the act of speaking – or rather to communicative interactions and language more generally – and strongly imply that unified brain activity governs both visible and audible output.

Language scholars as well as the general public have usually supposed these gestures incidental to speaking to be incapable of conveying the kinds of meaning found in spoken discourse. Nevertheless, such gestures continue to enhance the exchange of information – most people prefer a face-to-face conversation to a telephone conversation when important matters are discussed. Despite the usefulness of visible gestures, and probably because in comparison with spoken (and written) words visible gestures are much harder than words to study with strict, rigorous, logical, scientific scrutiny, the main intellectual tradition of the western world has focused on words, taken them as the only components of language, and left visible gestures in the twilight area of scientific investigation.

Anthropological linguists of an earlier generation (e.g. Bloch & Trager, 1942), who studied the cultural context as well as the language being used by a population, calculated that in normal conversation only a small fraction of the information exchanged is carried by the speech-hearing channel, and argued that the rest of the information is expressed by paralanguage (tone of voice but more than that), facial changes, posture and stance, the visible gestures just discussed, and other message systems.

Sign language gestures, in their linguistic function, are thus analogous both to spoken words and to the visible gestures that accompany speech. Sign language signs (that is, the words of signed languages) differ radically in physical structure from spoken words, and this difference reaches into syntax and meaning, as the next section will explain.

7.6 THE TREE IN THE SEED

The quaint metaphor once used for brain function and behavior, that a homunculus, a little man inside, runs the show, seems ridiculous today; but an equally venerable metaphor, that an oak tree lies compact in an acorn, turns out to be close to the truth. Genes in a seed and genes in a fertilized ovum not only guide the stages of growing to the mature organism but also determine what development is possible and what is not. A new metaphor (or paradox, "semantic phonology"), presented here almost for the first time (Stokoe, 1991) is that a visible gesture – a word of a sign language – may contain within itself not just a word but syntax and language in embryo.

It is quite obvious that visible gestures have a naming function, one possibly older than vocal naming (Kendon, 1991). But the common opinion is that the sign stopped there. The usual view of language origins tends to accept the visible gesture as an obsolete precursor of the spoken word, and to shelve it patronizingly alongside the hand-ax, the flint blade, and other exhibits of pre-history. That view is erroneous. In our view, the seed of language – the visible gesture – contains both word and syntax.

This apparent paradox is easily resolved and its truth can be seen in a simple demonstration – the reader is requested to perform the following and not just to read about it.

If you will, swing your right hand across in front of your body and catch with it the upraised forefinger of your left hand (Reverse these directions if you are left-handed).

What you have just done is not meant to be an actual gesture having a meaning in some existing gestural system but an action invented for this demonstration. Besides, what you have done – if you have really done it and not just read about it – is not a thing but an action. It is more: the dominant hand is the agent (it acts), its swinging grasp is the action (verb), and the stationary finger is the patient or object. The grammarians' symbolic notation for this is familiar: SVO. This order is also natural, as natural as the action itself. (From a limited perspective, things do get caught, e.g. "The mouse was caught by the cat," but on reflection or on closer inspection, the getting caught is seen to be the result of direct action by something or someone that catches.) Actions begin with and emanate from an actor.

All this depends, of course, on looking in a certain way at what was done with the hands and what appears to have happened. The grasping hand did not move itself; contractions of the muscles that rotate the humerus in its socket *moved* the whole arm and hand and fingers. Contractions of muscles also *had previously formed* the active hand into the configuration and the active and passive arms into the attitude needed for this particular action. The choice of tenses is crucial. The active part must be arranged first. All the muscular actions involved in forming the arms and hands into the required configurations, as well as those for performing the major movement here called "the action," are as much under control of regions in the left cerebral hemisphere as is the precise timing required to say "caught" (Kimura, 1993).

A second experiment in actual gestural production may make the importance of the priorities clearer. If the right hand is closed into a fist to begin with instead of being held open and spread, and if this hand springs open to present splayed fingers as it moves sharply forward (instead of across the front of the body), another event results, different from the first. The first action or event might be described thus: "The open hand catches and closes around an upright finger"; the second as follows: "The closed hand opens with a forward throwing motion." In both, the active hand had to be opened or closed perceptibly earlier (though the actual time is short) than the main action it performs.

This shaping of the acting (right) hand – precisely performed by brain-selected muscles – is crucial at a deeper level. The precise muscle timing (Kien's "presyntax") performed in the left cerebral hemisphere not only makes it possible to produce countless handshapes and actions that differ in great or small ways, but it is demonstrably a function of a particular part of the brain. According to Kimura (1991: 174): "The left cerebral hemisphere . . . is specialized for motor selection of both the oral and manual musculature." Whether syntax first emerged in vocal or in manual activity may still be in doubt, but there can be no doubt that the crucial matter of neural timing of what the muscles do is involved in both kinds of activity.

This discussion of arms and hands and actions and timing may seem to focus too much on unimportant matters: we do not have to think about what we do with our tongue and palate and larynx and lips when we make the vocal gestures of speech, and surely deaf people conversing in sign language do not focus their attention on the physical details of their actions. But this is precisely the reason for the caveat above. Visible gestures are not really looked at either by students of spoken languages, nor, paradoxically, by students of signed languages. It is natural to look at a gesture that one has performed or that someone else has performed as "a gesture," but doing so implies that it has a meaning, and one is likely to attend to the meaning and ignore the detail of the gesture. We expect that the gestures we and others make are made to signify and communicate; we seldom if ever look at them as having behind them as much complexity as lies behind the vocal tract gestures that result in speech.

One need not be familiar with a sign language to guess at the probable meaning of an unfamiliar gesture. The first manual exercise described above might mean 'catch' or 'arrest' or 'grasp.' Indeed, in some actual sign language it may mean one or all of these; but it could equally mean 'something captured something else' – or in suitable context, 'the hawk caught a gopher.'

Because the action has been described and performed simply as a demonstration of a possible action of the arms and hands, this particular action has no lexical meaning at all. But even if it is by definition meaningless, it possesses a structure: in it *something does something to something else,* or SVO – the seed of syntax.

The hands of the earliest recognizable hominids had a genuinely opposable thumb instead of a hand evolved for brachiation or knuckle walking. They could have performed gestural actions very similar to those described above, and it does not seem in the least unlikely that *Homo erectus*, whose skeletons show hands that qualify, and whose brains had already grown to three-fifths of the present average size (and were almost certainly lateralized), might have seen the similarity of such a finger-catching hand and its action to a predator seizing its prey. The perceived action and the gesture and the easily seen resemblance between them would have made a more natural pairing of sign with meaning than the "general grunt" for a "very broad idea" in the quotation above. But the important point here is not the ability of a visible gesture and the inability of a grunt to look like what they mean; the question of iconicity, transparency, and such physical resemblances will be discussed later. The importance of the early use of visible actions to signify and communicate is that they have, by their very nature, not only the potential to represent things or events, but they also have both the elements and the order – the structure of syntax – built into them.

There can be no doubt that early visible gestures would have functioned like words; they could have permanently named as well as temporarily pointed out things or persons. They still do this service for us and perhaps for chimpanzees. And, as many who study speech concede, visible gestures most probably were used by hominid populations, along with early spoken words, for naming things. But because gestures of this physical type contain the structure of the basic sentence – whether symbolized "SVO" or "NP + VP" – they also open the way to more sophisticated symbol use than naming; they permit language to begin; they symbolize relationships.

This section began with a look back at an outmoded epistemology. The homunculus inside satisfies few philosophers today, but a dominant theory of language postulates instead of the little man in every brain a few prime symbols and a finite set of rules; and modules that, operating with these symbols and rules, generate an infinite set of error-free symbol strings. Which is more in keeping with Occam's razor: having each brain contain S, NP, and VP; hence, S→NP + VP, and VP→V + NP (in other words, SVO); or having outside the brain, where any perceptive hominid can see in the same field of view, for example, a bird pecking at a berry and a thumb and forefinger plucking at a fingertip on the other hand?

7.7 THE OPENING OF THE SEED

It is not productive either to posit a stroke of luck or to suppose that syntax is a matter too simple to need explaining. Neither is it parsimonious to posit in all human brains a unique, highly complex, and identical or nearly identical neural hard-wiring dedicated exclusively to generating structures with syntactic relationships. The same is true of the suggestion that there are separate modules for managing regular and irregular morphology, syntax, and phonology. *Australopithecus* and *Homo* are primate genera. They belong to an order whose members are better at taking things apart than at putting them together, but to do that they need something to take apart. To see the rudiments of syntax, it is only necessary to look perceptively at the parts of a gesture like grasping a finger or miming throwing. Getting from consciously produced signs to syntax is a matter of analysis, not synthesis.

Given the gesture, with its acting element, its action, and (optionally) its surrogate for the thing acted on, the pioneers of the hominid progress toward sentence making seem more likely to have found syntax by taking the gesture apart than by making a lucky leap into the unknown and happening on a finite though very large set of logical categories – a set still being enlarged by grammarians. Even if we grant for the sake of argument that language requires a brain specifically configured to generate syntactic structures and to recognize and understand them, no biological theory to explain how the hard wiring could have come about has appeared; hence macro-mutation is invoked.

If theorists try to explain the systems for making (spoken or signed) words and for making sentences out of words as brain functions independent of other cognitive functions, they must then describe the particular behaviors from which such systems could have been selected. In the improbable chance that a sudden mutation equipped an individual human brain with the whole mechanism of grammar as described by the innatists, there would still be the problem of transmitting competence by these individuals to the rest of the species.

In the first place, the proponents of the theory of innate language competence insist that an infant must have such a brain in order to decode the utterances in its environment and later to compose its own. But language is a social as well as a biological system. A single brain mutationally so equipped might contain the competence to perform words and sentences, but performing them in the presence of others who lacked this competence is hardly likely to lead to the competent one's selection as a mate, and might well be deviant enough behavior to ensure that this unique, linguistically competent individual did not survive the experiment.

Allowing for sake of argument that the ability to create new words for things and events could have evolved from the general primate capability of associating vocalizations (and pointings and facial displays) with things and with states of the producer's emotions, leaves the trick of making words into sentences still unexplained. Putting spoken words, which have to be uttered one at a time, together to achieve syntax is not a matter for simple synthesis like fitting together bamboo poles to reach a banana, an operation that chimpanzees have been observed learning to do.

Suppose that words are the starting point: before they can be fitted into something resembling syntax as commonly understood, words must be sorted into categories — two categories at least to begin with: nouns and verbs, i.e. names for things that act and names for actions and states. But there is no way to do this sorting until the creature doing it has "seen" an SVO pattern in gesture and thus experienced an obvious demonstration that what acts and the action it performs are distinct but physically and temporally linked; nor can nouns that are subjects be distinguished from nouns that are objects without some notion that there exists something like an SVO pattern.

In gestural performance, hands can be agents or patients, and hands are not only logically different from the actions that they perform, but gesture makes actor and action visibly as well as proprioceptively distinct. Such differentiation at once yields the categories we call nouns and verbs, agents and actions, or subjects and predicates; but what they are called is of less importance (except to grammarians) than their differences in both the physical and semiotic domains. Without the pattern "SVO" provided by a simple manual gesture, the actual invention of language confronts a vicious circle: to categorize words requires syntax as the sorting principle; but to construct syntactic structure requires words already so sorted.

As writers have done for centuries, McCrone (1991) suggests that the SVO pattern of syntax is "a reflection of the patterns of cause and effect we see in the world around us." Earlier writers on sign language (e.g. Valade, 1854) pointed out that the order of signs in sign language sentences is a "natural order." In this they were quite correct, but they did not pursue this insight into the seminal nature of visible gestures.

One may easily suppose that hominids dimly saw this pattern in real world events; it is certainly out there, and anthropoid apes may also see it dimly. But it is one thing to see patterns and another to recognize that they are patterns and to symbolize them, either for the purpose of signifying to oneself or for communicating the insight to others. With words available only as associations between vocal actions and things or events, how would one go about fitting the words into a pattern or onto a pattern that did not already exist?[2] How would one *see* the pattern itself?

---

[2] This may explain Chomsky's belief that a human infant could not make sense of language heard without having a language system already complete in its brain.

Whether the starting point is one-at-a-time utterance of spoken words or the natural pattern of actor plus act, the next – the crucial – step, that of equating the relations in sentences with the relations in the outer world does not occur naturally from naming by vocal gestures. It is the pairing of visible events *with similarly structured visible gestures* that provides the relations, and the relations between relations, without which language and syntax are impossible. To transfer this to the Edelman scenario, the already primarily conscious hominid with symbolizing ability sees resemblance between things it is doing with its hands and events further away; reentrant mapping correlates in the brain the patterns in the near and the distant event, making them isomorphic in brain structure. In this regard, we are particularly excited by the discovery of Perrett and others (e.g. 1989) of elementary neuronal structures in macaque monkeys tuned to the detection of particular hand and forelimb configurations not unlike the handshapes of signed languages. We regard this as evidence for the existence of elementary neuronal groups that could provide the raw material for the construction of visible gestural "reentrant maps" along the lines of Edelman's TNGS.

Contrasted with the Herculean task of synthesizing (creating) syntax from words spoken alone, the cognitive act of focusing on part of the manual gesture to stand for part of the pattern does not seem as difficult. A manual-brachial gesture understood as representing a raptor seizing prey could be taken, in proper context, to stand for the raptor, or the prey, or the act of catching. Taking apart the manual gesture by focusing on the active hand in one situation, on the inactive target or object hand in another, and in still another on the action itself, would have resulted in an explosive multiplication of the lexicon of gestural words, and because of the syntactic pattern in the gesture, the visible words in it would already be effectively divided into nouns and verbs.

This brain-eye-limb activity, as was noted above, could have been equally as effective as speech in providing a selective factor for the rapid increase in human brain size and complexity in the last two million years. The social advantages such communication afforded would have contributed greatly to fitness of the population. But syntax, present in the gesture before it is taken apart, and involved in brain activity because of the relations in gestural actions seen, and in what the gestures signify, could have had an even more direct effect on brain evolution. Unlike words, which pair vocal or visible gestures with the (inner mapping of) things they name, syntax pairs relationships in the outside world with relationships within the brain; syntax deals in networks not nodes, neural matrices not modules.

7.8 LANGUAGE COEVOLVING WITH CULTURE

Whether a fully developed language using only visible gestures preceded a spoken language complete with syntax cannot be determined. Of course a vocally based language would have held great selective advantage for the species, once the ability to represent speech in alphabetic writing made spoken language vastly superior to signed language for preserving the culture of high civilizations. (Of course, one should not forget the mnemonic function of ritual, dance, and cave painting and other forms of early art that may have had close connections with visible gestural communication. Usually considered to be nonverbal, these art forms may well have had propositional uses if they were produced by people using a signed language.)

But writing is a very late development in the history of language, and signed and spoken languages both have their own advantages in pre-Neolithic cultures. Much of the aboriginal population of Australia still possess many elements of a hunting-gathering culture and hold tenaciously to an alternate sign language; the Warlpiri and other Australian peoples often choose, in various circumstances, to sign instead of speak (Kendon, 1989; Kwek, 1991).

Whether a complex language of visible signs or of vocal signs or a mixture of these two developed first is a question that does not need to be decided here. The important point is that syntax is already innate in visible gestures. Syntax is not being defined here, of course, as the standard T-G theory defines it – a finite set of logical categories, universal, governed by complex and interlocking rules of various types, capable of producing infinite combinations.

Syntax, in the evolutionary context, is the recognition, once things and events could be named, that certain relations obtain between the categorically different elements of events; i.e. actions and actors and things acted upon are effectively different. Syntax likewise implies recognition that names, like the things they name, can be sorted into actions and actors and patients. The actions of the upper body – once they have been seen to pattern exactly like other actions observed – bring about a special kind of pairing that might be symbolized as: svo⊃SVO or SVO⊃svo. (Whether the real-world event or its symbolization in language should be given the distinction of upper-case letters is debatable.) Here, of course, metaphor exerts its power in shaping the working of the brain, and of course the evolution of the brain. Naming itself is meta-phorical. When the metaphorical replacement of a real-world event by its miniaturization in gesture resulted in behavior that welded the social unit more closely and made its joint behavior more effective in surviving and improving the common lot of individuals, this kind of communicative behavior and the neural capacity behind it would have had a most powerful selective advantage.

7.9 ELABORATING THE PATTERN

The foregoing is far too simple a view of syntax, of course, to satisfy linguists. The subject and object nouns and the verb in this basic pattern of the sentence are only two of several "parts of speech." And, given the presence of S, V, and O in a gesture, the question arises: how did the simple SVO structure grow to admit adverbs and adjectives and to permit the subordination of one SVO structure, complete or truncated or altered, to another? Here again the power of vision and visible gestures suggests an answer. The producer of visible language gestures is not limited, as is the producer of a spoken utterance, to uttering one word, or one sound of a word, at a time.

Suppose the early user of signed language produces an action that both means and is understood by others as 'He [that one

188   *The origin of syntax*

there] caught it.' But suppose that the individual referred to, the one who caught something, is the least likely person in the group to be successful in a hunt. The signer of the signifying gesture may simultaneously be raising the eyebrows, a pan-cultural facial expression of surprise (Ekman & Friesen, 1978). A modern speaker of English, in some situations, can also simultaneously express astonishment that the one referred to could have been so lucky, simply by using "tone of voice," which is actually the use of several paralinguistic systems that speakers control. But facial expressions and tones of voice leave innatist grammarians nothing to do, because they have drawn the boundaries of language to exclude these kinds of "nonverbal" behavior from what they study. The modern speaker can, however, stick to spoken language "proper" and use an adverb, a phrase, a clause, a paraphrase or one of many other devices to modify meaning, e.g.:

'He somehow caught it.'
'By a lucky fluke, he caught it.'
'The guy with two left hands caught it.'
'After it fell down paralyzed, he caught it.'
'Yeah; Klutzy there caught it.'

This kind of elegant and inelegant variation on the underlying theme became possible, only after the simple SVO pattern had begun to be used in spoken form.

The possibility of modifying the basic signal, however, was there all the time in visible gesturing, because vision is not dimensionally limited as is hearing. The signer signing 'He caught it' can be at the same time expressing with face and posture any of the nuances of meaning in the paraphrases above and many others as well. Once again, visually signed language has furnished the seminal relationship between the basic symbolization of a complete idea and the means for modifying the idea. While the manual gesturing supplies the basic SVO structure, its producer's facial expression and posture changes add simultaneous adjectival or adverbial material.

The surprisingly rich development of this potentiality of gesture in a modern primary sign language was first described in a chapter ("written in collaboration with Carlene Canady Pedersen" [a native user of American Sign Language]) of *The signs of language* (Klima & Bellugi, 1979). Another breakthrough in the understanding of the grammar and syntax of signed languages is Supalla and Newport's "How many seats in a chair" (1978). Supalla (also a deaf native signer) shows how subtle adjustments in the action of an ASL sign mark the sign as either verb or noun.

Modification of the meaning of a visibly gestured sentence by other actions that the signer performs at the same time is by no means limited to adverbial modification, affective additions, or elegant variation. As early as 1960 it was shown that important signals about the intent of an ASL sentence – Is it a statement, a command, a question? And if a question, what kind? – are not primarily manual actions. Changes in facial expression, eye gaze, and head and body movement have such syntactic functions. Liddell (1980) explored some of these, as did Baker-Shenk (1983), who used the Ekman-Friesen *Facial Action Coding System* to make fine-grained analysis of the actions involved in this kind of syntax signaling in ASL.

The physical nature of visible gesture is determined by musculoskeletal anatomy of the human upper body, which fossil evidence shows has not changed significantly from the time of *Homo habilis* at least two million years before the present. Thus, the outward form of gestures would not have changed much either, from their earliest human use to their ultimate organization in modern signed languages. Darwin (1873) described the expression of basically adjectival meanings like 'good' and 'bad,' adverbial approval and disapproval, and a great deal more in the visible and vocal gesturing of animals. Once the modern observer gets past the stage of protesting that only speech can be the primary symbolization of language and begins really to look at the evidence, it becomes clear that in a language of visible signs, adjectives need neither to precede nor to follow nouns as physically distinct elements but can appear simultaneously as modifications in the performance of the sign language word. Likewise, adverbial modification of gesture action is a natural effect of the way that visible gestures are performed. Such visible "parts of speech" may be based in emotional states, a fact that renders them suspect to those who hold modular theories of language; but the possibility that intellect may have grown out of emotion – disregarding the compression and inadequacy of the terms *intellect* and *emotion* – is not unlikely.

This look into the syntax of a signed language used by a deaf population, possessing modern human brains, that is more or less fully integrated into a modern urban culture takes us far in one direction from the beginnings of language. It brings us closer, however, in another direction to the elements available to early members of our species and to other hominid species for inventing language. So much attention has been paid to the elements of spoken languages and so little to those of signed languages that it is important to see what potential the latter actually have.

Some of those who focus research on sign languages, as has been mentioned (Chapter 3), make much of the similarities of signed and spoken languages; and it can hardly be doubted that living in the modern world surrounded by written, printed, and projected language (although its primary form is inaudible to them), deaf persons in America have made changes in their signed language that reflect certain features of English while re-taining the natural structure of their language (Battison, 1978). But the human form – with its hands and arms and face and head and eyes – has been available for complex and rapid signaling at least as long as has the two-chambered vocal tract that made speech efficient, and probably for much longer.

A great deal remains to be found out about the modern sign languages that deaf populations use as their primary languages, and also about alternate sign languages used by hearing people who have a spoken language available to them. Our concerns here, however, are with the potential of visible actions to name things, and especially, to represent relations – not how this poten-tial became actual use by early humans, and when in the evolutionary time scale the breakthrough happened. Using the potential in visible actions could certainly have led to incremental brain evolution when more and more frequent and complex actions of the face and upper body for more than simple emotion display and danger signaling became part of everyday social life. In this respect, Corballis (1991: 186) notes the following:

Gestures may have provided the basis for propositional language, perhaps first in the form of pointing to people or things or indicating actions. . . . [V]ocalizations may have gradually become associated with actions . . .

7.10 GESTURE AND ICONICITY

It has become obvious in this discussion, if it was not already evident, that there are points of resemblance between, for example, a raptor snatching a sitting-up rodent and one hand snatching at an upright finger on the other. Many mammals are capable of seeing both of these actions, but seeing a resemblance between the members of the pairs in them (making the analogy "SVO: svo"[3]) might have been facilitated by a brain as large and complex as that possessed by *Homo habilis*. Nevertheless, this very resemblance between a visible gesture and what it is used to signify has been used to deny that sign languages belong in the class of *languages*. Such visible gestures are termed "motivated" by those who think that language signs must be arbitrary and that language is a human behavior independent of the cognitive functions shared with other animals. Others describe the signs of a modern sign language as "iconic" or "transparent." Many of these signs are iconic indeed, and this is a circumstance that could have led hominids to see a resemblance between external events and gestural actions. But in the tradition stemming from Saussure (or the lecture notes of his students), "motivation" has been used to deny that such signs can be signs of language. According to this tradition, language signs must be symbolic, arbitrary, unmotivated; i.e. without resemblance of any kind to what they denote.

The Saussurean is not the only semiotic tradition, however. Charles S. Peirce described several characteristics of signs. In his work, and semiotics generally, the word *sign* is used to mean anything that stands for something not itself. Peirce also laid down a critical definition of "the sign function": it consists of the sign vehicle and what it stands for, of course, but also an essential third

---

[3] Or in Langacker's terminology (1985), the semantic pole SVO and the phonological pole hand, action, acted upon.

thing that Peirce called the "interpretant." Signs, according to Peirce, relate to their meanings only through the interpretant, and they may relate as icons, indexes, or symbols, or a combination of these.

Peirce's insistence on an animate interpretant separates signs of this kind from the signals that the computer chips built into modern automobile engines send to the fuel injectors, the spark timing, the opening for intake air, and the crankcase ventilation valve. These latter are not signs because they do not need interpretation: if the sensor calls for more fuel, more fuel is pumped; if it calls for retarded spark, the spark is retarded. However, the gauges some manufacturers still include on the dashboard do qualify as signs: if the pointer on the fuel gauge points to "Empty," the driver can heed it and get more fuel, or can ignore it and risk the consequences.

Signs that have a large iconic component and quite obviously resemble what they mean are naturally rare in the world's spoken languages; there is an obvious limit to what sounds made by the voice can resemble; but Wescott (1971), Givens (1986) and others discuss some of the less obvious ways in which vocal symbols can relate to what they signify. Signs made visible by the body and its parts can much more easily resemble things and actions, and users of modern primary sign languages tend to modify their gesture-words until they lose both iconicity and transparency.

Signs of a sign language are also richly indexic; the users of signed languages point to what they mean, and not just with hand and arm direction; eyes, faces, heads, and even lips have pointing functions. Gestural signs can also have both iconic and indexic qualities; Peirce's definitions are not meant to be mutually exclusive. Thus, in the ASL sign **TEMPERATURE**, the right index finger moving up and down *points to* the rise and fall of a mercury or alcohol column, and the vertical left index finger *looks like* (perhaps) the stem of a thermometer. Thus, the ASL word is both index and icon, but neither sign nor thermometer would make any sense to a member of an isolated pre-Neolithic culture, and so it is symbolic; its iconicity or transparency is far from being a universal quality, as iconicity appears to be interpreted in the tradition after Saussure.

It is in such an isolated culture, however, that the iconic properties of signs in one primary sign language have been most fully examined. Rolf Kuschel (1973) found on a Polynesian outlier island, a man named Kangobai, deaf from birth, using a sign language with his family and companions. Kangobai was the first deaf infant in twenty-two generations believed to have survived to adulthood (in a culture where infanticide was formerly practiced), and so his is by definition an autochthonous sign system. Kuschel discovered also that what is iconic or not may depend largely on culture. He performed some of Kangobai's signs for natives of other Polynesian islands, for his Danish students, and for American colleagues. All groups immediately recognized what these signs were used to mean; they were, of course, signs for actions like eating, drinking, striking with a fist, throwing a small object, etc.

Other signs, however, only members of the first of these groups could understand, because these signs were iconic only within a particular culture. One of them, for example, Kangobai's sign for coconut was immediately understood by natives of distant Pacific islands, who knew nothing of Kangobai or the island he lived on. Although Polynesians understood the sign at once, Western observers drew a blank, or guessed that this sign might mean 'changing a light bulb.' Again, Western observers, to whom a gesture meaning 'fishing' mimes the use of a rod and line, could not guess Kangobai's perfectly transparent (to Polynesians) sign, because in their culture spear-fishing at night by torch light is the norm.

Still other of Kangobai's signs that Kuschel performed for these three different groups remained opaque to all except Kangobai's own companions. Only they knew that two of these signs, for example, meant 'father' and 'brother.' Until these signs had been generalized by Kangobai and his peers to become common nouns, the signs had been direct indexes: a finger pointed to a body part that figured importantly in the life story of Kangobai's own father or brother. Signs of this last group, beginning as indexic-iconic, were arbitrarily assigned to unique individuals to begin with, but they were fully symbolic when Kuschel encountered them.

This power of the visible gesture to resemble or point to what it represents has surely contributed to the lack of knowledge about visible gestures in many linguists' thinking, simply because they have been taught that linguistic signs must be unmotivated. It is, nevertheless, a most important power. Something a hominid can do, which can be seen by others and can also be seen by them to look like or point out something else that they can see, is motivated to be sure, but it can be the first step to signifying and to communicating with syntax, and hence to symbolizing. It constitutes a first step that is not mysterious, but exactly when in geological time it occurred still remains a question.

The natural composition of a such a gesture, containing as it does the essential elements of a sentence in addition to its iconic and indexic naming power, introduces, at the very moment of its first symbolic use, the germ of syntax, sure to grow in the fertile brain of a creature that has escaped, by this very act of symbolizing relationships, the hold of the immediate environment on perception, recognition, and memory.

7.11 SIGNALING SYNTAX

Another way that visible gesture takes a leading place in the emergence of syntax, and so of language, is in signaling the function of an utterance. Again iconicity is involved. In spoken language, a drop in the pitch of the voice followed by silence sends a signal. This signal marks the conclusion of an utterance or a sentence or even a conversational turn. Sustained, level pitch followed by silence sends a different signal; this signal indicates that the speaker will shortly resume speaking. A rise in pitch followed by silence sends a still different signal: the listener is expected to respond to the question just asked. But these descriptions are all metaphorical. Pitch, or the frequency of sound perceived, varies according to the number of changes in power per unit of time. Calling a faster rate of vibration "higher" and a slower rate "lower" is by now so common a way of speaking and thinking that we forget that these words are metaphors. There is nothing physically *up* or *down* in the actual phenomena – only more or fewer vibrations. We must look to signed languages to find *higher* and *lower* with literal and not metaphorical force.

When the analogous signals identifying this kind of utterance in sign languages are examined, the origins of the metaphors leap to the eye: the signer lowers hands at the end of an utterance or a sentence or a turn,[4] and the eye gaze moves down as well. The equivalent of a "comma pause" or level pitch in signing is signaled by keeping the hands in position for signing, not dropping them as at the end of a message. Corresponding with rising pitch for a question, a signer keeps the hands in place at the conclusion of the final sign or even pushes them forward toward the interlocutor, and at the same time intensifies eye gaze (by raising the upper lids) and lifts the gaze from the general face–neck area to make eye-to-eye contact with the one addressed.

If language complete with syntax and expressed by visible gestures antedated spoken language of the same completeness, that would explain the use of the metaphors "higher" and "lower" for language junctures. The head is up and the feet are down; the body and vision provide unmistakable bench marks for spatial reference. If spoken language syntax came out of nowhere (simply, or by lucky chance), the whole matter of how *up* and *down* came to be metaphors for voice pitch and loudness remains unexplained.

This discussion of juncture phenomena serves as a reminder that silence is an important element in spoken languages. Although it receives little attention in linguistic treatments of language, the way that the voice changes *to silence* – going up, down, or staying level in pitch – signals essential messages. In signed languages, at least in primary sign languages, silence and its contrast with sound have no part in the signaling system. Most users of a primary sign language cannot hear sound, even at "high" levels of intensity, and only some of them produce incidental vocal sounds while communicating with other signers. A speaker is either audible or has ceased vocalizing for a moment, but a signer remains visible whether actively engaged at the

---

[4] The lowered hands in most instances are in contact with each other and often rest on some part of the body (Baker-Shenk, 1983).

moment in producing lexical signs or not. Because of the difference of the perceptual systems employed by speakers and signers, the all important syntactic signals of signed languages must be attended to by direct visual attention; spoken language signals with the same functions can be heard whatever direction the listener to spoken language is looking.

Speakers, users of spoken language, have thus been freed from the necessity of looking directly at the signal source. Sound may reach the listener more satisfactorily if the two ears are equidistant from the source, but it can be heard even if they are not. This freedom from the necessity for visual attention is often noted as one of the advantages of spoken languages over signed languages, but it does not affect the argument about priority. If language began, and it must have, as a social adaptation, it was surely preceded by a long stage of paying very close visual attention to the activity of the others in the social group, particularly activity that places individuals face to face. This is exactly the kind of thing observers of chimpanzees in the wild find happening, and as the films they have made attest. Thus, as naming and syntax-containing gestures of hominids began to be used, they would have been simple though profound additions to the (primate) gestures already in use for command and control and interpersonal communication within the social group. Finally, as we pointed out above, there is evidence for the neurological substrate of arm and handshape recognition in nonhuman primates (Perrett et al., 1989).

The transfer from visible (literal) to vocal (metaphorical) gesturing of such messages as these juncture signals send may have taken place early in the hominid acquisition of spoken language. Hearing children in spoken language environments make excellent vocal imitations of sentence intonation envelopes – with dropping pitch, sustaining pitch, and rising pitch – several months before they acquire more than a few words. But all children, deaf children in signing families and other children as well, acquire from birth the visible-gestural management of face-to-face interaction by directly participating in it. A system as useful to a social species as language, with its tremendous adaptive advantages in the prehistoric world, a system that grew, moreover, out of already existing ways of behaving face to face, would seem more likely to have been in place sooner than a system that must map the four dimensions of acts in space and time into the limited dimensionality of vocal sounds.

Chen Kang Chai's chapter, "The character of human evolution" is the eighth and last in his *Genetic evolution* (1976). It begins with "A brief history of *Homo sapiens*" and discusses "... a few essential biological characteristics, such as bipedalism, expansion of brain size, development of self-consciousness, and the interplay between biological and cultural evolution" (p. 266). These characteristics are listed in the order of their emergence, but there can be no doubt that the earlier characteristics were fully involved with the later in the evolution of the species:

> It is known that the evolution of bipedalism began earlier than that of brain expansion in the hominids. But through transmission of brain impulses, bipedalism has stimulated the development of the brain. Thus, through the hands of man, the mental faculty was transformed into cultured expression. (Chai, 1976: 275)

We venture to say that the truth in Chai's last sentence has, for the most part, been interpreted metonymically. Hominid hands did shape tools for striking and piercing and cutting, did ignite and control fire, did fashion clothing and habitation, and did domesticate animals and cultivate plants. But with their hands and developed brain and greatly increased eye-brain-hand neural circuitry, hominids may well have invented language – not just expanding the naming function that some animals possess but finding true language, with syntax as well as vocabulary, in gestural activity. The development of self-consciousness would be a natural development from simple consciousness that a self-made gesture and an action observed have analogous structures. Thus, Chai's words apply to more than the metonymic or metaphoric sense of hands. To paraphrase and emend Chai:

Through the hands of man, the mental faculty was transformed *gesturally* into language, and through language into cultured expression.

CHAPTER 8

Language from the body: an evolutionary perspective

> When we no longer look at an organic being as a savage
> looks at a ship, as at something wholly beyond his com-
> prehension; when we regard every production of nature as
> one which has had a history; when we contemplate every
> complex structure and instinct as the summing up of many
> contrivances, each useful to the possessor, nearly in the same
> way as when we look at any great mechanical invention as
> the summing up of the labour, the experience, the reason,
> and even the blunders of numerous workmen; when we thus
> view each organic being, how far more interesting, I speak
> from experience, will the study of natural history become!
>
> Charles Darwin, *Origin of species*

If "language" were substituted for "organic being" and "natural
history" in the excerpt above, Darwin might be expressing the
perspective on the origin and evolution of language which we
have articulated in this book. We argue that language grows
out of a complex of primary human adaptations, including bipedal locomotion, social living, reproduction without an estrous
cycle, postnatal epigenesis, postreproductive longevity, and division of labor within the family. In addition, we argue that language grows out of more primitive primate and mammalian
neuro-behavioral complexes, including those that govern
face-to-face interaction, categorization, and symbolization.
Finally, we argue that the key to the transition from primate
vocal and visible gesture systems to language (that is, names
organized into sentences) is the introduction of iconic, visible
gestures at some point in hominid evolution. Perhaps the most
important point we make is that syntax, the *sine qua non* of *human*
language, emerges out of such visual-gestural systems, as we
argued, in depth, in the previous chapter.

8.1 THE HOMINID ADAPTIVE COMPLEX

Aristotle had it right. What sets humans apart from other mammals is bipedalism – humans are "terrestrial biped animals" (Barnes, 1984: 237). The fossil record establishes bipedalism as the fundamental human anatomical adaptation, preceding increases in brain size. The adaptive radiation that led to the divergence of the hominids from the African great apes (gorillas and chimpanzees – without doubt the closest living relatives of human beings), then, was characterized by a shift in life style that favored upright posture and bipedalism. Exactly what this shift in life style was has been the subject of a huge, and largely speculative, literature. We note of course that we are also engaged in speculation, so we will not be deterred from considering the main features of this literature. However, at this juncture, we are more interested in the other anatomical and behavioral changes that accompanied the shift to bipedalism, and we are referring to these as the "human adaptive complex" (see Clark, 1963).

At this point, we will not discuss language itself as part of this complex, because it is impossible to say with certainty when behavior sufficiently like modern human language arose; and, given our interest in gesture, we are not prepared to offer a definition of language precise enough to distinguish the last stage of prelanguage from the first stage of language. However, in making this last statement, we are already taking a theoretical position that distinguishes us from some theorists on this matter. Specifically, we take a Darwinian position that assumes there were gestural precursors of language that are logically and phylogenetically related to it. We do not support the position that it arose, *de novo*, probably in the Upper Paleolithic (that is, coincident with the appearance in Europe of creatures anatomically indistinguishable from modern humans roughly 40,000 years ago), with no real precursors (see, e.g., Dibble, 1989; Davidson & Noble, 1989; Milo & Quiatt, 1993). In any event, we will discuss this theoretical division in more detail later in this chapter.

What are the main features of the human adaptive complex? In addition to bipedalism, humans have some other anatomical peculiarities. Most notably, their hands have fully opposable thumbs, and, compared to the African apes, their fingers are much shorter. The hands in general are capable of much finer manipulation of objects – the hands of a tool maker and, we argue, a signer. The evolution of the human hand toward its current configuration appears to be fairly coincident with the evolution toward bipedalism and fully upright posture, thus Zihlman (1990: 193):

[B]ipedal locomotion was presumably the basis for the divergence of the hominid lineage, so that hominid hands from the time of divergence no longer functioned in bearing weight; instead natural selection favored hand mobility, flexibility, and power and precision grips.

In addition, humans exhibit handedness and an underlying cerebral asymmetry (see Chapter 4). The evidence suggests that it was probably already present in *Homo habilis* (Corballis, 1991: 86–188), perhaps earlier (Falk, 1980).

Human beings have generalized teeth and unlike other higher primates lack a pointed canine extending beyond the occlusal plane. The teeth in the upper and lower jaws are arranged in the form of a parabola or arch, rather than the parallel rows from the third molars to the canines characteristic of the apes; and the tongue is shorter, more massive and capable of greater flexibility in movement. All of this is characteristic of a pattern of chewing food in which the teeth form a flat grinding surface. This suggests that hominids had a diet that contained hard fibrous food. The lack of tearing and piercing teeth could, by inference, have been compensated for by the use of tools for cutting and piercing.

Humans have very large brains relative to their body size. Brain size increased relatively slowly during hominid evolution and the earliest hominids who were fully bipedal had brains that were similar in size to those of chimpanzees. Again, the evidence suggests that the adoption of bipedal locomotion, and the changes in life style that drove the evolution of the morphological changes needed for that pattern of locomotion, preceded increases in brain size and the undoubted increases in behavioral complexity that accompanied it.

The neurobiologist William Calvin has developed a detailed theoretical explanation for the expansion of the human brain that involves the presumed use of missiles in hunting (summarized in Calvin, 1990). Calvin observes that the act of throwing a missile at a distant target involves a sequence of judgments and actions so rapid that it could not benefit from self-correcting feedback during execution. He reasons that this would require development of massively parallel serial buffers, probably in the frontal lobes of the cerebrum. We find this argument plausible, but have several reservations. First, it is impossible to know what degree of importance ballistic hunting techniques may have assumed in the subsistence activities of hominids at various times in prehistory, although one might infer that they were very important in Ice Age Europe. Second, we believe that the elaboration of gestural communication along the lines we advocate here must certainly have been a concomitant driving force in brain expansion. Several strategic behavior patterns evolving in parallel would have contributed to increasing rapidity of brain expansion.

The human upper respiratory system is also quite different from that of other primates (Laitman, 1985; Lieberman, 1991). In most mammals, the passage from the mouth to the larynx is relatively straight and short, the larynx being high up in the neck. According to Laitman (1985: 282), "This high position permits the epiglottis to pass up behind the soft palate to lock the larynx into the nasopharynx, providing a direct channel from the nose through the nasopharynx, larynx and trachea to the lungs." Because of this arrangement, mammals can eat or drink and breathe at the same time. As there are two separate pathways for air and food, death by choking on food is rare. However, because this pattern results in a small supralaryngeal pharynx, only a small range of sounds can be produced. In adult humans, on the other hand, the larynx descends to a much lower level in the neck due to a flexing of the base of the cranium. This has two principal effects: it creates a common pathway for food and air, greatly increasing the risk of choking; and it creates a much larger supralaryngeal pharynx, increasing the range of vowel sounds that can be produced.

The reasons for this evolutionary change are problematic. To what extent is this pattern due to selection for hominids who could speak more efficiently and to what extent is it due simply to the hominid adaptation to upright posture? In quadrupeds, the head is slung forward, in front of the body, and the spinal column exits the skull through an opening, known as the foramen magnum, relatively far back on the skull. In a biped, the head balances on top of the spinal column, and the foramen magnum is at the base of a skull that has been flexed under.

Lieberman (1991) and Laitman (1985) have attempted to simulate the sounds that various hominids might have been able to make, based upon reconstructions of the upper respiratory tracts of fossil hominids. These results have sometimes been controversial. For example, results obtained by Lieberman and Crelin (1971) were widely interpreted to mean that the Neandertals (a subspecies of *H. sapiens*) of the Upper Pleistocene, who immediately preceded anatomically modern humans in Europe, were incapable of speech, although Lieberman himself (1991: 65) does not subscribe to this interpretation. Not the least of the problems associated with this interpretation, is the phylogenetic status of the European Neandertals. Laitman has summarized the results of this research as follows:

The crucial restructuring of the hominid upper respiratory tract may thus have begun some $1\frac{1}{2}$ million years ago with *Homo erectus*. The incipient degree of basicranial flexion in this group indicates that the larynx may have begun its descent into the neck, thus changing the basic mammalian upper respiratory pattern retained by our australopithecine ancestors . . . While change may have begun at this time, the first instances of full basicranial flexion similar to that of modern humans does not appear until the arrival of *Homo sapiens* some 300,000 to 400,000 years ago. (1985: 285–286)

We interpret these results as suggesting relatively gradual evolution of the effectiveness of speech as the medium of language and note that the human hand had reached its current configuration well before this time. Moreover, there continues to be controversy over interpretations of new fossil evidence. Arensburg and his associates (1989) report the discovery of the complete hyoid bone of a 60,000-year-old hominid at Kebara in

Israel. They claim that the bone is indistinguishable from that of a modern human, indicating that a fully modern upper respiratory tract had been achieved by this time. Lieberman, however, disputes this claim (1991 and see Houghton, 1993).

Evidence for all of the morphological changes in humans that we have thus far mentioned can be at least inferred from the fossil record as they are reflected in the skeleton and dentition. There are some other morphological peculiarities of humans that cannot be so recorded, thus one can only speculate about their time of origin, including most especially that humans are relatively hairless, with the exception of the head and face (in men), and the areas surrounding the genitalia. The hairlessness of humans is related to a system of cooling in hot weather that involves sweating, rather than panting, as the primary mechanism of heat transfer to the air. The evolution of this mechanism was presumably enabled by the ability of humans to use fire, to construct shelter, and to manufacture clothing and bedding as protection against death by hypothermia. This again reinforces the notion that the "hard" evidence for human evolution, some time after the adoption of upright posture and the freeing of the hands for manufacturing, followed a path that became increasingly *technological*. Maintenance of the hair in certain strategic locations may be plausibly (but controversially) linked to human sexual behavior, including lack of an estrous cycle so that the female is more or less continuously sexually active, and the adoption of social behavior that we will discuss below.

8.2 DARWINIAN THEORY: GRADUALISM, INCREMENTALISM, AND PUNCTUATION

Stephen Jay Gould has described a principal question in evolutionary biology – whether evolution by natural selection proceeds by the slow and fairly continuous accumulation of small adaptive changes ("gradualism") or by rapid "saltational" changes in structure, followed by long periods of relative stability ("punctuated equilibrium"):

Is our world (to construct a ridiculously oversimplified dichotomy) primarily one of constant change (with structure as a mere incarnation of the moment), or is structure primary and constraining, with change as a "difficult" phenomenon, usually accomplished rapidly when a stable structure is stressed beyond its buffering capacity to resist and absorb. (Gould, 1982: 383)

Note how strikingly the latter part of this dichotomy resembles the discussion of structural change in ontogeny given by William James (quoted in Chapter 5). It is the case, of course, that in the fossil record of the hominids we can find what appear to be examples of both parts of the dichotomy.

Gould (1982: 382) also makes the following observation:

At the levels of microevolution and speciation, the extreme saltationist claim that new species arise all at once, fully formed, by a fortunate macromutation would be anti-Darwinian, but no serious thinker now advances such a view . . .

This of course is exactly what Bickerton is advocating in the case of changes in the vocal tract and brain in the origin of *Homo sapiens*.

[S]yntax must have emerged in one piece, at one time – the most likely cause being some kind of mutation that affected the organization of the brain. Since mutations are due to chance, and beneficial ones are rare, it is implausible to hypothesize more than one such mutation. Several factors suggest, indeed, that just such a single mutation gave rise to our species. (Bickerton, 1990: 190)

Bickerton then goes on to assert that such a mutation might also have given rise to changes in the supralaryngeal vocal tract. However, despite presenting this critical comment by Gould, we take Bickerton's argument seriously. We have pointed out that a candidate mutational mechanism has been proposed by Greenhood (1992) in terms of a hypothetical homeotic gene. We have already presented an alternative to Bickerton's approach to the origin of syntax and here will present a more detailed critique of his evolutionary argument.

In the first section of this chapter, we presented a set of evidence that suggests *relatively* gradual evolution of the human vocal tract. The key word here is *relatively*. Clearly, it is possible to take a theoretical position that lies between single generation saltation and change by infinitely slow accretion. There is, however, a more fundamental sense in which Bickerton's assertion cannot be true within the current definition of species. Two populations are said to belong to different species if they are unable by inter-breeding to produce fertile offspring. This definition underlies one of the most important concepts in evolutionary biology: speciation follows reproductive isolation (Mayr, 1942). Bickerton's proposed mutation could not possibly have led to a *species* difference unless it also affected the reproductive system.[1]

This is not a trivial point, and it points to a fundamental misconstrual of the process of speciation. Speciation is the process by which *two populations* become reproductively isolated and then undergo suffficient morphological changes over time so as to become unable to interbreed productively. But the term is also loosely misapplied to the process whereby a single lineage under-goes change over time so as to appear sufficiently different from ancestral forms as to justify the creation of a new taxonomic category. As Gould points out, this does not and cannot occur in a single generation, as the macromutation would have to affect *all or nearly all of the members of the species*. In the evolution of a lineage, there is no point in time at which one can say that the original species has changed into the new species. For this reason, species such as *Homo erectus* and *Homo sapiens* that represent

---

[1] In attempting to imagine what, other than gross differences in the reproductive system, might have prevented Neandertals and anatomically modern humans from interbreed-ing, we cannot resist taking the reader on what we hope will be an amusing detour through ever more fanciful Paleolithic landscapes. It has been suggested that speaking anatomically modern humans might have rejected as mates inarticulate Neandertals. First, one imagines the tall, graceful Cro-Magnon maiden's repulsion at the brutish appearance of the short, rugged Neandertal man. Given the speculations about the speech of the Neandertals, one then imagines the inarticulate but importunate Neandertal, much like the proverbial stammering schoolboy on his first date, attempting to accomplish with a floral bouquet and choice joint of mammoth what he cannot achieve through speech. Finally, reflecting on the presumed ability of our Neandertal *inamorato* to sign, we imagine him pressing his suit eloquently with the universal signs of love, overcoming the objections of the maiden's anatomically modern relatives with his evident prowess as a hunter (remember the presentation of the mammoth joint). We are, thus, unable to find an unbreachable impediment to this union, however star-crossed it might seem.

different segments of a hominid lineage do not have the same biological status as coexisting species such as horses and donkeys.

It is clear from a reading of Bickerton's scenario for the appearance of syntax that he does not really mean that a single mutation "gave rise to the species," in the sense we just described. Rather, his scenario goes something like this: the favorable mutation he describes appeared in a local population of hominids (perhaps member of *Homo erectus*, perhaps another lineage descended from *Homo habilis*), probably somewhere in Africa, probably around 200,000 years ago. This mutation spread rapidly throughout the population, giving it a selective advantage over neighboring populations. It continued to spread throughout hominid populations either by replacement of those populations (note that this would be genocide, not speciation) or interbreeding or some combination of the two. The culmination of this vivid scenario is the elimination of the so-called classic Neandertals of Western Europe, considered to have been sufficiently isolated from other hominids to have become, in fact, a separate species.[2] This is not an implausible theory, and it is held by several prominent scholars, but in no sense does it support the notion that a mutation enabling syntax gave rise to our species, any more than the mutations enabling bipedalism did. It is not even clear how "saltational" it is. One man's saltational event may be another man's deflection in an otherwise gradual curve of change over time. An example from Bickerton's book will serve to illustrate this.

We have stated previously that both brain size and the configuration of the vocal tract appear to have changed relatively gradually ("incrementally" in the case of brain size) throughout hominid evolution, and that evidence for Broca's area dates at

---

[2] There is an essential difference between the claim that anatomically modern humans and Neandertals represented separate species and the claim that Neandertals made no genetic contribution to modern populations. Anatomically modern humans might well have been capable of fertile interbreeding with Neandertals, while nevertheless eradicating them totally. Genocide of this sort is not unknown in human history. It is simply impossible to prove whether or not such populations might have been physically capable of interbreeding. Note that the European Neandertals have been in and out of the modern human lineage numerous times, according to the dominant paleoanthropological theories of the time (Trinkaus & Shipman, 1993).

least from *Homo habilis*. All of these changes clearly enable *speech*. We contend that increases in brain size and lateralization of the brain enabled increases in the power of *language*. Clearly, we believe that speech is not necessary for language, but no one would deny the importance of increases in brain size and the lateralization of the cerebral hemispheres in its evolution. With respect to increases in brain size, Bickerton presents two figures (reproduced here as Figures 8.1 and 8.2) in support of his contention that there have been saltational events in human brain evolution. The first figure, representing increases in cranial capacity for putative human ancestors from *Australopithecus afarensis* to *Homo sapiens*, clearly supports the notion that brain expansion among the hominids has been incremental and gradual. Bickerton counters with a chart that shows increases in the encephalization quotient, which takes account of the fact that body size was also increasing during the course of evolution of the hominids. It is important to examine this metric, because it represents a measure

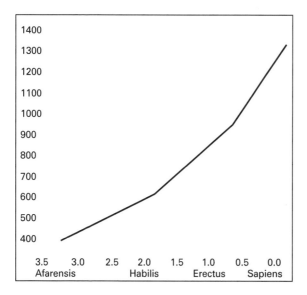

Figure 8.1 Gross hominid brain-size increase over time. Vertical axis = gross endocranial capacity in cubic centimeters; horizontal axis = time in millions of years, 0.0 = present (from Bickerton, 1990: 135)

Language from the body

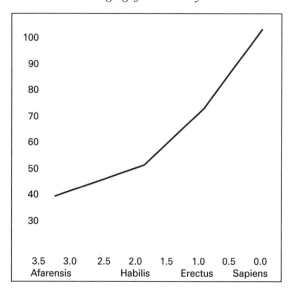

Figure 8.2 Encephalization quotient increase in real time. Vertical axis = EQ as a percentage of *h. sapiens* EQ; horizontal axis = time in millions of years, 0.0 = present (from Bickerton, 1990: 136)

of the *relative* growth of the brain and the expansion of brain power usable for functions unrelated simply to basic bodily control functions. This curve appears somewhat less linear than that for increases in simple cranial capacity. But an analysis by means of "eyeball least squares regression" suggests that a line could also be fitted to these data. There is also a suggestion of geometric increase, but again does that represent "saltational" or "catastrophic" change? We think not.

We have also stated that cerebral lateralization is probably a prerequisite for the acquisition of syntax, and we contend that a special evolutionary explanation is needed for this phenomenon. Could a mutation causing lateralization be Bickerton's brain reorganization mutation? We address that question in the next section, where we present an hypothesis for the origin of cerebral lateralization that implicates manual signing. In the course of considering the evolution of cerebral lateralization, we discuss models for the genetic causation of this trait. These models range from simple (which would support Bickerton's idea of a fairly simple mutation) to quite complex.

8.3 EVOLUTION OF CEREBRAL ASYMMETRY

As we mentioned in Chapter 4, the degree of cerebral asymmetry found in humans is a unique trait that requires a special evolutionary explanation, although neurological asymmetries are not uncommon in other primates (Bradshaw & Rogers, 1993; Falk, 1987; Kimura, 1993). Differences in function between the two hemispheres of the human cerebrum have been known for more than 100 years. Specifically, in the nineteenth-century Broca and Wernicke were able to show, in findings which have withstood criticism (Geschwind, 1970, 1972; Corballis, 1991; but see Rosenfield, 1988), that in most right-handed people the ability to produce and understand spoken and written language depends upon structures located in the cortex of the left cerebral hemisphere. They observed that injuries to certain parts (Wernicke's and Broca's areas) of the left temporal and frontal cortex resulted in disruptions of linguistic ability (aphasias); whereas comparable injuries to the right hemisphere did not ordinarily result in such impairments. Since it was well known that the left side of the brain also controls the right side of the body (and the vast majority of people are right-handed), it was natural to assume that speech and handedness are closely related phenomena, as it appeared that dominance for both is ordinarily a left-brain function. It also appeared that left-handed people are right-brain dominant for language. A necessary relationship between handedness and dominance for language has not proven to be the case, however; instances of mixed dominance for *left-handers* are now known to be the rule (Hecaen & de Ajuriaguerra, 1964; Milner, 1975). It remains the case, however, that the vast majority of people are left-brain dominant for speech and are right-handed.

A corollary of the theory that one side of the brain is responsible for language and skilled activity was that this side must also be dominant for most other intellectual functions as well. This has not proven to be the case, as the so-called minor hemisphere has recently been shown, through a variety of experimental techniques, to be predominant for a number of functions, such as aspects of musical ability, recognition of shapes and faces, and spatial orientation (Sperry et al., 1969; Bogen, 1973; Levy, 1974; Bever and Chiarello, 1974; Kinsbourne, 1978). Overwhelmingly, though, the primary function of the right hemisphere is visual cognition. Corballis (1991) includes a comprehensive survey of what is known about the separate functions of the two hemispheres. Furthermore, it is now known that the right hemisphere is not in all cases totally without linguistic ability, for example, it has been shown in split-brain patients that the right hemisphere can recognize spoken or printed words, especially nouns (Sperry et al., 1969; Levy et al., 1971).

More recently, the following terms have been applied to right hemisphere participation in language use: "connotative" (Armstrong & Katz, 1981); "semantic-lexical comprehension" (Gainnotti et al., 1981); "apprehension of complex linguistic materials" (Wapner & Gardner, 1981); "prosody" (Tompkins & Mateer, 1985); "metaphor" (Winner & Gardner, 1977); "verbal humor" (Brownell et al., 1983). Reviewing these and other findings, Armstrong (1987: 30) concludes that "[w]hat links all of these right hemispheric contributions to language use is the notion of context . . . and that interpretation of contextual cues is intimately related to visual perception . . ."

Evolutionary explanations for the functional significance of cerebral asymmetry are not lacking. One possible explanation involves the notion that lateralization removes the possibility of competition between the hemispheres for use of the vocal apparatus:

These interference effects support a rationale for the evolution of unilateral control of language expression, namely that such lateralization was an adaptation permitting control of the unique vocal apparatus, uncomplicated by competitive antagonism between the hemispheres. (Levy, 1969)

This hypothesis gains some strength in light of the fact that most of the muscles involved in speech are bilaterally innervated. For instance, the tongue is supplied by the two hypoglossal nerves, each of which receives axons from both hemispheres. It appears, in general, that each hemisphere is separately capable of running the vocal apparatus to the extent necessary for the production of intelligible speech (Smith, 1966; 1969), creating the possibility of competition between the hemispheres for control of this ability. One theory of the origin of stuttering relates this defect to incomplete lateralization of the speech function (Hecaen & de Ajuriaguerra, 1964: 770–80). Complete lateralization of the motor output system for this function should be sufficient to solve any possible problems related to hemispheric competition (see Corballis, 1980). Moreover, other animals, like songbirds that have complex vocal repertoires, also exhibit laterality (Bradshaw & Rogers, 1993; Corballis, 1991; Falk, 1987). Unfortunately, this explanation does not account for lateralization of the ability to *receive* language, except insofar as the receptive and expressive functions are necessarily bound to each other neurologically (Falk, 1980). That is, efficiency may be increased by topological proximity of the receptive and expressive mechanisms.

More generally, MacNeilage (1991) proposes that cerebral asymmetries are fairly common throughout the primate order. MacNeilage develops a general theory that these asymmetries are based on postural preferences in arboreal primates. The data supportive of the widespread distribution of asymmetries in primates remains somewhat equivocal.

Keeping in mind that a general relationship between language dominance and handedness (i.e. the great majority of people are left-hemisphere-dominant for speech and right-handed) may be fortuitous, it is natural to ask what selective advantage might accrue to individuals whose left hemispheres and right extremities were somewhat more active than the contralateral counterparts of those organs. Numerous explanations have been offered. Among these is the possibility of slightly more efficient circulation of blood to the left cerebral hemisphere and the right upper extremity (Hecaen & de Ajuriaguerra, 1964: 117–118). Both of these advantages favor right-handedness; whereas the first alone favors left-side dominance for language. Several caveats are in order here. As we have already pointed out, it now appears that a considerable division of labor exists between the hemispheres (Bogen, 1973; Sperry et al., 1969; Levy, 1969). It may be inappropriate, then, to assume that the left hemisphere and the right hand are normally more active than their counterparts. However it appears that, *in extremis*, some cognitive functions may be preserved at the expense of others – language, for instance (e.g. Levy, 1969).

Unfortunately, any attempt to produce evolutionary explanations for these phenomena is confounded by uncertainty surrounding the ontogeny of handedness and cerebral asymmetries in general (Annett, 1978, 1985; Corballis, 1991). Theories range from an environmental model stressing the importance of fetal position in the development of handedness or right-ear dominance (Churchill et al., 1962; Previc, 1991) to a dominant allele with incomplete penetrance model (Annett, 1978) to a two gene-four allele model (Levy, 1974). As Hecaen and de Ajuriaguerra (1964) have pointed out, the actual situation appears to be exceedingly complex. Particularly, it appears that lateralization of speech function may be somewhat unstable up to the time of puberty. This statement is due to research indicating that children recover speech more readily from lesions to the left hemisphere than do adults (Basser, 1962; Lenneberg, 1967).

Whether or not this is due to shifts in laterality is not clear, although it seems that such shifts can occur in the growing child (Hecaen & de Ajuriaguerra, 1964: 130–134). Furthermore, it appears that lateralization for speech presents a somewhat different picture in the left-handed than in the right-handed. In the lefthanded, language representation tends to be not as fully lateralized and more diffuse (Hardyck & Petrinovich, 1977; Hecaen et al., 1981); the left-handed with lesions to the "dominant" hemisphere (whether right or left) have a better prognosis for recovery of language function than do the right-handed (Hecaen & de Ajuriaguerra, 1964: 70–116; Hecaen & Sauguet, 1971).

The foregoing suggests that a simple genetic or environmental model is unlikely to account fully for the phenomenon of cerebral asymmetry. Twin research on the inheritance of cerebral asymmetry has been impeded by uncertainties regarding in utero effects peculiar to twins and by the fact that twins have a significantly higher frequency of left-handedness than single-tons (Carter-Saltzman et al., 1976). This latter fact is consonant with the supposition that in utero effects, such as positioning, are important, or to a lesser extent that "mirror-imaging" may occur in identical twins when the single fertilized ovum divides to form twins (Hicks & Kinsbourne, 1978: 32). Studies of the heritability of direction of laterality have yielded ambiguous results (e.g. Springer & Searleman, 1978).

The *behavioral* basis for the lateralization of aspects of language and handedness *generally* to the same hemisphere (usually the left) seems clear to us and to others (Kimura (1981, 1993) and Corballis (1991)). The behavioral similarity that links the two is praxis (Corballis, 1991), as we suggested in Chapter 4 – the ability to plan and assemble complex sequences of rapid motor actions. It is for this function that the left hemisphere seems specifically adapted. In this regard, we reflect on the derivation of the word "syntax." It comes from the Greek *syntaxis* – to arrange in order. As we have pointed out previously, there is a great deal more to syntax than arranging things in order – however, that ability is the most fundamental prerequisite for the development of syntax.

There is, in addition, an even more direct functional relationship between the lateralized functions of handedness and language. Kimura (1976) notes that manual signing and gesturing are skilled activities in which hand preference (that is, handedness) plays a key role. Moreover, Bonvillian and Richards (1993) provide evidence that, among children learning ASL as a first language, hand preference appears in signing before it does in object manipulation. This original preference is strongly correlated with the hand that eventually becomes the child's dominant hand – for example, eventual right-handers show strong initial preferences for using the right hand as the dominant hand in early signing. If signing developed early in the hominid lineage as a principal means of communication, it becomes relatively simple to see an evolving connection between the evolution of cerebral asymmetry for language and handedness. This would solve an enduring problem in understanding the evolution of the human nervous system. However, it appears unlikely that cerebral asymmetry could have resulted from a simple mutation of the sort proposed by Bickerton.

8.4 THE HOMINID LIFE STYLE

Anthropologists have engaged in a great deal of speculation about the change in life style, the movement into a new niche, that set in motion all of these morphological changes and the accompanying (or leading) behavioral changes that have made modern humans what they are. These speculative theories are quite diverse, even including one that posits an aquatic phase (see Morgan, 1982 – we are indebted to Corballis, 1991, for presenting this theory in a light that makes it seem almost believable – in fact, as part of a more general theory for the evolution of humans as *generalized* apes, habitation in wetlands might even add plausibly to the speculation). However, the preponderance of the evidence derived from naturalistic studies of primate behavior beginning in the 1960s seems to point to movement from exploiting a relatively rich and homogeneous forest environment, much like that of chimpanzees today, to exploitation of a more complex, open savanna type environment with relatively poorer and more widely distributed resources.

Again, there has been endless speculation as to why such an environment might have favored bipedalism, and it would be unreasonable to expect that there could be a simple answer – nothing could be more certain than that quadrupedalism is Nature's fundamental plan for the mammals (and for the land-dwelling vertebrates for that matter). So, in producing a bipedal mammal, natural selection had considerable morphological inertia to overcome. We will not attempt an exhaustive enumeration of the explanations that have been put forward, but will merely list some of the more plausible ones here:

- In such an environment, it would have been advantageous to have the hands free for carrying food over fairly long distances.
- Given a nomadic life-style, mothers (and fathers) could more easily transport their young.

- It would have been advantageous to see over tall grass, to
  spot food, predators, etc., from an upright posture.

If we accept the idea of the original hominid eco-niche as a
broken woodland/savanna, and we posit that the first hominids
were gatherers who gradually became more and more efficient
hunters, then we can begin to speculate on social structure, as we
will do in a later section. First, it would be profitable to consider
what sort of animal the earliest hominid might have been.

8.5 THE ANCESTRAL STOCK

In speculating about the supposed selective advantages of bipedalism, most theorists speculate on what aspects of bipedalism
might make it more advantageous than quadrupedalism. There is,
however, another way to think about this issue, and that is to
consider the *sort* of animal that might evolve into a biped (see
Leakey & Lewin, 1992: 90–91). When monkeys radiated into
such open environments, they produced quadrupeds such as
baboons, plantigrade with respect to all four limbs. On the
other hand, there are terrestrial vertebrate bipeds that inhabit
similar open environments – harking back to another observation by Aristotle, these are birds. What is significant about these
birds is that they evolved as free-ranging terrestrial bipeds from
animals whose forelimbs had been altered from the typical plantigrade locomotor function, that is, the forelimbs had become
wings. Moreover, birds have evolved into terrestrial bipeds, independently, in several geographically remote locations. The point
to be made here is that evolution is conservative and channeled
with respect to morphology. Once the plantigrade quadrupedal
pattern has been abandoned it is evidently unlikely that it will be
readopted.

   If we make the reasonable assumption that hominids evolved
from brachiator/knuckle-walkers, not too unlike contemporary
chimpanzees, it becomes easier to understand why a bipedal
mode of locomotion evolved. There are a number of reasons
to believe that the common ancestor was such an animal,
although fossil evidence to prove it is lacking (Zihlman, 1990).

First, chimpanzees and gorillas are the closest living relatives of modern humans. Second, genetic studies suggest that chimpanzees and humans are probably more closely related to each other than either is to the gorillas (see Weiss, 1987). This latter point is crucial to making the argument that the common ancestor was a brachiator/knuckle-walker. If gorillas, which are also knuckle-walkers, diverged from a common hominid/chimp line, then the common ancestor of humans and chimps must also have been a knuckle-walker. Third, the oldest fossils that are clearly hominids had brains similar in size to modern chimps. Finally, relatively small developmental differences might produce a biped out of a knuckle-walker. Zihlman (1990: 189) lists the following locomotor and postural capabilities of modern chimpanzees, all of which involve upright posture: "climbing, hanging, reaching, swinging, leaping, standing and walking bipedally."

If we assume that the hominid ancestor was a brachiator/knuckle-walker, what might have caused the divergence from the phylogenetic line leading to modern chimps? One could speculate, and many have, that the forest environment inhabited by climbing, knuckle-walking apes shrank and population pressure pushed some groups of animals out into the more difficult environment at the forest edge. The characteristic locomotor pattern of chimps involves movement about the forest floor over short distances by knuckle-walking or relatively inefficient, bipedal walking. Chimps are also, of course, adept at climbing and collecting food in trees. Presumably this locomotor adaptation would have been less efficient in a more open environment, and following the argument given above, we might speculate that bipedalism, rather than plantigrade quadrupedalism is the solution that such an animal adopts to solve its locomotor problems in this new environment. In this environment there would have been a premium on speed and endurance over long distances.

All that follows, then, hinges on the crucial fact that bipedalism becomes the predominant mode of locomotion. The hands are then freed for carrying, tool making and critically, from our point of view, for gesturing.

It is important for us to support further the notion that the common ancestor might have been fairly similar to modern chimps, because much is now known about the behavioral capacities of these animals. We recognize however that the chimp line has had equal time to evolve and diverge from the common ancestor. Here we speculate that the chimp line may have been relatively conservative in an evolutionary sense. If the common ancestor was adapted to a forest environment, and the chimps stayed behind, one might expect that they would have undergone less change than the hominids, behaviorally and morphologically. So the hypothesis that the common ancestor was quite similar to modern chimps is reasonable and plausible, although not subject to proof.

Perhaps most important from our point of view are the behavioral capabilities of chimpanzees, especially with respect to language-like behavior. We now have a wealth of information in this regard, information that has recently been summarized by some of the major investigators in this field (Premack, 1986; Gardner et al., 1989; Lord Zuckerman, 1991). There are areas of controversy, but several common themes emerge. First, and foremost, there can be little doubt that chimpanzees have well-developed abilities to communicate using signs (symbols, indices and icons) – whether gestured or manufactured. Second, they can form these signs into short strings. Third, they may have some ability to invent their own signs, although this ability is probably very limited. Fourth, they may be able to teach signs to other chimpanzees. Fifth, they are probably not capable of syntactic relations beyond a very rudimentary level. Sixth, they seem more capable of learning manual signs than of learning speech – but this may be due to the trainer's greater ease of physically molding the hands than of molding the vocal organs, rather than a reflection of some innate ability.

8.6 HOMINID SOCIAL BEHAVIOR

Again, much speculation has centered on the question of early hominid social life, and we have discussed briefly the speculation which has concerned its eco-niche. Social behavior is particularly important to us, because we propose that language grew out of hominid gestural systems, which would have had, as a primary purpose, coordination of group behavior. We stated above that the hominid adaptive complex became increasingly technological, and we would amend that to say, technological within a social context. Not surprisingly, we will consider inferences from both the behavior of modern humans and chimpanzees, in order to account for early hominid social behavior.

The primary problem for any speculative theory about the development of hominid social structure is to explain the origin of the family as the principle unit of social organization. Our reasons for being acutely interested in this phenomenon, within the context of a discussion of the origin of language, will become apparent later. Again, much of the recent speculation concerning the origin of the family has involved comparisons between the African apes and technologically primitive modern human populations – hunter/gatherers. We will concern ourselves here primarily with the reported behavior of chimpanzees, although some instructive contrasts can be drawn between chimps and gorillas. The model we discuss here has grown out of field studies that began in the 1960s, conducted by the great pioneers, including George Schaller, Jane Goodall, and Vernon Reynolds. This work was compared to the "man the hunter" studies of the same period (Lee & DeVore, 1968).

With respect to habitat, gorillas appear to be confined entirely to rain forest, although they occupy a wide range of altitudinal zones. Chimpanzees, while occurring largely in rain forest (as we suggested previously), do exist in significant numbers in open woodland and savanna areas. The wider distribution of chimpanzees seems to be related to their more diverse food base. Gorillas seem to be almost entirely herbivorous (Schaller, 1965; Reynolds, 1965), whereas chimpanzee populations, depending upon local habitat, range from primarily frugivorous (Reynolds & Reynolds, 1965) to omnivorous (Suzuki, 1969; Goodall, 1965). The diversified food base and ecological zones exploited by chimpanzees also lead to differences in range size and population density – more concentrated densities and smaller ranges occur in rain forest where resources are more concentrated.

As for social organization, there is relatively less to say about gorillas than about chimpanzees. Gorilla populations consist of lone males and bisexual groups of stable composition. Groups consist of one or more silverbacked (mature) males in association with varying numbers of female and young. If more than one silverbacked male is present in a group, one of these tends to be dominant over the others and the group as a whole. Schaller (1965: 344) stresses the cohesiveness of gorilla groups, asserting that "the diameter of a group rarely exceeds 200 feet as every animal remains attentive to the movements of others in the dense forest environment." Chance and Jolly (1970: 104) suggest that the attention of gorillas in groups is highly structured, with the dominant silverbacked male acting as a focus of attention and thereby governing group activities. These bisexual groups tend to be very stable over time.

With regard to chimpanzees, no such simple picture has been proposed:

In this species, most bands are so fluid and volatile that their constitution changes daily or hourly, as new animals join the band and others leave; or the band may split into two or more units which go their own ways and do not rejoin for a period of days, weeks, or months, if indeed they ever rejoin. (Reynolds, 1965: 695)

Reynolds distinguishes four major types of groups or "bands" among chimps: Mother groups, Adult male groups, Adult groups (both sexes), and Mixed groups (both sexes and all age groups). The first two of these groups are supposed to be the most permanent, although all are, ultimately temporary. Suzuki (1969), describing the behavior of chimps in a savanna woodland environment, identifies groups similar to those described by Reynolds; they are given in order of decreasing frequency of appearance: Mixed nomadic groups, Adult nomadic groups, Mother nomadic groups, Male nomadic groups. Larger groups of up to about seventy individuals may also come together on occasion, but they are not stable (Reynolds, 1965).

There has been speculation about the possible adaptive significance of the differences in social organization between chimps and gorillas, involving differences in eating habits (Reynolds, 1965; Suzuki, 1969). As herbivores, gorillas exploit a constantly available, evenly distributed food resource. Since their food resource is so evenly distributed, gorillas could, essentially, be grouped in almost any configuration and still exploit this resource efficiently. They are free, so to speak, to adopt a type of social structure that maximizes their ability to defend themselves against predators, while minimizing antagonism among adult males. Groups can be relatively large and stable, but the number of silverbacked males in any group is limited, and these are ranked in a strict dominance hierarchy. Chimpanzees, on the other hand, whether they live in rain forest or savanna woodland, exploit a resource base less evenly distributed, parts of which may be subject to seasonal variations. They require, therefore, a social structure that is capable of flux, allowing for the splitting of large into small groups and the merging of small into large groups. This splitting and merging must, in turn, be accomplished with a minimum of hostility among the animals, hence the larger groups with mutually recognizable and tolerant members. The smaller groups are formed, for foraging purposes, from these larger groups in some poorly understood manner, perhaps involving kinship ties – mother/child, or sibling/sibling.

It has occurred to several writers (e.g. Reynolds, 1968; Suzuki, 1969) that contemporary chimpanzee social organization is remarkably similar in gross terms to that described for certain hunter/gatherer groups, and might by extrapolation serve as a model for early hominid groups first venturing out of the rain forest. The configuration of a total chimpanzee group at any time appears to be determined largely by the pattern of distribution of resources at that time. If resources are concentrated in a particular area, groups there will be large, and if the resources are scattered, group size will be small. This is a pattern not unlike that of Mbuti pygmies described by Turnbull in the rain forest of the eastern Congo:

[F]lux appears as a systematic pattern . . . The focal point of the process is the honey season, during which net-hunters spread out into fragmented subbands, sometimes uniting siblings, sometimes dividing them, but always separating antagonistic elements. At the end of the honey season, the band begins to re-form, carefully avoiding any lines of fracture that remain unhealed. (Turnbull, 1968: 135)

It is interesting that Turnbull should mention sibling ties here, since Van Lawick-Goodall (1971) convincingly argues that sibling/sibling and mother/child cooperative behavior patterns and affectional ties are among the most important features of chimpanzee social life.

Reynolds (1966) has suggested that groups organized something like the large chimpanzee groups described above were important in the evolution of the hominids. Further elaborating upon this suggestion, he proposes that studies of chimpanzees and other anthropoids have revealed "the behavioral characteristics which may have preceded the development of hominid kinship and family patterns" (Reynolds, 1968: 212). These include:

1. an "open community" social system;
2. the matrifocal family of mother and immature offspring;
3. adult male bands;
4. the importance of ties of primary kinship;
5. predominance of mating outside the family.

The first three of these elements follow directly from suggestions made in the preceding section, as does the fourth to a certain extent. They follow, that is, if they are accepted as "primitive" traits in a phylogenetic sense. As to whether or not social traits such as these are very ancient, Reynolds makes a convincing argument for their priority. At some point in time, proto-hominids were, presumably, incapable of technological feats beyond the level of modern chimps, and since these two animals are closely related phylogenetically, it seems plausible, in a "cultural ecological" sense, to suggest that protohominids, who were adapting to environmental resources similar to those exploited by chimpanzees in certain areas, would have possessed societal elements similar to those of chimps.

The suggestion that mating outside the family would have been predominant receives support from studies of monkeys and apes. For example, Sade (1968) claims that matings almost never occur between females and their sons among the rhesus macaques of the Cayo Santiago colony. Van Lawick-Goodall (1971) suggests the existence of lasting relationships among chimpanzees between mother and son which seem to preclude or at least limit mating. During the past two decades there has been a continuing accumulation of evidence concerning kin recognition and incest avoidance in higher primates (Gouzoules, 1984; Cheney & Seyfarth, 1990). This suggests a firm biological foundation for the substrates of family life and their presence prior to the hominid split from the chimpanzees.

It seems plausible, then, that relatively large endogamous breeding units, which may only rarely have congregated for unified social activity, were the rule in protohominid populations and that nuclear families may have developed out of these. These larger populations could be regarded as the forerunners of social units corresponding to "tribes" in the anthropological literature.

How might the "nuclear family" have evolved out of these bands? Several writers (e.g. Reynolds, 1968; Morris, 1967) have suggested possible adaptive functions for pair bonding and the formation of nuclear families. These explanations revolve around the need for protection of mothers and their children in a hostile environment, but more importantly, in several cases, they stress the advantages of a system of division of labor by sex which could be facilitated by pair-bonding. The division of labor that is theorized, usually resembles that found in contemporary hunter gatherers. Males engage in both hunting and gathering, the relative importance of the two being determined by ecological zone and season. Again, upright hominids could be farther ranging and could carry food back to a base camp over a long distance (but see Binford, 1987 on the lack of evidence for either base camps or big-game hunting before the appearance of modern humans). Females would engage in gathering and caring for children. Kendon (1991) employs this notion of division of labor in a theoretical explanation of the elaboration of language. We will discuss that theory in more detail below.

Morris (1967) argues that the pair-bond is established and maintained through the sexual attraction between a continuously receptive female and an ever ready male. This argument is certainly open to caricature (see, e.g., Leakey & Lewin, 1992: 88 on Lovejoy, 1981), and the man as hunter and provider model has been subjected to feminist (e.g. Hrdy, 1981; Zihlman, 1981) and other critiques (Binford, 1987). But in its general form, the fore-going scenario seems to us (three males) to have the advantage of explaining many of the details of hominid evolution in a plausible manner. In its *most* general form, it suggests a strongly reciprocal relationship in which both sexes are essential to economic survival, females perhaps more than males.

Incest taboos proscribing various possible intrafamilial matings could then be seen as advantageous in that they would ensure the formation of new nuclear families, thereby providing for maximum dispersal of foraging units in difficult environments. As we have seen, incest avoidance may be relatively ancient among the primates, and it almost certainly also has beneficial genetic consequences. We will also discuss below the obverse of incest prohibition, namely marriage *preferences* for certain other types of relatives (cousins), and how both practices may also be implicated in the origin of language.

8.7 ORIGIN AND EVOLUTION OF LANGUAGE

We are arguing that language arose out of gestural communication primarily within emerging hominid extended families. Theories purporting to describe or explain the evolution of language can be divided into two broad categories. First, is a category of theories that see language as evolving slowly out of precursors in the communication systems common to the primates. These theories usually postulate an early emergence and continuous development of complexity. These theories also see language as developing primarily for the purpose of facilitating social communication. Clearly, a theory purporting to derive language from gesture will be most closely allied with this general perspective. Second, is a group of theories that see language as radically different from all other communication systems. These theories tend to derive their intellectual basis from the linguistic theory of Chomsky. Some theorists in this vein have even rejected a substantial role for natural selection in the evolution of language (Piattelli-Palmarini, 1989).

A recent exposition of the fundamental contrast between these theoretical types has been given by Burling (1993). Because

Burling so clearly epitomizes this contrast, we will consider his theoretical position in some detail.

Although he can see no evolutionary link between primate communication systems and language Burling (1993) has performed a signal service by confronting the major antinomies in language theory: innate vs. learned; digital vs. analog; conscious vs. instinctive. He also opens the discussion to all kinds of communication systems that animals use, recognizing two types: language and closely related signals, and nonverbal communication. He believes that nonverbal communication shows continuity from mammals to primates to humans – the last of these possessing what he terms "our 'gesture-call' system," but he believes that language could not have evolved from either the vocal calls or the visible gestures of pre-human primates.

His criteria for distinguishing between language and other communication systems are in the best traditions of anthropological linguistics, but he calls also on recent work of primatologists. His arguments and supporting evidence are well formed. Nevertheless, we do not subscribe to his conclusion that language did not evolve from the communicative behavior of other species but instead primarily from primate cognitive abilities.

Natural selection is a biological mechanism; it must operate on behavior not ability, on performance not competence. The ability to respond to information from the environment that reaches their perceptual systems is part of the genetic endowment of many creatures; but creatures with more complex neural systems are able to respond more flexibly and to process information from within the organism as well and to make comparisons and choices. It is not the cognitive abilities of the creatures but their actions, their widely varying actions, that make some of them more likely to survive and produce offspring and push succeeding populations toward still greater neural complexity.

Burling's conclusion seems to be presented more as a refutation of the proposition that animal calls evolved into human phonations and words than as a theory of language origin or evolution. The real issue is not a debate on this proposition, however, nor the debate between linguists and animal callists. It is a biological as well as a linguistic issue, and our second reservation about

Burling's conclusion is that despite use of both visible and audible signals in "nonverbal" communicating, the important neurological difference between hearing and sight requires that the actual characteristics of sign systems employing them be considered before lumping them into one "gesture-call system."

It should be made clear here that in our view the term "nonverbal communication" is not merely an oxymoron but an anomaly. Burling offers an anecdote to show that a smile, while not language-like, not contrastive but graded in form and meaning, and probably not consciously produced, nevertheless imparts enough information so that he knew (and immediately confirmed the knowledge) that the smile was directed to a male, not a brother but a boyfriend of the female smiler. Our view is that the smile and the message it sent both to its target and to Burling the onlooker indeed does not use the contrastive phonology, lexicon, and semantics of the English language, but the message it sends has been put clearly in words (verbally) by Burling and in the right circumstances the originator and the recipient of the signal could do so as well, though with variation in detail.

As creatures with language, all our communication can be verbalized – a claim to which the amount of literature on "nonverbal communication" bears witness – and much of our behavior can be rationalized, which also requires language that is "verbal" in the sense of using words and propositions not necessarily overtly vocal or gestural.

Possessed of higher-order consciousness, for which language is prerequisite, according to Edelman, our species cannot communicate precisely as do other mammals, even other primates, because the verbal part of our brain is never completely disconnected. The fact that not all of the signals we use are linguistic, digital, and in conscious awareness does not divide our minds into separate compartments. Human minds would appear to be formed as Edelman explains out of *cumulative increments* of rudimentary neural components, not by the sudden addition of radically new components.

It is useful to separate things that are not connected and to group things that are, but to understand language and mind and human nature it seems best to allow all the evidence in before judging the case. There is no logical nor biological barrier between language and other signal systems, as Burling's classification of gestures and vocalizations and language in fact shows. Within language, which is digital and contrastive, intonation is analog and graded. Burling quotes Bolinger:

> Intonation is part of a gestural complex whose primitive and still surviving function is the signaling of emotion . . . (1986:195)

Burling classifies iconic calls and gestures on the non-linguistic side and says they are not in contrast; earlier he says, "deaf signs form a contrastive system as do the words of a spoken language" (1993: 30).

The problem is to get from the signaling of emotion to the language side of the division, and Burling clearly recognizes that intonation, iconic signals, and sign languages are "doubtful cases" within the repertoire of communication systems. Carefully considering five of these, he places the first three on the language side: vocalizations like *oh-oh* for surprise and *mhm* for assent; conventional gestures; and deaf signing; but intonation and iconic calls and gestures he places on the other side. Our disagreement is with his statement about the last of these, the iconic signals:

> We use our hands to form a stream of iconic gestures. Since they are not in contrast, iconic signals are not, by the definition I have given, part of language and language-like communication. They also lack, by definition, one of the features that linguists have always regarded as an essential characteristic of words: arbitrariness. (1993: 31)

Two arguments may be laid against this classification. The minor is that arbitrariness, like many older pronouncements about language, is not absolute, as Peirce, Bolinger, and many others have demonstrated. More important, it is not at all clear that iconic, referential, visible signals are not in contrast. Burling has already put into the class of language and language-like systems the sign languages used by deaf people, all of which contain a great many iconic gestures; but it is not necessary to go to these languages to see that iconic gestures made by humans do indeed contrast.

Two pillars of the field (or discipline – Eco, 1979) of semiotics, Ferdinand de Saussure and Charles Sanders Peirce, differed on just this point. The former seems to have decided that language signs are always symbolic and arbitrary, while signs that resemble in some way what they mean cannot be language signs. The latter pointed out that all signs relate variously to what they denote in several non-exclusive ways (e.g. as indexes, icons, and symbols) and are not categorical but variable; moreover, that a sign vehicle denotes the sign meaning because of a third semiotic element: the sign interpretant – a human interpreter in the case of human sign use.

The contrast in iconic visible gestures can usually be seen both in the form and the meaning, or vehicle and denotatum. Thus, in any culture, among deaf as well as hearing people, gestures meaning 'go away' and 'come closer' are bound to contrast visibly even as the meanings are opposed. To be sure, the separation of the hands sending the message 'big' may vary along a graded continuum and not contrast in form as do the words *big* and *huge*. The degree of hand separation is also graded when the message the hands are signaling is 'small'; but there is sharp contrast in the neural and muscular as well as the visible actions between the 'big' and the 'small': the former requires moving the arms outward from the sides (abduction); the latter requires the opposite action (adduction) – the physiological contrast is stark.

In primary sign languages it will be hard if not impossible to find sign verbs with the general semantic values 'liking' and 'loathing' that do not contrast in form and do not use, respectively, limb flexion vs. extension, or forearm supination vs. forearm pronation, or both. As far back as Darwin's time it was known – to the rhetoricians of the ancient world as well – that human and animal expressions of emotion shared such fundamental bodily contrasts, and Ekman's recent work shows that facial actions also contrast, though the detail, like the facial musculature, is highly complex.

Because "iconic" visible gestures do contrast, just as do the concepts they represent, they make literally obvious sources for the contrastiveness characteristic of language and language-like communication. Because these gestures also present – to the master perceptual-cortical system in primates – visible resemblance between concept and expression, they provide an excellent basis for forming a vocabulary of signs-for-things.

Possession of a set of signs for naming things, both to oneself and to others, seems to us a critical stage in the evolution of language. We have devoted much attention to the argument that the hominids diverged from an ancestral stock much like (clever) chimpanzees. Recent accounts of primates in the wild and of experiments with free-ranging, captive, and home-reared chimpanzees suggest strongly that our nearest relatives in the primate order are almost at the threshold of, or on the next to last step up to, this stage. To the questions why didn't chimpanzees then continue toward the evolution of language, and why did the hominid branch do so, Kendon (1991) has a persuasive reply: in their ecological niche, chimpanzees do not need and never have needed a more evolved complex system of communication than those they still possess; hominids, however, met all kinds of new environmental challenges that "forced" them to take the next step.

It is a long way, a giant step up, to the next stage. This is the stage at which contrast of one kind or another is used not just for naming and sorting classes of things and events but also for expressing and signifying and communicating the contrast of perceived and conceived relationships among things and events.

Using visible gestures iconically to express concepts of first importance in their lives, hominids would have become even more dependent on social solidarity, although it can with equal justice be argued that a more human-like social living arrangement would have exerted pressure for developing more communication of all kinds. Far from agreeing with Burling that gesture-call communication is separate from language and language-like communication, we see it as the basis of language – the essential word-forming subsystem of language.

Word forming does not fully qualify as language, of course, because language needs more than contrastiveness, conscious awareness, and learning. Despite the differences in kinds of human communication, all are centered in and are manifestations of the working of the same organ unique in the animal world, the human brain.

To be a language a system needs syntax as well as words. We agree with Burling that vocal calls of animals provide little material for building a vocabulary of signs-for-things and none at all for inventing a sentence-forming system. We have seen, though, that iconic visible signals have an advantage: they provide enough resemblance between sign and what it denotes to communicate to others the linkage or association that may be in the brains of sign producer and sign interpreter, and so be on the borderline between unconscious and conscious knowledge. Kendon has found (and Burling does not disagree) in the recent literature on chimpanzees convincing evidence that these animals' gestures show some naming capability. Indeed iconic gestures – audible as well as visible – may provide the transition between largely arbitrary call systems and genuine language by providing needed flexibility and open-ended progress toward conventionalization.

The next question is whether iconic upper-body gestures, having been exploited as the highly convenient and useful way to express a conceptual sorting of the immediate (social as well as external) environment, could have led to the evolution of a signaling system incorporating syntax. We believe they could.

A socially cooperating species, becoming more skillful, not only at coping with the environment but also at devising new techniques for doing so, would certainly find communicating with more or less transparent, easily interpretable gestures a great advantage. Engaged in such communication, their attention would become more and more closely focused on the signals as well as the messages, and at some stage, we propose, they began to see that iconic visible gestures depict abstract relationships as well as concrete things and actions. The crucial step up is simple: iconic gestures made with the arms and hands and faces (by a creature with cerebral, visual, and manual specialization) are more than icons; they are animated representations – instant replays as it were – of something doing something to something else: a pattern we recognize as subject-verb-object (see Chapter 4).

8.8 LANGUAGE AND LONGEVITY AS EVOLUTIONARY
PROBLEMS

We have presented the argument made by Kendon (1991) that a division of labor and something to talk about might have been sufficient to start the hominids down the road toward fully realized languages. Problems remain, however. Premack (1986: 133) puts one of the problems in these terms: language is "an embarrassment for evolutionary theory because it is vastly more powerful than one can account for in terms of selective fitness." Kendon implies that hominids in a new niche would have needed to communicate in increasing complexity about their environment and its resources; Premack's suggestion is that this sort of communication would not have necessitated something as powerful as modern languages. This point may also be implicit in Burling's argument. A similar point is made in arguments that relate the emergence of language to the rapid development of technologies beginning in the Upper Paleolithic (e.g. Davidson & Noble, 1989; Dibble, 1989). The problem with these late-onset, unused capacity arguments is that the brain had already become very large by the time of the appearance of *Homo erectus*, the hands were modern, and the vocal apparatus had begun to evolve toward its modern configuration (Laitman, 1985). Something must have been going on that was not evident in the archeological record of the development of material culture.

Responding to Davidson and Noble (1989), Armstrong (1989: 138) put it in these terms: "The selective advantage accruing to users of human languages must lie elsewhere than in the material culture, precisely in the abilities to develop and elaborate complex social structures, plans, and strategies that belong to all those who live in human social groups. It is difficult to conceive that these things do not have a very long evolutionary history" (cf. Pinker & Bloom, 1990). This suggests that our position is not entirely at odds with Burling's assertion that enhancement of cognitive capacities must have been an important selective advantage in the evolution of language, but it must have been cognitive enhancement within a social context.

Katz and Armstrong (1994) provide a rationale for speculating about such a context, in which the evolution of both language and longevity are linked to the management of genetic transmission within small social groups comprised of close relatives – certainly, as we have argued, the most likely candidate for the social groups in which hominids have lived for most of their evolutionary history. We suggested above that the evolution of language poses particular problems for Darwinism, and longevity does also. Longevity is a problem for traditional evolutionary theory, because the mechanism of natural selection can only with great difficulty deal with the maintenance of large numbers of non-reproductive individuals.

In order to deal with this phenomenon and to show that its evolutionary relationship to language is one of positive feedback, Katz and Armstrong invoke a modified version of what has come to be known as the "grandmother hypothesis," an explanation for the development of postmenopausal life span in women (e.g. Gaulin, 1980; Hamilton, 1966). The "grandmother hypothesis," in turn, invokes the concept of kin investment. According to Hill (1991), the grandmother hypothesis posits increased fitness to women at some age through social investment in grandchildren rather than through continued care for children of their own. In other words, grandmothers with no young children of their own to care for can "invest" in their grandchildren by assisting in their care. The grandchildren, in turn, have a high probability of having the grandmother's genes. In its most general form, the grandmother hypothesis is relatively nonspecific with respect to the mechanics of kin investment. Katz and Armstrong (1993) suggest that storage of knowledge is clearly a key attribute that would facilitate this process, in this case knowledge about the physical environment and about the relationships of kin to each other.

Knowledge about kinship relations is particularly critical to the argument of Katz and Armstrong. Noting the asymmetrical transmission of the sex chromosomes they show that a certain pattern of cousin marriage, matrilateral cross-cousin marriage, coupled with patrilocal residence rules, greatly increases a longlived grandmother's chances of making an investment in succeeding generations who will have her x-chromosome. Noting also that a gene controlling a crucial developmental hormone, DHEAS, which may have important functions in the timing of the human lifecycle, is coded on the x-chromosome, they argue that, from an evolutionary perspective, language and longevity are in a positive feedback relationship.

By emphasizing this argument, including its information storage component, are we not endorsing Burling's mentalist argument for the evolution of language? Clearly, we are suggesting that language has important implications for cognition, but information storage of the kind we are discussing is only optimized when it can be retrieved and communicated to a fellow creature, in this case a descendant. Enhancement of communication within the family, then, may be an evolutionary goal of the development of language, through the enhancement of survivability of the group. This communication would clearly partake, among the earliest hominids, of the gestural communication systems of pre-hominid primate ancestors.

Having advanced the argument that there was a stage in the development of language during which it was primarily signed, we must also account for how it eventually came to be primarily spoken. Armstrong (1983), following Hockett (1978), presents a list of possible adaptive advantages for speaking over signing, most of them following basic principles of common sense:

- Communication could occur while the hands were otherwise occupied, for tool use or carrying.
- Speech could occur in the dark and when sight lines were interrupted.
- Speech may be more energy efficient.
- Reception of a spoken message does not require directed visual attention.

These and similar advantages could easily account for such an hypothesized shift. In any event, we do not hypothesize a "mute" stage during which there was no communication involving vocal gestures. Rather, we hypothesize that complexity was increasing in both modalities, the visual system taking the lead for a time.

Other aspects of language, in addition to syntax and use of the vocal-auditory channel, have been said to pose special problems in the evolution of language, have been said to represent discontinuities between human language and non-human communication systems. We will mention only one more of these special problems – the problem of duality of patterning or double articulation (e.g. Pulleyblank, 1986).

Stated in its simplest form, duality of patterning can be defined as the property of all languages, including signed languages, whereby meaningful units (morphemes, words, sentences) are built up by rules of assembly from a stock of meaningless units (phonemes). This also implies that the relationship between words and the objects they refer to is arbitrary – that is, words are symbols.

Different languages select for use different phoneme classes from among all the possible sounds that the human vocal tract is capable of emitting, and it is recognized that the rules governing assembly of the meaningless units (phonology) are independent of those governing the rules of assembly of the meaningful units (syntax). All of this is fundamental to the central dogma of structural linguistics, and Pulleyblank sees a strict discontinuity between human languages and all previous communication systems in this regard, hypothesizing that it was introduction of duality, again around the beginning of the Upper Paleolithic, that launched the linguistic revolution. In particular, Pulleyblank sees no way to derive duality gradually, through stages from primate communication systems, as others (including two of the present authors – Stokoe, 1992; Armstrong, 1983) have argued.

In fact, Pulleyblank presents our argument very effectively, in attempting to refute it with a formalist argument of his own:

If this claim can really be sustained, it obviously has important consequences for the origin of language. It might indicate that the achievement of duality of patterning in the vocal medium was not such a crucial step as has been assumed (Hockett, 1960; Pulleyblank, 1983). The kind of duality that one finds in the sign languages can rather easily be imagined to have arisen as a gradual process in which separate iconic gestures derived from mimicry and pantomime have been conventionalized and through being rapidly combined with one another, shaped so as to conform economically to natural constraints on hand and body movement and visual perception. (Pulleyblank, 1986: 104–105)

We would extend this argument to include conventionalizing of vocal gestures as well – by extension, denying Pulleyblank's claim that there must be discontinuity, the same argument with respect to syntax, that we have already considered. Of course, neither discontinuity, implying "punctuated" evolution, nor gradualism can be proved from existing evidence. We believe, however, that our incremental argument has biology and plausibility on its side.

Several general observations follow from the arguments we have made so far.

First, the earliest linguistic units were derived from visible and vocal gestures – primarily visible gestures in the earliest stages of hominid evolution.

Second, the earliest linguistic units are likely to have been relatively large and semantically complex – that is, they were sentence-like rather than word-like – smaller units have since been analyzed out of these.

Third, direct actions of the physical body provided early hominids with a useful metaphor for the hierarchical structure of language.

8.9 LANGUAGE FROM THE BODY: FINAL METAPHORS

We began this book with the wave-particle metaphor of physics. We begin our ending with a metaphor from Coleridge:

Is *thinking* impossible without arbitrary signs: and how far is the "arbitrary" a misnomer? Are not words, etc., parts and germinations of the plant? And what is the law of their growth? In something of this sort I would endeavor to destroy the old antithesis of words and things; elevating, as it were, words into things and living things too. (Coleridge, quoted in Shattuck, 1985)

This suggests, again, that arbitrariness and symbolization are not necessarily as important as de Saussure and other linguists have suggested. In fact, Pavlov's seminal experiments showed that the ability to respond to arbitrary symbols is far from restricted to humans. It is the ability of the individual to conceptualize and of the group to conventionalize that are fundamental. And, as we have suggested previously, it is gestural communication within societal groups that permits this organic growth to occur.

If pure thought runs all our trains, why should she run some so fast and some so slow, some through dull flats and some through gorgeous scenery, some to mountain heights and jewelled mines, others through dismal swamps and darkness? – and run some off the track altogether, and into the wilderness of lunacy? (William James, quoted in Laughlin & D'Aquili, 1974: 100)

Our mental life is run by metaphor, and, some would argue, so is the structure of our languages (Lakoff & Johnson, 1980), as metaphorical representations of our own bodies and their interactions with the environment. We have argued that syntax is metaphorically *embodied* in the direct actions, that is gestures, of our hands and other parts of our bodies. We see also that its hierarchical structure may be inherent as well in our representations of the body politic, in this case the extended family. Few things could be more concrete than our physical relationships with close kin, and few things more abstract than representations of our relationships with them.

We may be misled into believing that the metaphors of language are the only metaphors; and that thought is impossible without language, the question that Coleridge poses. The mathematician Roger Penrose answers this question in the negative – thought is not impossible without language. Penrose (1989: 424) quotes Einstein as follows:

The words of the language, as they are written or spoken, do not seem to play any role in my mechanism of thought. The psychical entities which seem to serve as elements of thought are certain signs and more or less clear images which can be "voluntarily" reproduced and combined . . . The above mentioned elements are, in my case, of visual and some muscular type. Conventional words or other signs have to be sought for laboriously only in a second stage, when the mentioned associative play is sufficiently established and can be reproduced at will.

What is constant about the metaphors of human thought and of human language is that they employ symbols (one thing stands for another) and syntax (symbols recombined to form novel relationships).

There is also a deeper sense, then, in which Penrose may be wrong. The biochemical/neurological events that generate conscious behavior, nonverbal thought, and language must all belong to the same category of cerebral activity. We believe that we have shown that this cerebral activity ultimately derives from the body's (muscular) interactions with the visible world.

References

Abeles, M. 1991. *Corticonics: neural circuits of the cerebral cortex.* Cambridge University Press

Allan, K. 1977. Classifiers. *Language* 53: 285–311

Annett, M. A. 1978. Genetic and non-genetic influences on handedness. *Behavior Genetics* 8: 227

1985. *Left, right, hand and brain: the right shift theory.* London: Erlbaum

Arensburg, B., A. M. Tiller, B. Vandermeersch, H. Duday, L. A. Schepartz & Y. Rak. 1989. A middle Paleolithic human hyoid bone. *Nature* 338: 758–760

Armstrong, D. F. 1983. Iconicity, arbitrariness, and duality of patterning in signed and spoken languages: perspectives on language evolution. *Sign Language Studies* 38: 51–69

1984. Scientific and ethical issues in the case for American Sign Language. *Sign Language Studies* 43: 165–184

1986. Comment on Pulleyblank, The meaning of duality of patterning and its importance in language evolution. *Sign Language Studies* 51: 121–134

1987. Word, sign, and object. *Journal of the Washington Academy of Sciences* 77(1): 26–31

1989. Comments on Davidson and Noble, The archaeology of perception: traces of depiction and language. *Current Anthropology* 30(2): 137–138

Armstrong, D. F. & S. H. Katz. 1981. Brain laterality in signed and spoken language: a synthetic theory of language use. *Sign Language Studies* 33: 319–350

Baker-Shenk, C. 1983. A microanalysis of the nonmanual components of questions in American Sign Language. Unpublished doctoral dissertation, University of California, Berkeley

Baker, C. & C. Padden. 1978. *American Sign Language: a look at its history, structure, and community.* Washington, DC: Gallaudet University Press

Barnes, J. 1984. *The complete works of Aristotle.* Princeton University Press

Basser, L. S. 1962. Hemiplegia of early onset and the faculty of speech with special reference to the effect of hemispherectomy. *Brain* 85: 427–460

Bateson, G. 1979. *Mind and nature: a necessary unity*. New York: Dutton

Battison, R. 1978. *Lexical borrowing in American Sign Language*. Silver Spring, MD: Linstok Press

Bellugi, U. 1980. How signs express complex meanings. In C. Baker & R. Battison (eds.), *Sign language and the deaf community: essays in honor of William C. Stokoe*. Silver Spring, MD: National Association of the Deaf

Bellugi, U. & E. S. Klima. 1982. From gesture to sign: deixis in a visual-gestural language. In R. J. Jarvella & W. Klein (eds.), *Speech, place, and action: studies of language in context*. New York: Wiley

Bernstein, N. 1967. *The coordination and regulation of movements*. Oxford: Pergamon

Bever, T. G. & R. J. Chiarello. 1974. Cerebral dominance in musicians and nonmusicians. *Science* 185: 537

Bickerton, D. 1985. *Roots of language*. Ann Arbor, MI: Karoma
    1990. *Language and species*. University of Chicago Press

Biederman, I. 1990. Higher-level vision. In D. N. Osherson, S. M. Kosslyn, & J. M. Hollerbach (eds.), *Visual cognition and action*. Cambridge, MA: MIT Press

Binford, L. R. 1987. American Association of Physical Anthropologists Annual Luncheon Address, April 1986: The hunting hypothesis, archaeological methods, and the past. *Yearbook of Physical Anthropology* 30: 1–9

Birdwhistell, R. L. 1970. *Kinesics and context: essays on body motion communication*. Philadelphia: University of Pennsylvania Press

Bloch, B. & G. L. Trager. 1942. *Outline of linguistic analysis*. Special publication of the Linguistic Society of America

Bloomfield, L. 1933. *Language*. New York: Holt

Blount, G. & W. Kempton. 1976. Child language socialization: parental speech and interactional strategies. *Sign Language Studies* 12: 251–277

Bogen, J. E. 1973. The other side of the brain: an appositional mind. In R. Ornstein (ed.), *The nature of human consciousness*. New York: The Viking Press

Bolinger, D. 1972. *Degree words*. The Hague: Mouton

Bonvillian, J. D. & H. C. Richards. 1993. The development of hand preference in children's early signing. *Sign Language Studies* 78: 1–14

Bradshaw, J. L. & L. Rogers. 1993. *The evolution of lateral asymmetries, language, tool use, and intellect*. San Diego: Academic Press

Browman, C. P. & L. Goldstein. 1985. Dynamic modeling of phonetic structure. In V. Fromkin (ed.), *Phonetic linguistics*. New York: Academic Press

1986. Towards an articulatory phonology. *Phonology Yearbook* 3: 219–252

1989. Articulatory gestures as phonological units. *Phonology* 6: 201–251

1990a. Gestural structures: distinctiveness, phonological processes, and historical change. In I. G. Mattingly & M. Studdert-Kennedy (eds.), *Modularity and the motor theory of speech perception*. Hillsdale, NJ: Lawrence Erlbaum

1990b. Gestural specification using dynamically-defined articulatory structures. *Journal of Phonetics* 18: 299–320

Brownell, H. H., D. Michell, J. Powelson, & H. Gardner. 1983. Surprise but not coherence: sensitivity to verbal humor in right-hemisphere patients. *Brain and Language* 18: 20–27

Bullowa, M. 1977. From performative act to the performative utterance: an ecological perspective. *Sign Language Studies* 16: 193–218

Burling, R. 1993. Primate calls, human language, and nonverbal communication. *Current Anthropology* 34(1): 25–53

Bybee, J. 1985. *Morphology: a study of the relation between meaning and form.* Amsterdam: John Benjamins

1988. Morphology as lexical organization. In M. T. Hammond & M. P. Noonan (eds.), *Theoretical morphology*. San Diego: Academic Press

1992. Cognitive/functional phonology. MS

Calbris, G. (tr. O. Doyle). 1990. *The semiotics of French gestures*. Bloomington: Indiana University Press

Calvin, W. 1990. *The cerebral symphony*. New York: Bantam Books

Carroll, J. B. 1961. Review of W. C. Stokoe, *Sign language structure*. *Exceptional Children*, October, 113–116

Carter-Saltzman, L., S. Scarr-Salapatek, W. F. Barker, & S. H. Katz. 1976. Left-handedness in twins: incidence and patterns of performance in an adolescent sample. *Behavior Genetics* 6(2): 189

Chafe, W. 1970. *Meaning and the structure of language*. University of Chicago Press

Chai, C. K. 1976. *Genetic evolution*. University of Chicago Press

Chance, M. & C. Jolly. 1970. *Social groups of monkeys, apes and men*. New York: Dutton

Cheney, D. L. & R. M. Seyfarth. 1990. *How monkeys see the world*. University of Chicago Press

Chomsky, N. 1959. Review of B. F. Skinner's *Verbal behavior*. *Language* 35: 26–58

1965. *Aspects of the theory of syntax*. Cambridge, MA: MIT Press

1966. *Cartesian linguistics*. New York: Harper and Row

1980. *Rules and representations*. New York: Columbia University Press

1986. *Knowledge of language: its nature, origin and use*. New York: Praeger

Chomsky, N. & M. Halle. 1968. *The sound patterns of English*. New York: Harper and Row

Churchill, J. A., E. Igna, & R. Senf. 1962. The association of position at birth and handedness. *Pediatrics* 29: 307–309

Churchland, P. 1986. *Neurophilosophy*. Cambridge, MA: MIT Press

Clark, W. E. 1963. *The antecedents of man*. New York: Harper and Row

Condon, W. 1976. An analysis of behavioral organization. *Sign Language Studies* 13: 285–318

Corballis, M. C. 1980. Laterality and myth. *American Psychologist* 35(3): 284–295

1991. *The lopsided ape: evolution of the generative mind*. Oxford University Press

Critchley, M. 1953. *The parietal lobes*. London: Arnold

1975. *Silent language*. London: Butterworth

Daniloff, R. & R. Hammarberg. 1973. On defining coarticulation. *Journal of Phonetics* 1: 239–248

Darwin, C. 1873. *The expression of the emotions in man and animals*. New York: D. Appleton and Company

1909. *Origin of species by means of natural selection, or the preservation of favored races in the struggle for life*. New York: P. F. Collier (org. pub. 1859)

Davidson, I. & W. Noble. 1989. The archaeology of perception: traces of depiction and language. *Current Anthropology* 30 (2): 125–155

Deane, P. D. 1991. Syntax and the brain: neurological evidence for the spatialization of form hypothesis. *Cognitive Linguistics* 2(4): 361–367

1993. *Grammar in mind and brain: explorations in cognitive syntax*. Berlin/New York: Mouton de Gruyter

DeLong, M. R., G. E. Alexander, A. P. Georgopolos, M. D. Crutcher, S. J. Mitchell, & R. T. Richardson. 1984. Role of basal ganglia in limb movements. *Human Neurobiology* 2: 235–244

Denny-Brown, D. 1958. The nature of apraxia. *Journal of Nervous and Mental Disorders* 126: 9–32

Deuchar, M. 1985. Implications of sign language research for linguistic theory. In W. Stokoe & V. Volterra (eds.), *Proceedings of the III. international symposium on sign language research*. Silver Spring, MD: Linstok Press

Dibble, H. 1989. The implications of stone tool types for the presence of language during the Lower and Middle Paleolithic. In P. Mellars and C. Stringer (eds.), *The human revolution: behavioural and biological perspectives on the origins of modern humans*. Edinburgh University Press

Eco, U. 1979. *A theory of semiotics*. Bloomington: Indiana University Press

Edelman, G. M. 1987. *Neural Darwinism: the theory of neuronal group selection.* New York: Basic Books

1988. *Topobiology.* New York: Basic Books

1989. *The remembered present: a biological theory of consciousness.* New York: Basic Books

1992. *Bright air, brilliant fire: on the matter of mind.* New York: Basic Books

Edmonson, W. 1987. Segments in signed languages: do they exist and does it matter? Paper at IV International Symposium on Sign Language Research, Helsinki

Efron, D. 1941. *Gesture and environment.* Morningside Heights, NY: King's Crown Press

Ekman, P. & W. V. Friesen. 1978. *The facial action coding system.* Palo Alto, CA: Consulting Psychologists' Press

Falk, D. 1980. Language, handedness, and primate brains: did the Australopithecines sign? *American Anthropologist* 80: 364–367

1987. Brain lateralization in primates and its evolution in hominids. *Yearbook of Physical Anthropology* 30: 107–125

Feyereisen, P. & J.-D. de Lannoy. 1991. *Gestures and speech: psychological investigations.* Cambridge University Press

Fodor, J. 1983. *The modularity of mind.* Cambridge, MA: MIT Press

Fok, A., K. Van Hoek, E. S. Klima, & U. Bellugi. 1991. The interplay between visuospatial language and visuospatial script. In D. S. Martin (ed.), *Advances in cognition, education, and deafness.* Washington, DC: Gallaudet University Press

Fowler, C. 1985. Current perspectives on language and speech production: a critical overview. In R. Daniloff (ed.), *Speech science.* San Diego: College Hill Press

1986. An event approach to the study of speech perception from a direct-realist perspective. *Journal of Phonetics* 14: 3–28

1987. Perceivers as realists, talkers too: commentary on papers by Strange, Diehl et al., and Rakerd & Verbrugge. *Journal of Memory and Language* 26(5): 574–587

Fowler, C. A., P. Rubin, R. E. Remez, & M. T. Turvey. 1980. Implications for speech production of a general theory of action. In B. Butterworth (ed.), *Language production (Vol. I: Speech and talk).* London: Academic Press

Fowler, C. A. & M. R. Smith. 1986. Speech perception as "vector analysis": an approach to the problems of invariance and segmentation. In J. S. Perkell & D. H. Klatt (eds.), *Invariance and variability in speech processes.* Hillsdale, NJ: Lawrence Erlbaum

Frishberg, N. 1975. Arbitrariness and iconicity. *Language* 51: 696–715

Fromkin, V. 1979. *Errors in linguistic performance: slips of the tongue, ear, pen and hand.* San Francisco: Academic Press

Gainnotti, G., C. Caltagirone, G. Miceli, & C. Masullo. 1981. Selective semantic-lexical impairment of language comprehension in right-brain-damaged patients. *Brain and language* 14: 201–211

Gardner, H. 1983. *Frames of mind: the theory of multiple intelligences.* New York: Basic Books

1985. *The mind's new science: a history of the cognitive revolution.* New York: Basic Books

Gardner, R.A., B.T. Gardner, & T.E. Van Cantfort. 1989. *Teaching sign language to chimpanzees.* Albany, NY: State University of New York Press

Gaulin, S.J. 1980. Sexual dimorphism in the human post-reproductive lifespan: possible causes. *Journal of Human Evolution* 9: 227–232

Gazzaniga, M.S. 1992. *Nature's mind: the biological roots of thinking, emotions, sexuality, language, and intelligence.* New York: Basic Books

Geschwind, N. 1965. Disconnexion syndromes in animals and man. *Brain* 88: 237–294; 585–644

1970. The organization of language and the brain. *Science* 170: 940–944

1972. Cerebral dominance and anatomic asymmetry. *New England Journal of Medicine* 287(4): 194–195

Gibson, J. J. 1966. *The senses considered as perceptual systems.* Boston: Houghton Mifflin

Gibson, K. 1983. Comparative neurobehavioral ontogeny and the constructionist approach to the evolution of the brain, object manipulation and language. In E. de Grolier (ed.), *Glossogenetics: the origin and evolution of language.* Paris: Harwood Academic Publishers

Givens, D. 1986. The big and the small: toward a paleontology of gesture. *Sign Language Studies* 51: 145–170

Givón, T. 1984. *Syntax: a functional–typological introduction volume I.* Amsterdam: John Benjamins

1989. *Mind, code and context: essays in pragmatics.* Hillsdale, NJ: Lawrence Erlbaum

Goldin-Meadow, S. & H. Feldman. 1977. The development of language-like communication without a language model. *Science* 197: 401–403

Goldsmith, J. 1976. An overview of autosegmental phonology. *Linguistic Analysis* 2: 23–68

Goodall, J. 1965. Chimpanzees of the Gombe Stream Reserve. In I. DeVore (ed.), *Primate behavior.* New York: Holt, Rinehart and Winston

Gopnick, M. 1990. Feature-blind grammar and dysphasia. *Nature* 344: 715

Gould, S. J. 1982. Darwinism and the expansion of evolutionary theory. *Science* 216(3): 380–387

1992. A humongous fungus among us. *Natural History* July

Gouzoules, S. 1984. Primate mating systems, kin associations, and cooperative behavior: evidence of kin recognition? *Yearbook of Physical Anthropology* 27: 99–134

Greenfield, P. M. 1991. Language, tools and brain: the ontogeny and phylogeny of hierarchically organized sequential behavior. *Behavioral and Brain Sciences,* 14: 531–595

Greenfield, P. M. & E. S. Savage-Rumbaugh. 1991. Imitation, grammatical development, and the invention of protogrammar by an ape. In N. A. Krasnegor, D. M. Rumbaugh, R. L. Schiefelbusch & M. Studdert-Kennedy (eds.), *Biological and behavioral determinants of language development.* Hillsdale, NJ: Lawrence Erlbaum

Greenhood, W. 1992. Homeotic genes and the origin of syntax. Paper presented at annual meeting of Language Origins Society. University of Cambridge, UK

Haiman, J. 1985. Introduction. In J. Haiman (ed.), *Iconicity in syntax.* Amsterdam: John Benjamins

Hall, E. T. 1959. *The silent language.* New York: Doubleday

Hamilton, W. D. 1966. The moulding of senescence by natural selection. *Journal of Theoretical Biology* 12: 12–45

Hardyck, C. & L. F. Petrinovich. 1977. Left-handedness. *Psychological Bulletin* 84: 385–390

Hebb, D. O. 1949. *The organization of behavior: a neuropsychological theory.* New York: Wiley

Hecaen, H. & J. Sauguet. 1971. Cerebral dominance in lefthanded subjects. *Cortex* 8: 19–25

Hecaen, H. & J. De Ajuriaguerra. 1964. *Left-handedness: manual superiority and cerebral dominance,* translated by E. Ponder. New York: Grune and Stratton

Hecaen, H., Deagostini, M., & A. Monzon-Montes. 1981. Cerebral organization in left-handers. *Brain and Language* 12: 261

Heine, B., U. Claudi, & F. Hünnemeyer. 1991. *Grammaticalization: a conceptual framework.* University of Chicago Press

Hewes, G. 1973. Primate communication and the gestural origin of language. *Current Anthropology* 14: 5–24

1974. Language in early hominids. In R. Wescott, G. Hewes & W. Stokoe (eds.). *Language origins.* Silver Spring, MD: Linstok Press

Hewes, G. W. 1976. The current status of the gestural theory of language origins. *Annals of the New York Academy of Sciences* 280: 482–504

Hicks, R. E. & M. Kinsbourne. 1978. Human handedness. In M. Kinsbourne (ed.), *Asymmetrical function of the human brain.* Cambridge University Press

Hill, J. 1974. Hominoid proto-linguistic capacities. In R. Wescott, G. Hewes & W. Stokoe (eds.). *Language origins.* Silver Spring, MD: Linstok Press

Hill, K. 1991. The evolution of premature reproductive senescence and menopause in human females: an evaluation of the "grandmother hypothesis." MS

Hines, M., L. Chiu, & L. McAdams. 1992. Cognition and the corpus callosum: verbal fluency, visuospatial ability, and language lateralization related to midsagittal surface areas of callosal subregions. *Behavioral Neuroscience* 106: 3–14

Hockett, C. F. 1960. The origin of speech. *Scientific American* 203: 89–96
1978. In search of Jove's brow. *American Speech* 53: 243–315

Holloway, R. 1981. Culture, symbols and human brain evolution. *Dialectical Anthropology* 5: 287–303

Hopkins, W. D. & R. D. Morris. 1992. Hemispheric priming by meaningful and nonmeaningful symbols in language-trained chimpanzees (Pan troglodytes): further evidence of a left hemisphere advantage. *Behavioral Neuroscience* 106: 575–582

Houghton, P. 1993. Neandertal supralaryngeal vocal tract. *American Journal of Physical Anthropology* 90: 139–146

Hrdy, S. B. 1981. *The woman that never evolved.* Cambridge, MA: Harvard University Press

Hymes, D. 1971. Foreword. In M. Swadesh, *The origin and diversification of language.* Chicago: Aldine

James, W. 1961. *Psychology: the briefer course.* Edited by G. Allport. New York: Harper and Brothers [originally published in 1892]

Jespersen, O. 1924. *The philosophy of grammar.* New York: Norton [1965 edition]

Johnson, M. 1987. *The body in the mind: the bodily basis of meaning, imagination and reason.* University of Chicago Press
1992. Philosophical implications of cognitive semantics. *Cognitive Linguistics* 3–4: 345–366

Kantor, R. 1980. The acquisition of classifiers in American Sign Language. *Sign Language Studies* 28: 193–208

Katz, S. H. & D. F. Armstrong. 1994. Cousin marriage and the evolution of longevity, language and the X–chromosome. In D. Crews & R. Garruto (eds.), *Biological anthropology and aging: an emerging synthesis.* Oxford University Press

Kegl, J. & R. Wilbur. 1976. When does structure stop and style begin? Syntax, morphology, and phonology vs. stylistic variation in

American Sign Language. In S. Mufwene, C. Walker & S. Steever (eds.), *Papers from the twelfth regional meeting, Chicago Linguistic Society.* University of Chicago Press

Kelso, J. A. S., E. L. Saltzman, & B. Tuller. 1986. The dynamical perspective on speech production: data and theory. *Journal of Phonetics* 14: 29–59

Kendall, A. 1864. Introductory address at the inauguration of the College for the Deaf and Dumb. In *History of the College for the Deaf, 1857–1907,* by E. M. Gallaudet. Washington, DC: Gallaudet College Press (1983)

Kendon, A. 1975. Gesticulation, speech, and the gesture theory of language origins. *Sign Language Studies* 9: 349–373

  1980. Sign language of the women of Yirendumu. *Sign Language Studies* 27: 101–112

  1988. How gestures can become like words. In F. Poyatos (ed.), *Crosscultural perspectives in nonverbal communication.* Toronto: Hogrefe

  1989. *Sign languages of aboriginal Australia.* Cambridge University Press

  1991. Some considerations for a theory of language origins. *Man* 26: 199–221

Kien, J. 1992. Temporal segmentation in the motor system, symbolization, and the evolution of language. Paper presented at the Annual Meeting of the Language Origin Society, Cambridge, UK

Kimura, D. 1976. The neural basis of language qua gesture. In H. Whitaker & H. A. Whitaker (eds.), *Studies in neurolinguistics, Volume 2.* New York: Academic Press

  1979. Neuromotor mechanisms in the evolution of human communication. In H. D. Steklis & M. J. Raleigh (eds.), *Neurobiology of social communication in primates.* New York: Academic Press

  1981. Neural mechanisms in manual signing. *Sign Language Studies* 33: 291–312

  1988. Book review of *What the hands reveal about the brain,* by H. Poizner, E. S. Klima & U. Bellugi, Cambridge, MIT Press, 1987. *Language and Speech* 31(4): 375–378

  1992. Sex differences in the brain. *Scientific American* 267(3): 118–125

  1993. *Neuromotor mechanisms in human communication.* Oxford University Press

Kimura, D. & Y. Archibald. 1974. Motor functions of the left hemisphere. *Brain* 97: 337–350

Kinsbourne, M. (ed.) 1978. *Asymmetrical function of the human brain.* Cambridge University Press

Klima, E. S. 1991. Panel discussion: the motor theory and alternative accounts. In I. G. Mattingly & M. Studdert-Kennedy (eds.),

Modularity and the motor theory of speech perception. Hillsdale, NJ: Lawrence Erlbaum

Klima. E. & U. Bellugi. 1979. *The signs of language.* Cambridge, MA: Harvard University Press

Kuhl, P. K. & A. N. Meltzoff. 1982. The bimodal perception of speech in infancy. *Science* 218: 1138–1144

Kuhl, P. K., K. A. Williams, F. Lacerda, K. N. Stevens, & B. Lindblom. 1992. Linguistic experience alters phonetic perception in infants by 6 months of age. *Science* 255: 606–608

Kuschel, R. 1973. The silent inventor: the creation of a sign language by the only deaf-mute on a Polynesian island. *Sign Language Studies* 3: 1–28

Kwek, J. 1991. Occasions for sign use in an Australian aboriginal community. *Sign Language Studies* 71: 143–160

Laitman, J. 1985. Evolution of the hominid upper respiratory tract: the fossil evidence. In P. V. Tobias (ed.), *Hominid evolution: past, present and future.* New York: Alan R. Liss

Lakoff, G. 1987. *Women, fire, and dangerous things: what categories reveal about the mind.* University of Chicago Press

Lakoff, G. & M. Johnson. 1980. *Metaphors we live by.* University of Chicago Press

Lane, H. 1976. *The wild boy of Aveyron.* Cambridge, MA: Harvard University Press

1984. *When the mind hears.* New York: Random House

1992. *The mask of benevolence: disabling the deaf community.* New York: Alfred A. Knopf

Lane, H., P. Boyes-Braem, & U. Bellugi. 1976. Preliminaries to a distinctive feature analysis of handshapes in American Sign Language. *Cognitive Psychology* 3: 263–289

Langacker, R. W. 1987. *Foundations of cognitive grammar volume I: Theoretical prerequisites.* Stanford University Press

1988. An overview of cognitive grammar. In B. Rudzka-Ostyn (ed.), *Topics in cognitive linguistics.* Amsterdam: John Benjamins

1991a. *Foundations of cognitive grammar volume II.* Stanford University Press

1991b. *Concept, image, and symbol: the cognitive basis of grammar.* Berlin: Mouton de Gruyter

Laughlin, C. & E. D'Aquili. 1974. *Biogenetic structuralism.* New York: Columbia University Press

Leakey, R. & R. Lewin. 1992. *Origins reconsidered.* New York: Doubleday

Lee, R. & I. Devore (eds.). 1968. *Man the hunter.* Chicago: Aldine

Lenneberg, E. H. 1967. *Biological foundations of language.* New York: John Wiley and Sons

Levy, J. 1969. Possible basis for the evolution of lateral specialization of the human brain. *Nature* 224: 614

1974. Psychobiological implications of bilateral asymmetry. In S. Dimond & J. G. Beaumont (eds.), *Hemisphere function in the human brain*. London: Paul Elek, Ltd

Levy, J., R. Nebes, & R. Sperry. 1971. Expressive language in the surgically separated minor hemisphere. *Cortex* 7: 49–58

Liberman, A. 1982. On finding that speech is special. *American Psychologist* 37(2): 148–167

Liberman, A. & I. G. Mattingly. 1985. The motor theory of speech perception revised. *Cognition* 21: 1–36

Liddell, S. K. 1980. *American Sign Language syntax*. The Hague: Mouton
1984. THINK and BELIEVE: sequentiality in American Sign Language. *Language* 60: 372–399

Liddell, S. K. & R. E. Johnson. 1989. American Sign Language: the phonological base. *Sign Language Studies* 64: 195–277

Lieberman, P. 1985. On the evolution of human syntactic ability. *Journal of Human Evolution* 14: 657–668
1991. *Uniquely human: The evolution of speech, thought and selfless behavior.* Cambridge, MA: Harvard University Press

Lieberman, P. & E. S. Crelin. 1971. On the speech of Neanderthal man. *Linguistic Inquiry* 2: 203–222

Locke, J. 1971. *An essay concerning human understanding.* Edited by A. D. Woozley. New York: The World Publishing Company. (First published 1690)

Lovejoy, O. 1981. The origin of man. *Science* 211(4480): 341–350

Lunde. A. 1956. The sociology of the deaf. Paper presented at the American Sociological Meeting, Detroit, MI

Lyons, J. 1981. *Language and linguistics: an introduction.* Cambridge University Press

Maccoby, E. C. & C. N. Jacklin. 1978. *The psychology of sex differences.* Oxford University Press

MacNeilage, P. F. 1991. The "postural origins" theory of primate neurobiological asymmetries. In N. A. Krasnegor, D. M. Rumbaugh, R. L. Schiefelbusch & M. Studdert-Kennedy (eds.), *Biological and behavioral determinants of language development*. Hillsdale, NJ: Lawrence Erlbaum

MacNeilage, P. & P. Ladefoged. 1976. The production of speech and language. In E. C. Carterette & M. Friedman (eds.), *Handbook of perception: language and speech*. New York: Academic Press

Maestas y Moores, J. 1980. Early linguistic environment interactions of deaf parents with their infants. *Sign Language Studies* 26: 1–13

Marshack, A. 1984. The ecology and brain of two-handed bipedalism: an analytic, cognitive and evolutionary assessment. In H. L. Roitblat, T. G. Bever, & H. S. Terrace (eds.), *Animal cognition*. Hillsdale, NJ: Lawrence Erlbaum

1992. Language origin: a multidisciplinary approach. In J. Wind, B. Chiarelli, B. Bichakjian, A. Nocentini, & A. Jonker (eds.), *The origin of language: an anthropological approach*. Dordrecht: Kluwer

Mayr, E. 1942. *Systematics and the origin of species*. New York: Columbia University Press

1982. *The growth of biological thought*. Cambridge, MA: Harvard University Press

McClave, E. 1991. Ph.D. dissertation, Georgetown University, Linguistics

McCrone, J. 1991. *The ape that spoke: language and the evolution of the human mind*. New York: William Morrow and Company

McNeill, D. 1985. So you think gestures are nonverbal. *Psychological Review* 92: 350–371

1987. *Psycholinguistics: a new approach*. New York: Harper & Row

1992. *Hand and mind: what gestures reveal about thought*. University of Chicago Press

McNeill, D. & P. Freiberger. 1993. *Fuzzy logic*. New York: Simon and Schuster

Mead, G. H. 1970. *Mind, self and society* (edited and with an introduction by C. W. Morris, originally published 1934). University of Chicago Press

Milner, B. 1975. Psychological aspects of focal epilepsy and its neurosurgical management. In D. P. Purpura, K. J. Penry, & R. D. Walter (eds.), *Advances in Neurology*. Vol. 8. New York: Raven Press

Milo, R. G. & D. Quiatt. 1993. Glottogenesis and anatomically modern Homo sapiens: the evidence for and implications of a late origin of vocal language. *Current Anthropology* 34(5): 569–581

Mitchell, S. J., R. T. Richardson, F. H. Baker, & M. R. DeLong. 1987. The primate globus pallidus: neuronal activity related to direction of movement. *Experimental Brain Research* 68: 491–505

Morgan, E. 1982. *The aquatic ape: a theory of human evolution*. New York: Stein and Day

Morris, D. 1967. *The naked ape*. New York: McGraw-Hill

Morton, J. 1970. What could possibly be innate? In J. Morton, *Biological and social factors in psycholinguistics*. Urbana, IL: University of Illinois Press

Mowrey, R. & W. Pagliuca. 1988. The reductive character of phonetic evolution. MS

Mowrey, R. A. & I. R. A. MacKay. 1990. Phonological primitives: electromyographic speech error evidence. *Journal of the Acoustic Society of America* 88: 1299–1312

Myers, R. 1976. Comparative neurology of vocalization and speech: proof of a dichotomy. In S. Harnad, H. Steklis & J. Lancaster (eds.), *Origin and evolution of language and speech*. New York: New York Academy of Sciences

Neisser, A. 1983. *The other side of silence: sign language and the deaf community in America*. New York: Alfred A. Knopf

Neisser, U. 1967. *Cognitive psychology*. New York: Appleton–Century–Crofts

1976. *Cognition and reality: principles and implications of cognitive psychology*. New York: Freeman

Neville, H. J. 1977. Electroencephalographic testing of cerebral specialization in normal and congenitally deaf children: a preliminary report. In S. J. Segalowitz & F. A. Gruber (eds.), *Language development and neurological theory*. New York: Academic Press

Padden, C. 1990. Rethinking fingerspelling. *Signpost*, October: 2–4. International Linguistics Association. University of Durham, UK

Padden, C. & T. Humphries. 1988. *Deaf in America: voices from a culture*. Cambridge, MA: Harvard University Press

Parker, S. 1985. A social–technological model for the evolution of language. *Current Anthropology* 26: 617–639

1993. Comment on Robbins Burling, Primate calls, human language, and nonverbal communication. *Current Anthropology* 34(1): 41–42

Penrose, R. 1989. *The emperor's new mind: concerning computers, minds, and the laws of physics*. New York: Penguin Books

Perlmutter, D. 1988. A mosaic theory of American Sign Language syllable structure. Paper presented at Second Conference on Theoretical Issues in Sign Language Research. Gallaudet University, Washington, DC

Perrett, D. I., M. H. Harries, R. Bevan, S. Thomas, P. J. Benson, A. J. Mistlin, A. J. Chitty, J. K. Hietanen, & J. E. Ortega. 1989. Frameworks of analysis for the neural representation of animate objects and actions. *Journal of Experimental Biology* 146: 87–113

Perrett, D. I., A. J. Mistlin, & A. J. Chitty. 1987. Visual cells responsive to faces. *Trends in Neuroscience* 10: 358–364

Petitto, L. A. & P. F. Marentette. 1991. Babbling in the manual mode: evidence for the ontogeny of language. *Science* 251: 1493–1496

Piaget, J. 1970. *Structuralism*. New York: Harper & Row

Piaget, J. & B. Inhelder. 1969. *The psychology of the child*. New York: Basic Books

Piattelli-Palmarini, M. 1989. Evolution, selection and cognition: from "learning" to parameter setting in biology and in the study of language. *Cognition* 31: 1–44

Pike, K. L. 1993. *Talk, thought and thing: the emic road toward conscious knowledge*. Dallas, TX: Summer Institute of Linguistics

Pinker, S. 1991. Rules of language. *Science* 253: 530–535

Pinker, S. & P. Bloom. 1990. Natural language and natural selection. *Behavioral and Brain Sciences* 13(4): 707–765

Poizner, H., E. S. Klima, & U. Bellugi. 1987. *What the hands reveal about the brain*. Cambridge, MA: MIT Press

Premack, D. 1976. *Gavagai! or the future history of the animal language controversy*. Cambridge, MA: MIT Press

Previc, F. H. 1991. A general theory concerning the prenatal origins of cerebral lateralization in humans. *Psychological Review* 98(3): 299–334

Pulleyblank, E. G. 1983. The beginnings of duality of patterning in language. In E. de Grolier (ed.), *Glossogenetics: the origin and evolution of language*. Paris: Harwood Academic Publishers

1986. The meaning of duality of patterning and its importance in language evolution. *Sign Language Studies* 51: 101–120

Quine, W.V. 1961. *From a logical point of view*. New York: Harper and Row

Reilly, J. S., M. L. McIntire, & H. Seago. 1992. Affective prosody in American Sign Language. *Sign Language Studies* 75: 113–130

Reynolds, V. 1965. Some behavioral comparisons between the chimpanzee and the mountain gorilla in the wild. *American Anthropologist* 67: 691–705

1966. Open groups in hominid evolution. *Man* 1: 441–452

1968. Kinship and the family in monkeys, apes, and man. *Man* 3: 209–223

Reynolds, V. & F. Reynolds. 1965. Chimpanzees of the Budongo Forest. In I. DeVore (ed.), *Primate behavior*. New York: Holt, Rinehart and Winston

Ricklan, D. 1990. The precision grip in Australopithecus africanus. In G. H. Sperber (ed.), *From apes to angels: essays in honor of Philip V. Tobias*. New York: Wiley-Liss

Rosenfield, I. 1988. *The invention of memory*. New York: Basic Books

Rumelhart, D. E. & J. L. McClelland. 1986. Learning the past tenses of English verbs: implicit rules or parallel distributed processing? In B. MacWhinney (ed.), *Mechanisms of language acquisition*. Hillsdale, NJ: Erlbaum

Rymer, R. 1992a. A silent childhood–I. *The New Yorker*. April 13: 41–81

1992b. A silent childhood–II. *The New Yorker*. April 20: 43–77

Sacks, O. 1985. *The man who mistook his wife for a hat.* New York: Summit Books

Sade, D. S. 1968. Inhibition of son-mother mating among free-ranging rhesus monkeys. *Science and Psychoanalysis* 12: 18–38

Sandler, W. 1986. The spreading hand autosegment of American Sign Language. *Sign Language Studies* 50: 1–28

Sarles, H. 1974 Could a Non-H? In R. Wescott et al. (eds.), *Language origins.* Silver Spring, MD: Linstok Press

Satz, P. 1973. Left-handedness and early brain insult: an explanation. *Neuropsychologia* 11: 115

Savage-Rumbaugh, S., R. A. Sevcik, & W. D. Hopkins. 1988. Symbolic cross-modal transfer in two species of chimpanzees. *Child Development* 59: 617–625

Schaller, G. 1965. The behavior of the mountain gorilla. In I. DeVore (ed.), *Primate behavior.* New York: Rinehart and Winston

Shattuck, R. 1985. Words and images: thinking and translation. *Dædalus* 114(4): 201–214

Singleton, J. L. & E. L. Newport. 1989. When learners surpass their models: the acquisition of American Sign Language from impoverished input. In *Proceedings of the 14th Annual Boston University Conference on Language Development.* Vol. 15. Boston: Program in Applied Linguistics, Boston University

Siple, P. 1978. Visual Constraints for Sign Language Communication. *Sign Language Studies* 19: 95–110

Skinner, B. F. 1957. *Verbal behavior.* New York: Appleton–Century–Croft

Smith, A. 1966. Speech and other functions after left (dominant) hemispherectomy. *Journal of Neurological and Neurosurgical Psychiatry* 29: 467–469

1969. Nondominant hemispherectomy. *Neurology* 19: 442–445

Smith, H. L., Jr. 1967. The concept of the morphophone. The Inglis Lectures

Sperry, R., M. Gazzaniga, & J. Bogen. 1969. Interhemispheric relationships: the neocortical commissures: syndromes of hemisphere disconnection. In P. J. Vinken & G. W. Bruyn (eds.), *Handbook of clinical neurology.* Amsterdam: Wiley

Springer, S. P. & A. Searleman. 1978. The ontogeny of hemispheric specialization: evidence from dichotic listening in twins. *Neuropsychologia* 16(3): 269–281

Steklis, H. 1985. Primate communication, comparative neurology and the origin of language reexamined. *Journal of Human Evolution* 14:157–173

Stokoe, W. C. 1960. Sign language structure: an outline of the communication systems of the American deaf. *Studies in Linguistics, Occasional Papers*, 8

1976. Sign language autonomy. *Annals of the New York Academy of Sciences* 280: 505–513

1980. Sign language structure. *Annual Review of Anthropology* 9: 365–390

1991. Semantic phonology. *Sign Language Studies* 71: 107–114

1992. Review of Calbris (1990) & Feyereisen (1991). *Sign Language Studies* 75: 183–188

Stokoe, W. C., C. Croneberg & D. Casterline. 1965. *A dictionary of American Sign Language on linguistic principles.* Silver Spring, MD: Linstok Press

Strange, W. 1987. Information for vowels in formant transitions. *Journal of Memory and Language* 26(5): 550–557

Studdert-Kennedy, M. 1985. Perceiving phonetic events. In W. H. Warren & R. E. Shaw (eds.), *Perspectives and change.* Hillsdale, NJ: Lawrence Erlbaum

1986. Two cheers for direct realism. *Journal of Phonetics* 14: 99–104

1987. The phoneme as a perceptuomotor structure. In D. A. Allport (ed.), *Language perception and production: relationships between listening, speaking, reading and writing.* London: Academic Press

Studdert-Kennedy, M. & H. Lane. 1980. Clues from the differences between signed and spoken languages. In U. Bellugi & M. Studdert-Kennedy (eds.), *Signed and spoken languages: biological constraints on linguistic form.* Basel: Springer–Verlag

Supalla, T. & E. Newport. 1978. How many seats in a chair? The derivation of nouns and verbs in American Sign Language. In P. Siple (ed.), *Understanding language through sign language research.* New York: Academic Press

Suzuki, A. 1969. An ecological study of chimpanzees in a savanna woodland. *Primates* 10: 197–225

Swisher, M. V. 1990. Developmental effects on the reception of signs in peripheral vision by deaf students. *Sign Language Studies* 66: 45–60

Swisher, M. V., K. Christie, & S. Miller. 1989. The reception of signs in peripheral vision. *Sign Language Studies* 63: 99–125

Taylor, J. R. 1989. *Linguistic categorization: prototypes in linguistic theory.* Oxford: Clarendon Press

Ten Houten, W. 1976. Discussion and criticism: more on split-brain research, culture and cognition. *Current Anthropology* 77: 503–506

Terrace, H. S., L. A. Petitto, R. J. Sanders, & T. G. Bever. 1979. Can an ape create a sentence? *Science* 206: 891–900

Tobias, P. V. 1987. The brain of Homo habilis: a new level of organization in cerebral evolution. *Journal of Human Evolution* 16: 741–761

Tomblin, J. 1989. Familial concentration of developmental language impairment. *Journal of Speech and Hearing Disorders* 54: 287–290

Tompkins, C. A. & C. A. Mateer. 1985. Right hemisphere appreciation of prosodic and linguistic indication of implicit attitude. *Brain and Language* 24: 185–203

Trinkaus, E. & P. Shipman. 1993. *The Neandertals*. New York: Alfred A. Knopf

Turnbull, C. 1968. The importance of flux in two hunting societies. In R. Lee and I. DeVore (eds.), *Man the Hunter*. Chicago: Aldine

Valade, Y.-L. 1854. Remy. *Etudes sur la lexicologie et la grammaire du langage naturel des signes*. Paris

Van Lawick-Goodall, J. 1971. *In the shadow of man*. Boston: Houghton Mifflin Company

Varela, F. J., E. Thompson, & E. Rosch. 1991. *The embodied mind: cognitive science and human experience*. Cambridge, MA: MIT Press

Volterra, V. & C. Erting. 1990. *From gesture to language in hearing and deaf children*. Berlin: Springer-Verlag

Wallman, J. 1992. *Aping language*. Cambridge University Press

Wapner, W., S. Hamby & H. Gardner. 1981. The role of the right hemisphere in the apprehension of complex linguistic materials. *Brain and Language* 14: 15–33

Washabaugh, W. 1986. *Five fingers for survival*. Ann Arbor, MI: Karoma Publishers

Watson, J. 1976. *The molecular biology of the gene* (3rd edition). Menlo Park, CA: W. A. Benjamin

Weiss, M. L. 1987. Nucleic acid evidence bearing on hominid relationships. *Yearbook of Physical Anthropology* 30: 41–73

Wescott, R. 1971. Linguistic iconism. *Language* 47: 416–428

Wescott, R., G. Hewes, & W. C. Stokoe (eds.). 1974. *Language origins*. Silver Spring, MD: Linstok Press

White, L. 1979. *The science of culture*. New York: Farrar, Strauss

Wilbur, R. 1979. *American Sign Language and sign systems*. Baltimore: University Park Press

  1987. *American Sign Language: linguistic and applied dimensions*. Boston: College Hill Press

Wilcox, S. 1990. The structure of signed and spoken language. *Sign Language Studies*. 67: 141–151

  1992. *The phonetics of fingerspelling*. Amsterdam: John Benjamins

Wilcox, S. & S. Wilbers. 1987. The case for academic acceptance of American Sign Language. *The Chronicle of Higher Education*. Opinion. July 1

Winner, E. & H. Gardner. 1977. The comprehension of metaphor in brain-damaged patients. *Brain* 100: 717–729

Woodward, J. C. 1973. Implication lects on the deaf diglossic continuum. Unpublished doctoral dissertation. Georgetown University, Washington, DC

Zeki, S. 1992. The visual image in mind and brain. *Scientific American* 267(3): 68–76

Zihlman, A. 1981. Women as shapers of the human adaptation. In F. Dahlberg (ed.), *Woman the gatherer*. New Haven: Yale University Press

    1990. Knuckling under: controversy over hominid origins. In G. H. Sperber (ed.), *From apes to angels: essays in honor of Phillip V. Tobias*. New York: Wiley-Liss

Lord Zuckerman. 1991. Apes "R" not us. *The New York Review of Books* 38(10): 43–49

Author index

Abeles, M., 131
Allan, K., 14
Annett. M.A., 212
Arensburg, B.A., 202
Armstrong, D.F., 12, 18, 80, 82, 104–105, 132, 152, 210, 230–233

Baker, C., 86
Baker-Shenk, C., 90, 189, 195
Barnes, J., 199
Basser, L.S., 212
Bateson, G., 90
Battison, R., 190
Bellugi, U., 14, 28–29, 31, 64, 69, 78, 84, 90, 99–101, 104
Bernstein, N., 44
Bever, T.G., 210
Bickerton, D., 23, 159, 204–209, 214
Biederman, I., 49
Binford, L.R., 222–223
Birdwhistell, R.L., 177
Bloch, B., 178
Bloom, P., 230
Bloomfield, L., 68
Blount, G., 150
Bogen, J.E., 210, 212
Bolinger, D., 176, 226
Bonvillian, J.D., 213
Boyes-Braem, P., 78
Bradshaw, J.L., 116, 209, 211
Browman, C.P., 9, 32, 44–45, 54, 74
Brownell, H.H., 210
Bullowa, M., 151
Burling, R., 38–39, 88, 223–229
Bybee, J., 32, 35, 40, 54, 135–138

Calbris, G., 66
Calvin, W., 116, 201

Carroll, J.B., 69
Carter-Saltzman, L., 213
Casterline, D., 72
Chafe, W., 12
Chai, C.K., 197
Chance, M., 158, 219
Cheney, D.L., 164, 222
Chiarello, R.J., 210
Chomsky, N., 30, 93, 122, 168, 173, 184
Churchill, J.A., 212
Churchland, P., 51
Clark, W.E., 80, 83, 199
Claudi, U., 40
Condon, W., 151
Corballis, M.C., 94, 96, 99, 115, 190–191, 200, 209–214
Crelin, E.S., 148, 202
Critchley, M., 60
Croneberg, C., 72

D'Aquili, E., 105, 235
Daniloff, R., 8
Darwin, C., 156, 189, 198
Davidson, I., 18, 199, 230
de Ajuriaguerra, J., 209–212
de Lannoy, J.-D., 67
Deane, P.D., 35–36, 59–60, 103, 105
DeLong, M.R., 59
Denny Brown, D., 94
Deuchar, M., 125
DeVore, I., 218
Dibble, H., 18, 199, 230

Eco, U., 227
Edelman, G.M., 16–19, 23, 30, 49–51, 53, 59, 80, 89, 99, 119–120, 138–139, 144–147, 149, 155–160, 163, 166–173, 185, 225

255

Subject index

Hours : 1/22 - 7:35 - 8:35 - Reading
9:45 - 10:45 · Internet & calls
12:30 - 1:30 → Reading & call

12-17 => AM   Am Assoc for the Adv of
                      Science
        202-326-6450

Philadelphia Convention Center -
   Marriott =>

complete information =>

   AAAS =>   www.aaas.org

                  membership & meetings =>

            scope
            ═══════════

Darwinian
   Sat Feb 14 => 3-6 Marriott.

Judy Kegl
250 Morris Ave
Summit, NJ 07901

(908) 598-9475

kegl@andromeda.rutgers.edu

716-271-3611